WI...YN

"THE KEY TO ST... ...SS,"

say the experts, "is not luck, or even skill, but understanding." How much do *you* understand about—

- The floor of the New York Stock Exchange
- How the "bulls" and the "bears" operate
- Performance funds
- Fields of investment—bonds, mutual funds, science and technology
- Investing abroad
- The psychology, economics and politics of the market
- Analyzing and forecasting stock prices
- Brokers' loans
- Selling against the box
- Dow Theory

These are but a few of the areas covered in this readable, concise and complete book for the investor who is in the market for consistent profits.

Among the contributing specialists are Eliot Janeway, outspoken economist; Armand G. Erpf, well-known Wall Street executive; Walter Maynard, Vice Chairman, Shearson, Hammill & Co., Inc.; Kurt I. Lewin, Vice President of Bache & Co.; and many others.

With charts, tables and
a glossary of technical
terms.

Here is what the reviews said about
THE ANATOMY OF WALL STREET:

"If ever a single book could mean all things to all investors, this would be it." —*Buffalo Courier-Express*

"Readers will come away from the book with a greater understanding of the investment business gleaned from some of Wall Street's most prominent thinkers."
—*Library Journal*

"It provides a lot of solid information, it's well indexed and it has a glossary that may even make it possible to understand market letters." —*Wall Street Journal*

"A candid approach to the manifold problems of the investor that will enable him to fully understand the basic value of a stock." —*Minneapolis Star*

"A book for the serious investor . . ."
—*London Economist*

"The book offers more reliable and up-to-date knowledge than more amusing volumes recently published."
—*Minneapolis Tribune*

The Anatomy
of
Wall Street

Edited by

Charles J. Rolo and George J. Nelson

AWARD BOOKS
NEW YORK

TANDEM BOOKS
LONDON

FIRST AWARD PRINTING 1969

The editors acknowledge with thanks the permission of The Financial Analysts Federation to include two chapters first published in the *Financial Analysts Journal:* Chapter 14, "Economics and Investment Management" by Edmund A. Mennis, published in the November–December, 1966, issue of the *Financial Analysts Journal,* Copyright 1966 by The Financial Analysts Federation; and Chapter 16, "Price/Earnings Ratios: A Critical Reappraisal" by Nicholas Molodovsky, published in the May–June, 1967, issue of the *Financial Analysts Journal* under the title "Recent Studies of P/E Ratios," copyrighted © by The Financial Analysts Federation, 1967.

"Performance Is the New Name of the Game" is copyright © 1967 by Kennington Publishing Corporation and is used by permission.

Published by arrangement with J. B. Lippincott Company

Library of Congress Catalog Card No.: 67-25899

AWARD BOOKS are published by
Universal Publishing and Distributing Corporation
235 East Forty-fifth Street, New York, N. Y. 10017

TANDEM BOOKS are published by
Universal-Tandem Publishing Company Limited
14 Gloucester Road, London SW7, England

Manufactured in the United States of America

Contents

PART III: ANALYTIC APPROACHES

PART IV: AN OVER-ALL VIEW

APPENDIXES

Charts and Tables

ABOUT THE EDITORS:

Charles J. Rolo was born in Egypt and educated in England, with an honors degree from Oxford in politics, philosophy and economics. He later received a master's degree in journalism from Columbia University in New York. Since 1960, Mr. Rolo has been a senior security analyst with H. Hentz and Company.

George J. Nelson was born in Russia and, after attending schools in Copenhagen and Berlin, entered the London School of Economics and Cambridge University. In 1955 he formed his own mutual fund, The Nelson Fund, Inc. In 1963 Mr. Nelson formed The Tokyo Fund, of which he is president today.

Foreword

By Charles J. Rolo and George J. Nelson

Readers of this book are offered an unusual guarantee—they will not find in it a single formula, recipe or watertight system for making a fortune on the stock market or even "instant profits" of a more modest nature. The record shows that a given formula or system has, once in a while, produced spectacular results for its creator (usually after a harrowing and expensive period of trial and error). But the annals of Wall Street are strewn with sad little stories of speculators who lost their stake, or most of it, following pat systems for success in the stock market. In 1966, one of these unfortunates anonymously committed his saga to print in a book entitled *Wiped Out*. It is an authentic and edifying horror story.

Our most serious objection to the "how-to-get-rich-quick" books is twofold. They encourage greed, perhaps the most dangerous failing for an investor; and what may be worse, they also encourage a simplistic approach to the stock market, whereas most investors would benefit from a keener awareness and understanding of the market's complexities. Indeed the complexities of the investment world are such that few men would consider themselves experts on all or even most of its facets. Thus a symposium on investments has this to commend it: topics that call for specialized knowledge are treated by the appropriate specialists.

Professionals in the audience will recognize the names of some or many of the contributors, and they will find the table of contents self-explanatory. But readers who are not well traveled in the world of investments may be helped by a few words of orientation—a briefing on the tour which the editors have prepared for them.

Part I concerns itself largely with "how things work" in Wall Street. It begins where the action is, where the happenings happen—on the floor of the New York Stock Exchange —and describes the functioning of the nation's leading securities market. It then catalogues and comments on the innumerable sources of information available to investors, and goes on to show how this information is processed, evaluated and translated into recommendations by a Wall Street Research Department. Thus by the end of Chapter 3, the reader has visited three key places in the world of investments—its chief market place, its library without walls, and its Intelligence department.

Chapter 4 is an introduction to a subject the average investor tends to neglect: the tactics, defensive and aggressive, which can be used when one expects the general market or individual issues to decline. And the last chapter of Part I focuses on a relatively recent phenomenon which has had a dramatic impact on security markets and is therefore of considerable significance to all owners of equities. We refer to the competitive pursuit of high "performance" by traditionally conservative institutional portfolio managers, especially those of the mutual funds.

Part II focuses on some of the main fields of investment: bonds, mutual funds, growth companies, science and technology stocks, and foreign securities.

Part III might have been loosely headed, "Investment Strategy." It deals with the various approaches to the stock market, and to individual issues, used by security analysts and portfolio managers: the fundamental approach, which concerns itself essentially with value; the technical approach, which concerns itself with price changes and trading volume; the psychological approach, which concerns itself with the irrationality of the market place, the emotions of the crowd. The subject of investment strategy is rounded out with studies of the major external forces that influence the movement of stock prices and have a vital bearing on investment decisions: the trends in the economy and the political situation.

Part IV is an illuminating analysis of the present-day structure of American capitalism. It breaks down our corporate universe into meaningful categories, discusses their investment characteristics, and concludes with a trenchant survey of the long-term investment outlook.

The contributors to this book—their biographical sketches appear in an appendix—come from varied sectors of the financial world. The majority are top-flight Wall Street professionals—among them some of the "cardinals" of the Wall Street hierarchy. Several are leading financial journalists. Two are investment counselors.

To whom is this somewhat diversified faculty addressing itself? Not to a kindergarten, certainly, nor to the deans of the securities industry. This book is not a primer and it is not a workshop course for specialists seeking to explore the stratosphere of stock-market theory and practice. The level of discourse ranges between these two extremes. Some chapters are clearly of an introductory nature; some belong to the "intermediate" category; and a number are quite advanced. It is the editors' belief that such a conspectus of Wall Street and the world of securities will inform, instruct, stimulate and occasionally provoke a variety of people who take, or wish to take, a serious interest in the stock market. Our contributors have something of value to say to a heterogeneous audience —thoughtful and inquiring investors, large and small; students of business and finance; and stockbrokers and security analysts who feel they still have something to learn.

ACKNOWLEDGMENTS

The chapters by Nicholas Molodovsky and Edmund A. Mennis first appeared in the *Financial Analysts Journal* and are copyrighted by The Financial Analysts Federation. Charles Rolo's Introduction and the chapter by Dan W. Lufkin have been published by *Finance Magazine*. The chapter by George J. W. Goodman has appeared in *The Institutional Investor*.

The editors wish to thank George Bookman, Director of Public Information of the New York Stock Exchange, for his helpful cooperation.

Introduction

A Portrait of the Ideal Investor

By Charles J. Rolo

A friend of mine—an astute, hard-working and very successful stockbroker—confessed to me on one occasion that he was baffled by the current behavior of the market and could not decide whether he should be buying or selling. "Whenever this has happened to me before," he said, "I've fallen back, as a last resort, on two customers of mine who have a record of being invariably *wrong*. The trouble now is that one is bearish and the other is bullish."

Elementary logic suggests that one of our friend's two customers must at this point have been right, at least temporarily. Nonetheless, it is an observable fact that there are certain investors who do the wrong thing with almost uncanny regularity and even manage to lose money in bull markets. It is equally demonstrable that there are certain people who, over the long pull, consistently make money in the stock market. Things may go against them badly for several months; they may even run into a losing year; but in due course they come out on top and their capital keeps growing.

Now the intriguing thing is that the losing group is by no

means entirely composed of naïve and uninformed investors; it includes otherwise successful businessmen and quite a few people who are professionally employed in the investment business. It would seem that success in the stock market—while it unquestionably depends to a very large degree on information, knowledge and hard work—is also quite intimately related to certain traits of personality, perhaps to a particular character structure. Is it then possible to draw, in psychological terms, a portrait of the ideal investor?

We can begin our inquiry on firm ground by sketching a portrait of his opposite, the chronic loser; for the varied literature on the stock market has copiously catalogued the failings and impulses that lead investors on the road to error. The chronic loser is intellectually lazy, gullible, greedy, irrational, indecisive, prone to extremes of optimism and pessimism, and readily infected by the emotions of the crowd. Examine this portrait for a moment and you will recognize that it is the portrait of an archetype—our old friend *Homo sapiens*. In other words, the traits that make for failure in the stock market are the normal traits of Everyman; they are altogether human. From which it follows that the traits which make for success in the stock market must be, in a loose sense, somewhat *inhuman*. This is implicit in maxims enshrined in the folklore of Wall Street: "Never sell on strike news," or "Sell when the good news is out." Clearly these maxims enjoin us to resist the spontaneous human response; they tell us to do what does *not* come naturally. (Unfortunately, widespread acceptance has robbed them of some of their original force. The pseudo-sophisticated investor who makes it a rule to sell on good news is in effect doing what now comes naturally—he is surrendering to a new brand of "group think.")

We can now attempt to define the ideal investor in more positive terms. He is, to begin with, a person who has lost all of his innocence about the stock market. He is insistently aware of the follies committed by otherwise intelligent human beings when they become part of a crowd, and he has trained himself to scrutinize his own behavior for symptoms of irrationality and involvement in crowd psychology. By temperament, or by virtue of rigorous discipline, he is armored by a strong sense of inner direction against the influences which surround him; and he has the self-confidence —the sheer intestinal fortitude—to persist in a course which in the short run may appear wrong and may not be proved right for a considerable period of time.

A suggestive clue to the most deep-seated characteristic of the ideal investor is contained in an essay on "The Nature of Genius" by the late Ernest Jones, one of the pioneers of psychoanalysis. Starting with Pascal's observation that greatness consists of a union between two extremes, Jones examines the lives of several men of scientific genius—notably Copernicus, Newton and Freud—and shows that each of them exhibited a singular combination of two seemingly opposite traits—skepticism and credulity. This insight, we believe, is peculiarly applicable to the world of investments, where success essentially results from a process of discovery—a perception of future values and potentialities not discounted in present market prices. Extremes of credulity and skepticism, when these traits are separated—as they usually are—constitute severe liabilities for the investor. For credulity puts one at the mercy of rumors, tipsters and stock touts; and chronic skepticism inexorably leads to inertia, to a sterile passivity. On the other hand, a degree of skepticism is the prerequisite for independent thinking about the stock market; and it certainly takes considerable credulity—one may prefer to call it vision, imagination or faith—to believe in the long-term potentialities of a Xerox or a Polaroid when such companies are in their infancy, or even in their early youth. Thus a counterpoint, a balance, an inner "dialogue" between skepticism and credulity produces a dynamic fusion of doubt and belief which may well be the crucial ingredient in the makeup of the ideal investor.

Most experienced and sophisticated investors are fully aware of the importance of psychology in the investment process. They know how they should handle themselves in the market place; and often they handle themselves well. But even in the sharpest of professionals there is an amateur howling to be let out—witness the behavior of so many brilliant managers of "performance funds" in the market break of 1966. They stampeded to dump their glamour stocks, even though in most cases the fundamentals were sound; and they rushed to buy them back a few months later, for the most part at considerably higher prices. Yet these selfsame managers unquestionably have fine performance records, and in spite of their mistakes in 1966 the funds they manage did much better than the general market. We are back to the point we made earlier—that ordinary human frailty is a major source of error in the stock market.

At this point, we should also emphasize a more obvious and inescapable source of error—the fact that investors are dealing with imponderables and unknowns. The wider and timelier dissemination of corporate information and the refinement of the art of security analysis have together made estimates of future company earnings more readily available and more reliable than they used to be. But even corporate managements often cannot accurately foresee what may happen one year or even six months ahead; and security analysis, though it is emulating the scientific method, is forced to concern itself in part with the human factor and with major imponderables and to make certain judgments which are necessarily subjective. After all, you cannot put a stock in a test tube. And the staggering capabilities of the computer, though they can be helpful to investors, still fall far short of clairvoyance.

Thus the stock market is likely to remain an area in which the individual pits his reason, his knowledge, his vision and his guts against a variety of forces: his own human impulses; the large and varied uncertainties of the future; and the collective wisdom and irrationality of other investors. The contest is a tough one but to the victor the rewards are hand-some—and they are within the reach of all. This is what gives the stock market its seductive challenge and its endless fascination.

Part I

Inside Wall Street

1

Inside the New York Stock Exchange

By Myron Kandel and Philip Greer

Every business day of the year, at precisely 10 A.M., a brass bell peals out across the barnlike floor of the New York Stock Exchange—and the world's largest organized securities market swings into frenzied action. Five and one-half hours later, when the same bell signals the end of the trading day, an average of $300 million worth of stocks and bonds has changed hands in more than 100,000 separate public transactions and an additional $100 million has been bought and sold for the accounts of Exchange members.

From its site at Wall and Broad streets in lower Manhat-

Myron Kandel is the editor of the *New York Law Journal*. Philip Greer is the New York Financial Correspondent of the *Washington Post*.

tan, near the spot where George Washington took the oath of office as the first President of the United States, the Exchange spreads its influence into virtually every home, office and factory across the nation. Nearly 13 million people directly own shares in corporations whose securities are listed on the Big Board and many millions more own shares indirectly through mutual funds, pension and profit-sharing plans, insurance companies and bank deposits.

At the end of 1967, the market value of the 11.6 billion shares in the 1,275 companies listed on the Exchange amounted to the staggering total of $586 billion, equal to more than $2,900 for every man, woman and child living in the United States. During that year alone, more than 2.2 billion shares valued at $125 billion were traded on the Exchange. The value of the stocks traded on the Big Board was nearly four times that of all other United States exchanges combined.

But the New York Stock Exchange did not always stand in this dominant position. When the nation was young, and its political, economic and financial institutions were taking root, Philadelphia was the financial center of the country, just as it was the political capital from 1790 until the seat of government was moved to Washington in 1800. In New York, a group of traders gathered daily next to a buttonwood tree on Wall Street to deal in government securities and bank stocks. In 1792, the traders banded together and signed the famous Buttonwood Tree Agreement, in which they pledged to trade only among themselves and charge outsiders a commission. The New York Stock Exchange traces its start to this agreement.

The following year the brokers moved indoors into the newly built Tontine Coffee House, where they conducted their business in a room high up under the eaves. But trading in New York, despite the flurry of speculation that resulted from the War of 1812, lagged behind that in Philadelphia, which had had an organized exchange since 1790. It was not until 1817 that the New York brokers set up a formal organization, called the New York Stock and Exchange Board, modeled after the Philadelphia Exchange, and they moved to larger quarters at 40 Wall Street. A constitution was drawn up, officers were elected and trading rules established. The scale of the operation, however, was reflected in the fact that the initiation fee was set at $25. (In 1929, a record price of $635,000 was paid for a seat on the Exchange.)

From those humble beginnings, the Exchange kept pace with the growth of the nation whose expansion it helped to finance. It survived good times and bad, panics and booms, speculative fevers and investment apathy. In 1863, its official name was changed to the New York Stock Exchange, and the end of the Civil War two years later opened up a period of unprecedented growth. The West was being settled, railroads began spreading into every corner of the country and large-scale manufacturing took hold. As interest in the stock market accompanied the expansion of business and industry, colorful figures like Jay Gould, Jim Fisk, Russell Sage, Commodore Cornelius Vanderbilt and Daniel Drew made and lost millions in speculations, while promoters like Edward H. Harriman, James J. Hill and William C. Whitney made fortunes in the railroads.

The Exchange had growing pains, but new technological developments, such as the introduction of the first stock tickers in 1867 and of telephones in 1879, helped to spur its growth. In the generation spanning the turn of the century, the rise of giant corporate trusts—among them United States Steel, Standard Oil, Eastman Kodak and Du Pont—brought industrial stocks to a level of equal importance with railroad equities, which previously had dominated the market. The great names of the era included J. Pierpont Morgan, Andrew Carnegie, Charles Schwab and John D. Rockefeller. It was during this period, on April 22, 1903, that the Exchange moved into its present building, a solid, unpretentious structure that was designed by James Renwick, the architect of Grace Church and St. Patrick's Cathedral, and cost nearly $2 million to build.

World War I brought the Exchange its greatest jolt. When the war started and exchanges all over the world shut down, the New York Stock Exchange, too, was forced to suspend trading. It closed its doors on July 31, 1914, and did not re-open them until November 28. It was only the third time in its history that the Big Board had been forced to close down, and it still remains the longest suspension of trading. (The two previous suspensions resulted from a fire in 1835 and from the gold panic of 1873.) As the war raged overseas and orders flooded into the nation's industry, the reopening of the Exchange was soon followed by a major bull market.

The entry of the United States into the war in 1917, how-ever, was to provide unexpected and lasting benefits to the se-curities market. To pay for the conduct of the war, Washing-ton vigorously promoted the sale of Liberty Bonds, which were bought by the public in large numbers. Thus, as Profes-sor Robert Sobel has pointed out: "The hard sell of 1917–19 led the general public to participate in securities offerings, many for the first time. This experience led many to the Stock Exchange, where they bought war stocks in odd lots. In this way, the wartime financial and monetary necessities helped create the broad-based bull market of the 1920s."

That "golden" period ended in the crash of 1929. By that year, annual trading volume had risen from 173 million shares in 1921 to 1.1 billion shares. On Tuesday, October 29, a total of 16.4 million shares changed hands, a record that stands to this day. The country slid into the Great Depression and Wall Street fell into disfavor. A Senate investigation of the securities market and the New York Stock Exchange un-covered flagrant abuses and led to the creation in 1934 of the Securities and Exchange Commission (SEC), which for the first time set up federal controls over the securities industry.

The Commission immediately instituted a series of restric-tive rules on trading and demanded a reorganization of the Exchange's administrative structure. This was resisted by most of the membership, which felt that the Exchange itself could provide whatever regulation was necessary. But in 1937, William O. Douglas, newly appointed chairman of the SEC, blasted the Exchange as a "private club" and added: "For a business so vested with public interest, this traditional method has become archaic. The task of conducting the large exchanges (especially the New York Stock Exchange) has become too engrossing for those who must also run their own business. . . . Their management should not be in the hands of professional traders but in fact, as well as nominally, in the charge of those who have a clearer public responsibility."

Opposition to Douglas' proposals melted suddenly in 1938, when Richard Whitney, five times president of the Big Board, who had told the Senate investigators five years earlier that the Exchange "is a perfect institution," was involved in a scandal that eventually sent him to prison. After that, the overhaul of the Exchange was rapid. Its first paid president, William McChesney Martin (who later became chairman of the Federal Reserve Board), took office in June, 1938.

Despite the reorganization and the watchful eye of the SEC, public participation in the stock market remained at a low ebb. In fact, it sank even lower with the advent of World War II. So small was public interest in securities trading at that time that in 1942 a membership on the Exchange sold for $17,000—less than the $20,000 which the Exchange is committed to pay a member's heirs on his death.

Wage and price controls held stocks in check throughout most of the war, but once peace came, and the postwar depression that some feared did not materialize, Americans found themselves with more spendable money than they had ever had before. Long pent-up consumer demand and the development of new products by revolutionary technologies generated dreams of vast expansion for American business. In the nineteen fifties and sixties, these forces and others (such as the Exchange's campaign to broaden share ownership and the big rise in equity ownership by institutions) helped to push stock prices to unprecedented heights, and activity soared on the New York Exchange.

To keep up with the rapidly expanding pace of trading, the Exchange began moving into the electronic age. In 1964, a new high-speed ticker was installed. The following year, computers started taking over a large part of the mountainous paperwork that previously had been handled by an evergrowing army of clerks. In June, 1966, this Electronic Systems Center also enabled the Exchange to produce for the first time a half-hourly index of the prices of all the common stocks listed on the Big Board, the broadest stock market indicator yet compiled.

The heart of the Exchange's operations remains, of course, the trading floor. Orders reach the floor from 2,000 private telephone and teletype wires from the more than 3,700 offices maintained by member firms throughout the United States and abroad. The orders are relayed by telephone clerks to floor brokers, who take them to the place on the floor, called a trading post, assigned for trading in each particular stock. (Bonds are traded in a separate room by different brokers.)

At one of the eighteen trading posts the floor broker with an order to buy or sell joins "the crowd," which consists of other brokers who also have orders to buy or sell the same stock. Bids and offers are made aloud (the rules require them to be announced in a voice loud enough to be heard by every one in the immediate vicinity) and the highest bid and lowest offer have priority over all the others.

When a trade is made, the buying and selling brokers make note of each other's firm name, the number of shares and the price. No written contracts are exchanged between parties to the trade on the floor. Each broker then reports the trade to his own telephone clerk, who relays the information back to the home office.

At the trading post the auction in each stock is conducted by an Exchange member called a "specialist." Because the market in the stock revolves around him, the specialist is the key element in the entire Exchange operation. He is charged with maintaining a "fair and orderly market" in the stocks under his supervision. In discharging this responsibility, he acts in two different capacities—as broker and as dealer.

As a broker, the specialist executes orders for other brokers. For example, a client may give his broker an order to sell 100 shares of ABC Corp. at a price one point higher than the current price. Since the firm's floor partner must execute orders for many, if not all, of his firm's customers, he cannot wait in the trading crowd to see whether the price of ABC Corp. will rise to the specified level. So he gives the order to the specialist, who enters it in his book. Since the specialist is permanently stationed at his post, and since he does not do any business directly with the public, he will be able to execute the order when and if the stock reaches the specified level. For this service, he receives a part of the commission. Many orders are written "at the market," which means the best price available at the time the order reaches the floor. In those cases, or when the specified limit is very close to the current market, the floor broker executes the order himself, but he still must do it at the specialist's post.

In his function as a dealer, the specialist buys and sells stock for his own or his firm's account, absorbing stock in sell-offs and supplying shares when buying picks up. He is required by Exchange rules to make 70% of his trades for stabilizing purposes. In other words, 70% of his trades must be against the market, that is, buying when the price of a stock is going down and selling when it is going up. He is not expected to prevent fluctuations in a stock but only to see to it that *stocks do not fluctuate abnormally in relation to the amount of buying and selling.* In his trading, the specialist takes the same risks as any other broker, except for the fact that, since he has a record of orders from other brokers, he has a better picture of the buying and selling interest in his stocks than anyone else. After a trade is made, the selling broker must see to it that an Exchange reporter—reporters are stationed around each of the 18 trading posts on the floor —notes the number of shares, the ticker symbol of the stock and the price. The reporter then marks the information on a card and drops it into an optical scanning machine, which electronically "reads" the information and feeds it into a central computer, whence it is flashed to the Exchange's worldwide ticker system. The current ticker, installed in 1964, can print up to 900 characters a minute and is able to keep up with the pace of trading on the floor, except during extraordinarily active periods. Under normal conditions, it takes less than a minute from the time of execution for a trade to be printed on the ticker tape.

If the floor broker is especially busy, he can call for a page to pick up orders from his telephone clerk, deliver reports to the clerk for transmission back to his office, or do other errands. The rules of the Exchange state that no member may make a trade unless he has a written order in his possession, so the floor brokers (or the pages) are constantly going back and forth to the telephone clerks.

When a telephone clerk wants his floor broker to come to the telephone booth, he can call him by posting his number on the large annunciator boards at either end of the trading floor. The annunciator boards are operated by switches at each telephone booth. If the clerk is in a hurry, he flips the switch back and forth, making the number flap on the board to attract the broker's attention. Only Exchange members have full run of the trading floor. Telephone clerks, reporters, pages and clerks all must stay within prescribed areas unless they are sent on errands by a member. Visitors to the floor must always be in the company of a member or an Exchange official.

The only other person permanently located at the trading post, aside from the specialist and his clerks, is the odd-lot dealer. Stocks normally trade in the regular auction market in units of 100 shares, called "round lots." Any order for 1 to 99 shares is handled by the odd-lot dealer, who buys round lots and breaks them up for odd-lot buyers. The odd-lot dealer keeps track of all trades in the stocks at his post and buys and sells stock based on the prices of round-lot trades. Unlike the specialist, who may or may not take a part in a trade, the odd-lot dealer must be involved in every odd-lot transaction. For his service, he makes a charge of 12½ cents per share for stock selling under $55 and 25 cents per share for stock selling at $55 or higher. Approximately 99% of the odd-lot trading on the New York Stock Exchange is done by two firms, which date back to one founding firm started in the late nineteenth century.

Another class of member is the registered trader, who trades in stocks on the floor for an account in which he has an interest. Many of the registered traders also act in the capacity of specialists, commission brokers for their firms, or "two-dollar brokers." The floor trading rules bar a registered trader from effecting a transaction for an account in which he has an interest and handling a public order in the same stock on the same trading day. As a result of the SEC's Special Study of Securities Markets in 1963, the requirements for permission to trade on the floor for one's own account have been sharply increased and the number of registered traders—formerly called floor traders—has been drastically reduced. Registered traders are free to roam the floor and—within the guidelines of Exchange rules—to trade in any stocks they choose. Among the rule limitations applicable, no more than three traders may be active in any stock at one time; they must have initial working capital of $250,000 (and a minimum of $175,000 at all times); they must pass a test on floor trading rules; and they must make at least 75% of their trades in a cushioning manner against the trend of the market.

Some brokers work for small member firms which do not generate enough business to keep them busy all day. Others are not affiliated with any firm, but help out other brokers when the market is busy. These Exchange members, called "two-dollar brokers," execute orders for member firms and receive a portion of the commission.

The entire floor operation at the Exchange is supervised by 59 officials, who may be either Exchange governors, members of the Exchange or staff members. The floor officials interpret the rules, settle disputes and oversee the activities on the floor.

The Exchange itself is run by a Board of Governors elected by the membership. The board has 33 members, including the Exchange President and three members of the public. All policy decisions must be originated or approved by the board, which meets regularly after the close of the market on Thursdays.

Projections of the growth in Exchange trading in the decade ahead suggest that it could well equal or exceed the tremendous rate of expansion of the past two decades. Thus it is certain that the future will bring significant new problems and challenges. Two that already loom importantly on the horizon are demands for new patterns of regulation and a virtual revolution in the mechanics of handling transactions.

Regulation will be a two-sided affair—one side resulting from the ever-increasing public participation in the stock market and the greater governmental supervision which this will bring; the other, from the securities industry's own desire to police itself and thus keep outside interference to a minimum. The core of the problem is that the Exchange is required to serve the public interest, yet its members are private businessmen seeking to make a profit from their efforts. The specialist, the central figure in the Big Board operation, epitomizes the problem in the conflict between his public obligation to conduct a fair and orderly market and his private desire to make a profit in his business. The Exchange must somehow resolve this conflict in such a way that the public interest is served while at the same time sufficient financial incentive is provided to keep the specialist in business.

If activity on the Exchange doubles by 1975, as forecast, it will be necessary to continue to upgrade requirements for specialists even further in order to ensure their ability to operate properly under increased stresses. Much of the foundation for this tightened self-supervision already exists in the Big Board's rules.

The Exchange will also have to resolve a number of other ticklish problems with which it has been wrestling for some time. These include the questions of whether member firms should disclose more fully their financial affairs and, if so, how much information should be made public; should they sell stock in their own firms to the public; and should there be changes in the commission structure, in particular a lower rate for large orders.

In the mechanical area, the tremendous increase in trading volume expected in the next decade demands the full automation of day-to-day trading procedures. Many tests are currently under way at the Exchange aimed at eliminating or at least further automating the vast piles of paperwork required for securities transactions. Already computers are to a large extent handling such areas as record-keeping, dissemination of trading information, and surveillance procedures. Odd-lot dealers, who presently employ armies of clerks to transact their detail-laden business, are experimenting in cooperation with the Exchange with methods to turn over much of their work to machines.

One of the more controversial issues stems from a recommendation made in 1963 by the SEC's Special Study of Securities Markets, which suggested that some of the functions of the specialist could be taken over by computer. This step, the study suggested, would eliminate the human factor and allow for speedier and possibly more accurate execution of orders. Both the Exchange and the specialists have strongly opposed such a change. However, should the Big Board's own projection of a doubling in daily share volume by 1975 prove correct, some type of automated assistance to specialists and others involved in floor operations would become a necessity.

Any appraisal of the future of the New York Stock Exchange must also focus on the SEC. As we have seen, the establishment of the Commission by the Securities Exchange Act of 1934 was bitterly opposed by most of the brokerage community. Brokers, fearful of government encroachment, direly predicted that "grass will grow in Wall Street." Today most brokers admit that the high degree of public acceptance enjoyed by the securities industry is in part due to confidence engendered by the surveillance of the SEC, which in turn has spurred self-regulation and self-policing on the part of the industry. Even so, most of the major steps taken by the Commission in recent years have met with varying degrees of resistance. The conflict stems basically from the Wall Streeter's desire to run his own business and the Commission's obligation to see that that business is run without damage to the public interest. But many in Wall Street complain that the spreading encroachment of SEC activities has exceeded the growth of both the securities industry and Big Government in general. It is certain that the Commission's reaching for additional authority, and the Exchange's ability to negotiate compromises and to live with new controls, will strongly influence the Big Board's future development. It is equally certain that the New York Stock Exchange will continue to play a central role in the American economy as the nation's leading securities market. Indeed, the Big Board is without question the world's leading securities market—the largest, the most active and by far the best organized.

2

Wall Street's "Knowledge Industry"

By Louis Stone

Full disclosure of financial information in connection with the sale of corporate securities is now the accepted rule in Wall Street, owing partly to government regulation, partly to Stock Exchange requirements, and partly to the liabilities that are inherent in the common-law rules of equity. 'Twas not always thus. Indeed until the early 1900s, financial information of any kind was hard to come by. The prevailing attitude was that a public corporation was in fact a private club, with no obligation except to its own stockholders.

Today's giant financial publishing industry has achieved most of its growth in the past 30 years, but its birth dates back to 1860, when Henry Varnum Poor started publishing the *History of the Railroads and the Canals of the United States*, later known as *Poor's Manual*. This appeared annually, and was followed by *Poor's Directory of American Officials* (1886) and *Poor's Handbook of Investment Securities* (1890). Poor's manuals and other financial services were absorbed in 1961 by Standard Statistics, which—along with Moody's *Manuals*, inaugurated in 1900—had become the third major publisher of financial statistics. Originally started

Louis Stone, the Economist of Hayden Stone, Inc., is the author of his firm's *Monthly Letter*.

in 1906 by Luther Lee Blake as a card service, the present Standard & Poor's—which became a subsidiary of McGraw-Hill, Inc., in 1966—is by far the largest financial publisher in the world, employing about 800 people and billing about $27 million a year in statistical and investment services. A brief description of Standard & Poor's is perhaps the best introduction to the nature of today's highly developed corporate reporting system.

At the basic statistical level, corporate news does not come from the digging of some inquiring reporter; it is presented by the corporations themselves in the form of official releases to the news agencies and reports to stockholders, to the stock exchanges, to the Securities and Exchange Commission, and to various other federal and state agencies. Standard & Poor's basic function is to collect all of this corporate news and present it to subscribers in convenient and up-to-date form. Its *Corporation Records* service is a six-volume loose-leaf alphabetical compendium containing fairly complete data on nearly 7,000 publicly owned companies; current news and revisions of basic data are accumulated in an additional loose-leaf section every two months. Supplementing this is a *Daily News* loose-leaf section, summarizing all news subsequent to the basic *Records,* with the daily issues indexed cumulatively twice a week. The professional researcher, of course, must often go back to original sources, but for most purposes Standard's *Corporation Records* are an adequate authoritative reference.

Second most important of Standard & Poor's publications are the single-sheet, loose-leaf *Stock Reports*, which provide ready summaries of the basic data on about 4,500 issues, listed and unlisted, with a brief appraisal in the case of listed issues. Supplementing these basic publications are a wide variety of other publications and services, some of them purely factual, such as *Dividend Records* and the *Called Bond Record,* some of them advisory, such as *The Outlook,* which comments weekly on the economy and the stock market and on the prospects for particular stocks. The widely used *Indus-*

try Surveys present basic data on particular industries, with valuable comparative figures on leading issues in the industry, which are brought up to date periodically. And in the technical field, Standard & Poor's puts out the *Trendline* "Daily Basis Stock Charts," which chart the market action and volume of about 600 listed stocks, with 200-day moving averages and summarized per-share earnings statistics. Standard & Poor's issues about a dozen other publications, ranging from the daily *Facts and Forecasts* to the bimonthly *Municipal Bond Selector,* a comprehensive tabulation of U.S. and Canadian municipal issues, with pertinent statistical data and the all-important bond ratings, which compete with Moody's ratings for institutional acceptance.

Standard & Poor's has also moved into a more sophisticated area of financial intelligence with its computerized tapes and cards that contain basic long-term data on over 1,000 leading companies. This new "Compustat" service, together with a computerized pricing service for updating portfolio values, is expected to find increasing acceptance among institutions, particularly since the growing mass of corporate data is becoming more and more unmanageable. Clearly, we have come a long way from the time when corporate figures were the exclusive preserve of the "insiders."

Although Standard & Poor's is by far the largest concern of its kind, it has competitors, large and small, including the well-known Moody's Investors Service, originally started in 1900 by John Moody and now owned by Dun & Bradstreet. Moody's *Manuals* are issued annually in five volumes (supplemented twice a week) containing very comprehensive basic data. The *Manuals* are broken down into five categories: industrials, public utilities, railroads and other transportation companies, banks and financial institutions, and municipal and government issues. In addition, Moody's publishes weekly stock and bond surveys and a variety of advisory and investment services. Moody's bond ratings, both for corporates and for municipals, are generally accorded the highest acceptance by professional and institutional bond buyers.

Moody's parent company, Dun & Bradstreet, originally established in 1841, is another big repository of business statistics. Geared largely to credit information, it covers some three million ratable business concerns.

Next in importance to Standard & Poor's and Moody's as a tool for security analysts, portfolio managers and serious investors is *The Wall Street Journal,* published daily by Dow, Jones & Co., Inc., now publicly owned but still controlled by the heirs of Clarence W. Barron, a Boston financial publisher who bought Dow-Jones in 1902. As a result of the broad concept of news coverage introduced by the present management over the past twenty years, *The Wall Street Journal* now enjoys the second largest *daily* circulation in the United States—over 1 million, a figure surpassed only by the New York *Daily News. The Wall Street Journal* is a "must" for professionals in the securities industry because it is often an original source of business news as well as an excellent compiler of background material in its feature articles.

The single most important source of spot news for the financial community is the Dow-Jones news ticker—generally referred to as "the broad tape"—which is installed in brokerage houses, banks, clubs, newspapers and broadcasting stations all over the country. The commanding position long enjoyed by the Dow-Jones news ticker has helped to make the Dow-Jones Averages—Industrial, Rail and Utility—by far the best known of the indices used to measure the movements of the stock market.

Despite the confusion that surrounds the Averages, there is actually nothing particularly complicated or mysterious about them. The Dow-Jones Industrial Average, for example, is a simple, unweighted, arithmetical average of the prices of 30 leading industrial stocks, all big and all representative of their particular industries. To be sure, their collective action on a given day is not always representative of the total market, since the 30 stocks do not embrace a number of major industries—for example, drugs, office equipment, banks and insurance, and electronics, as well as numerous other groups that are periodically in the limelight. However, the total value of the 30 components of the Industrial Average accounts for about 30% of the aggregate value of all common stocks listed on the New York Stock Exchange.

Part of the confusion about the Dow-Jones Industrial Average stems from its high level, which has ranged since 1962 from 525 to 995, whereas the actual average price of the 30 stocks has ranged from about 53 to about 75. This seeming discrepancy is due wholly to the stock splits and stock dividends that have tended to mar the consistency of the Average over the past 60 years. Obviously, an adjustment has to be made each time a stock splits; otherwise, the Average would go down because of the split rather than an actual decline in stock prices. To prevent this, the divisor has been periodically reduced from its original level of 30; it was 2.163 at the end of 1967, and it will contine to be adjusted downward as further splits occur. This procedure is perfectly correct arithmetically, but it is not readily understood, either by the investing public or by Wall Street's sales personnel, most of whom are not too sharp on mathematical theory.

The New York Times's 25-stock Industrial Average includes 18 of the 30 stocks in the Dow-Jones Industrial Average, but instead of adjusting the divisor for splits, the Times multiplies the split stock by the split component, which is correct but cumbersome. The Standard & Poor's 500-stock Average is more representative of the general market than the Dow-Jones, particularly because each stock is weighted for the number of shares outstanding, a procedure which also eliminates the problem of splits. In spite of these differences, all three Averages have in actual fact tended to conform rather consistently over a period of time. Whatever their shortcomings, the Dow-Jones Averages will continue to be the dominant indices, largely because of their exclusive use on the ubiquitous "broad tape."

Aside from the basic statistical and news services described above, there are a great number of financial publications, some of which are required reading for professionals. Foremost of these is *Barron's,* a weekly with a national circulation in the neighborhood of 210,000. Published by Dow-Jones, *Barron's* offers a highly respected combination of factal news, comment and opinion—on the economy, on particular industries, and on individual companies. Also important to the security analyst is *The Commercial & Financial Chronicle,* established in 1839 and now published weekly in two sections, one statistical, the second editorial. The second section (circulation about 10,000) specializes in reprinting fully the texts of important speeches and articles dealing with business and finance.

Forbes (bimonthly: circulation 445,000) was established in 1917 and is now going stronger than ever under the lively direction of Malcolm Forbes. A magazine of business reportage, comment and opinion, it publishes profiles of corporate personalities and of companies; annual surveys of industry prospects, company performance and mutual fund performance; and stock market commentaries by several leading Wall Street analysts.

The *Financial Analysts Journal* (bimonthly: circulation about 16,000) is the official publication of the Financial Analysts Society. Edited and written by professionals for a strictly professional audience, it is a "high-brow" journal which seeks to advance the art of security analysis by publishing original work and providing a forum for scholarly controversy.

United States Investor (weekly: circulation 17,000), long respected for its analytical treatment of financial topics, has high-level readership among institutional investors and professional trustees.

The Institutional Investor (monthly: circulation about 18,000) was founded in March, 1967, with the novel concept that a highbrow financial magazine should be visually attractive and readable. Lavishly produced and elaborately illustrated, *The Institutional Investor* is addressed to institutional portfolio managers and investment officers. It is not available to the general public, but persons employed full time in the investment business may subscribe to it.

It is, of course, impossible to read systematically all of the regular financial periodicals. The best that any serious student can do is to skip more or less lightly from one source to another in order to be aware of what's going on in opinion-making circles and, more importantly, in the hope of finding "leads" for serious study. In this connection, it should be realized that the U.S. government is the greatest data-collector in history. It spends about $150 million a year for all kinds of economic data—some of them nonsense, some of them mere guesswork, some of them exceedingly valuable to specialists in one field or another—and it turns out some 4,500 daily, weekly, monthly and annual reports containing information about every subject known to economic man. Detailed lists of government publications, whose multiplicity is truly outstanding, are available from the U.S. Superintendent of Documents. A somewhat less overwhelming source of information is the *Monthly Bulletin* of the Federal Reserve Board, which presents the Board's own figures on money, banking, and industrial production, along with selected statistics from the Commerce Department and monetary data from The Treasury Department. For the economist who is primarily concerned with the business cycle, the Commerce Department's monthly *Business Cycle Developments* is an invaluable working tool; and for students of employment and unemployment, the Department of Labor's monthly *Report on the Labor Force* is a basic statistical compilation which also carries useful articles on current trends.

Perhaps the most interesting and certainly the most readable continuing commentaries on the economic questions of the day are presented in publications of the three leading New York City banks—the First National City Bank's *Monthly Economic Letter*, the Chase Manhattan Bank's bimonthly *Business in Brief*, and the Morgan-Guaranty's monthly *Survey*. While there are a considerable number of well-prepared bank letters all over the country—notable among them are those offered by the regional Federal Reserve Banks—the three New York City bank letters are of special importance in that they command a broad audience and represent the combined efforts of the large economic staffs of these three mammoth institutions. The First National City Bank *Monthly Economic Letter,* for instance, which dates back to 1904, has a circulation of about 350,000 and is widely read in high and medium-high financial circles. Continued study of the articles presented in these bank letters could prove equivalent to a graduate course in economics and one with an unusually practical application to the present-day economic scene. The banks, unfortunately, do not award degrees.

There are more than a dozen large Wall Street brokerage firms, known in the trade as "wire houses" because of their network of branch offices extending around the country, that spend $300,000 a year and up on their research departments. Although a considerable number of junior analysts devote much of their time to servicing the huge flow of routine inquiries from Registered Representatives and clients around the circuit, a good deal of valuable research work is done by the senior analysts, many of whom get $25,000- to $30,000-a-year salaries for their combination of specialized knowledge, experience, insight and flair. Because of the present-day size of institutional portfolios, a million-dollar shift from one stock to another is a fairly common occurrence, with the resultant brokerage commissions averaging about $18,000 on each such trade. Thus research costs are still low in relation to the profit potential, and the high pay-off explains the volume of serious research material that comes out of Wall Street. In fact, it is quite impossible for any analyst or any investor to keep up with the flood of research studies that are available, free-for-nothing, to clients and prospective clients. Most of this material is now conveniently assembled in a 40- to 50-page, well-indexed publication, the *Wall Street Transcript,* published twice a month at a cost to subscribers of $180 a year. Many people poke fun at Wall Street's so-called guessing game and consider the whole business of research reports and market letters just a "come-on" aimed at the sucker public. Nothing could be further from the truth in the present-day environment. Readers capable of winnowing out the grain from the chaff can get from *The Wall Street Transcript* a valuable insight into industry developments and into the record of and prospects for particular stocks. The old days when Wall Street research was largely consigned to low-paid statistical hacks are long since gone. The opinions of today's leading industry specialists are not just market comment; they often are the stuff that *makes* markets. A well-researched buy or sell recommendation from one of the big brokerage houses, or from a firm noted for its institutional research, may well influence the price of a particular stock for months to come. In addition to brokerage house research reports, the *Transcript* also publishes the full text of speeches made by corporate officials to meetings of security analysts. These texts often contain new and authoritative information about company developments and prospects.

For the very reason that so much brokerage house material can be had for the asking, many people who distrust what is free prefer to be guided by one or more of the "advisory services" that are extensively advertised in the daily press. There are all kinds of such services, some completely irresponsible, some very worthwhile. *United Business Service,* for example, or *Babson's Reports,* incorporate excellent background information in their well-researched recommendations. *Value Line* offers a fairly comprehensive loose-leaf statistical service and attempts to project actual values for some years ahead. *Capital Gains Research Bureau* focuses on particular stocks that have become the object of buying or selling pressure from institutional portfolios. *Argus Research* has a long record of conscientious research, mainly oriented toward quality stocks or at least well-established issues. Its service also includes a searching and outspoken analysis of economic and monetary trends and other factors that could influence the stock market. *Equity Research* specializes in trying to find undervalued issues of good quality and makes forthright recommendations.

In addition, there are a host of services that offer forecasts, sometimes sensational, on the future of business and the market. Some of the better known are the *Dines Letter, George Lindsay's Opinions,* the *Drew Odd-Lot Studies,* the *Granville Market Letter,* the *Magee Service, Dow Theory Forecasts,* the *Indicator Digest, Forbes' Investors' Advisory Institute* and Leo Cherne's *Research Institute of America.*

The total amount of money spent on all these services, and on others less well known, must be tremendous, and nobody can say whether it is well spent or not. The right advice is worth a fortune on Wall Street, but there is no accepted measure of what is right and what is wrong. If you follow a recommendation to buy a stock that goes down from 20 to 15 and then gradually goes up to 40, who was right and who was wrong? Most of the people who subscribe to the advertised services want "instant money"; even when a recommendation specifies long-term investment they are disappointed if the particular issue does not start rising immediately.

The foregoing discussion of some of the multitude of services available to the inquiring investor has not included what is probably the most important of all—professional investment counsel. There are in this country about 50,000 investors with capital resources of $1 million and up. Many of these substantial investors are people who are too busy, or who lack the necessary knowledge, to plan and supervise their investments—for example, executives running a business, professional men, or hapless widows. And some of them feel that an experienced investment counselor, working on a fee basis, will devote more attention to their portfolio and manage it with greater objectivity than a stock-broker working on a commission basis and handling a large number of clients. There is obviously no way of comparing the performance of investment counselors and that of stockbrokers, and anyhow the over-all performance is irrelevant because each investor is dealing with an individual. All that can be said is that in both fields there are conscientious and astute men who do well for their clients and others who perform poorly. In any event, the investment counseling profession fills an important need on the part of wealthy investors who can afford to pay for continuing disinterested advice (on top of the brokerage charges that accrue on all transactions). These advisory fees are generally set at about ½% a year of the principal amount involved, with a customary minimum of $500 a year. This means, as a practical matter, that about $100,000 is the starting point for this kind of service. There are numerous variations, of course, both in the minimum amounts of principal accepted and in the rates of charge; some counseling firms will not accept less than $500,000 and their minimum fee is $5,000. It is clear that the profession as a whole has thus far been the rich man's helper, not the poor man's, though now there is increasing interest in providing advisory service to smaller accounts. Many investors are reluctant to pay out ½% of the principal as a fee, particularly when stocks yield less than 4%, but the more discerning of the rich realize that this is a small price to pay for able professional counsel in a period of increasingly rapid change. Moreover, the tremendous build-up of inherited wealth is creating an increasing fun of "idiot money" in the hands of heirs, many of whom have not the slightest notion of how to increase or even conserve the loot that their grandfathers accumulated. Such people may be saving themselves from serious loss when they place their fortune in the hands of a top-notch investment counselor.

The quality of the counsel given over a period of time is, of course, the determining factor in assessing the merits of investment counseling as a profession. The Investment Counsel Association of America has rigorous requirements for membership; its 1966–67 directory lists only 48 member firms out of a total of several thousand individuals and organizations that offer their services to the investing public for a fee. Among the better-known member firms with more or less national coverage that specialize *primarily* in straight investment counsel work (although they may have related functions such as mutual fund management) are the following: E. W. Axe & Co.; David L. Babson & Co.; Brundage Story & Rose; Eaton & Howard, Inc.; Lionel D. Edie & Co.; Loomis Sayles & Co.; Naess & Thomas; T. Rowe Price & Associates; Scudder Stevens & Clark; Stein Roe & Farnham; Templeton Dobrow & Vance; Trainer, Wortham & Co.; Van Cleef, Jordan & Wood.

The Investment Counsel Association's standards do not apply to the profession as a whole, which is regulated by the Investment Advisers Act of 1940. Any investment adviser with 15 clients or more who solicits accounts from the public must register under the Act with the Securities and Exchange Commission, supplying fairly complete information as to his education and business background, and stating the basis of his intended compensation. He may not share in his client's projected profits, and he may not assign or transfer his contract to others without the client's consent. Moreover, he must agree to maintain detailed records, available to the Commission upon request. On the whole, the federal government's regulation has not been too restrictive or heavy handed, but the mere existence of the Act and the Commission has helped to keep outright fraud from developing to any significant extent.

Supplementing the work of the larger investment counsel organizations are a large number of smaller firms, some of which provide highly specialized service to a select group of wealthy clients. Meyer Handelman & Co., for example, is a relatively small aggregation of experts whose services include investment counsel, tax work, insurance advice, and even the handling of business and personal affairs, right down to the hiring and payment of service personnel. At the other end of the investment advisory spectrum are the big statistical services, like Standard & Poor's and Moody's, which have literally billions of dollars of clients' funds on which they provide continuing counsel, in some cases on an impersonal basis, in other cases working closely with the client.

By far the largest volume of advisory service is, of course, provided by the nation's banks, mostly on a formal fee basis, but sometimes on the basis of more flexible arrangements. The U.S. Trust Co. in New York City, for example, is a leading trust and counseling concern, reputed to be handling something like $10 billion in investment funds, although its deposit accounts total only $250 million. Other banks such as the Bankers Trust have long specialized in the handling of trust funds and, in recent years, of pension funds, the total of which has grown to tremendous proportions and is still growing at a rate which makes the bank-administered funds the largest single influence in the security markets today. For the individual investor, one of the best starting points for an inquiry into the professional management of his money is probably a chat with the trust officer of one of the larger banks.

In the period extending from 1950 through November of 1967, the Dow Industrial Average rose from 200 to 876, or more than four-fold. Very few speculative or investment accounts can show a comparable percentage appreciation over the same period. The Dow Average is a fair measure of the general market, and the reasons for individuals' failure to match its performance are many, but the most common is the search for fast gains through in-and-out trading, which generally results in missing a large part of a major upmove in a stock. Short-term trading can be very profitable from time to time, and it accounts for a good part of the tremendous daily activity on the stock exchanges, but it cannot compete with the gains that have accrued to the patient investor who has the fortitude to sit through occasional 100- or ever 200-point declines in the general market. At any rate, this had been true in the past. There is, of course, no guarantee that it will be true in the future.

In sum, it appears that there is no such thing as an easy investment policy of sitting back and watching your money show constant growth in the nation's top equities. The only way of achieving long-term success is to follow closely the major trends in the economy and the stock market and the fortunes of the companies in which you own stock, and to keep searching, all the while, for situations with strong growth prospects. This is the reason why Wall Street's "Knowledge Industry" is of crucial importance to all serious investors.

3

Inside the Research Department

By Walter Maynard

Basically the duties of the research department of a Wall Street firm are not unlike those of Intelligence in a military organization. In both cases, they consist in collecting information from all available sources, evaluating it and, it is hoped, reaching a correct conclusion with respect to future capabilities and performance. The information-gathering of Wall Street is directed toward the whole of our corporate and economic activity.

The first problem in assembling a Wall Street research organization is that of personnel. The director of the operation must be mature, experienced, possessed of a broad range of knowledge of economics, banking and industry. He must also be imaginative, a good editor, and able to write about complex subjects simply and persuasively.

Of these qualities, imagination deserves especial emphasis. The most valuable part of the output of a research department is not its statistical compilations and recapitulations of the record, but its appraisals of the future, that is, its forecasts. And a lively but disciplined imagination is an essential ingredient in the mental makeup of a successful research director, and in senior analysts as well.

In addition, the director of a research department must

Walter Maynard is Vice Chairman of Shearson, Hammill & Co., Inc.

possess a talent for recruiting and training able analytical personnel. He therefore must not only have an attractive personality, but must be able to instill in the analysts on his staff the needed qualities of imagination and creativity.

A typical Wall Street research department will have, in addition to the director, a number of senior analysts who are industry specialists. Some firms have only a handful of senior analysts, each of whom tries to cover several industries. The larger brokerage houses—and also smaller ones which specialize in high-quality research—may have upwards of 15 senior research men, some of whom may be partners. These analysts are generally graduates of business schools; they must have inquiring and persistent habits of mind; and they should have the kind of personality that makes them welcome visitors in corporate offices. Nowadays these men to a certain extent perform double duty, in that they are not only responsible for evaluating securities in the area of their specialty, but are also required to call upon important institutional clients—mutual funds, insurance companies, pension funds, banks—in a sales capacity. Institutions are no longer content to receive all of their information and advice via reports or through a salesman's account of an analyst's figures and opinions. They insist on in-depth interviews with the men on the analytical firing line.

A senior analyst must have pursued his specialty long enough to have acquired a thorough knowledge of its operations and economics: size of the market and traditional growth rate; prevailing profit margins in good years and bad; average return on invested capital; characteristic dividend payout; prospective growth in the years ahead; and many other matters. He must also be alert to the implications for his industry of changes in the political situation and the regulatory environment. Most importantly, he must have earned the confidence of a wide range of persons in the industry or industries in which he specializes. He achieves this relationship by visits to corporate executives in their offices, by attendance at industry conventions, by participating in group industry tours, and the like. A close personal relationship of this kind is desirable for two reasons. First, it is the soundest method of gaining insight into the qualities of management, which, after all, are a force even more important than economics in the success or failure of businesses. Second, it lays the basis for getting prompt information via telephone concerning such developments as price changes, rumored mergers and acquisitions, new contracts and personnel changes, which can have an important effect on day-to-day security price movements.

The senior analyst usually has a junior analyst as an assistant. This assistant maintains industry data in tabular form; he keeps up-to-date comparative information of all kinds on companies within the industry; he answers routine questions from Registered Representatives and stands in for the senior analyst while the latter is away from his office visiting corporations or clients. The junior analyst may also be charged with the responsibility for following the smaller and less important companies in an industry.

In addition to the analytical staff, many Wall Street research departments also employ a professional economist, who, among other things, makes over-all forecasts of the probable course of the economy and seeks to anticipate how prospective economic changes will affect specific industries. Many research departments also employ outside economic consultants, who not only assist in forecasting but may also perform specialized tasks such as econometric studies. In addition, some firms retain outside technical consultants to advise them in such areas as drugs, electronics, and antitrust matters.

Large research departments often include an editor, who rewrites or condenses analysts' stories and assembles research material for publication. They also usually have a "wire desk," which answers questions submitted by wire from the firm's branch offices. Finally, brokerage houses which deal with the public on a large scale have to maintain a sizable portfolio section, which reviews the portfolios of clients or prospective clients (submitted to the research department by

Registered Representatives) and makes buy, sell or hold recommendations.

A properly equipped research department should have an extensive library. In addition to filing annual reports, manuals, publicity handouts, government publications, and the like, the library staff also answers routine questions about dividend declaration dates, stock splits, and so on.

A tool coming into increasing use in research departments is the computer. Generally speaking, the computer has so far achieved its greatest usefulness as a compiler of detailed information in comparative form—a calculator of such statistics as returns on equity and invested capital and of data of a routine nature, which would occupy a great deal of the analyst's time. Some firms and advisory services have programed computers to make forecasts of future price action. Most of the programs used so far have been based on price changes and trading volume. That is to say, the "input" consists of data used by the technical analyst. However, a few firms have also harnessed the computer to fundamental analysis. One of the most complex methods in use employs the computer to ascertain—essentially on the basis of the historical record and projections of anticipated earnings growth—the so-called present value of securities. A comparison of this "present value" with the current market price theoretically indicates whether the stock is overpriced, correctly priced or undervalued.

It cannot be said as yet that these programs have been outstandingly successful. In my view, it is unlikely that the computer will displace the informed judgment of the trained analyst, partly because of the crucial problem, alluded to earlier, of evaluating the personal qualities of the management team.

The research departments of the larger firms are, in effect, in the publishing business and they put out several kinds of publications. To begin with there are so-called institutional reports—detailed studies of industries or individual companies, sometimes running to 50 or more pages, containing much statistical and background material, and usually but not invariably ending with an optimistic forecast concerning the subject of the story. Much of the same material generally appears in abbreviated form—reports of one to six pages—for distribution to individual clients. The larger firms also keep their Registered Representatives posted, via wires or "flashes," on new developments concerning companies whose securities have been recommended; the Registered Representative is supposed to relay this information to clients who hold, or have expressed an interest in, the securities in question. The research department of a very large brokerage firm may produce as many as 20 to 30 separate documents of varied length and detail in a single day.

A great many firms issue monthly publications for general distribution to clients. These include lists of recommended securities, market "letters," and sometimes elaborate glossy-paper brochures with illustrations and multicolored covers.

An account of a successful research operation will help to illustrate how a research department functions. The subject of this operation is the New York Central Railroad. New York Central (ticker symbol CN) had exhibited a spectacular flash of earning power in 1955 and 1956 ($8.03 and $6.02 per share respectively), but thereafter earnings declined through 1961, when a net loss of $1.92 per share was reported. This disappearance of earnings power, and the failure to declare a dividend in 1961, caused the stock to drop irregularly from its 1955 high of about $50 per share to a low of $11 in mid-1962. Nevertheless, a number of favorable changes were beginning to be apparent. A relatively new and competent operating management was beginning to produce visible results, and it seemed possible that in the near future real progress could be made with the problem of feather-bedding, especially via the elimination of firemen on diesel locomotives. At this time, the research director of a large brokerage firm suggested to his senior transportation analyst that a careful study of New York Central might be worth undertaking. A list of questions was drawn up, and a number of significant facts emerged from the answers.

First, the New York Central, as the result of a large cash flow partly generated by sales of unneeded property, was in a strong financial position, and there were no bond maturities within the next ten years that could present a problem. Second, as the result of new methods of traffic control, considerable trackage could be eliminated without impairing services, resulting in substantially reduced costs. Third, demand for utilization of New York Central's real estate in New York and other cities was strong and a substantial increase in revenues from this source could be expected in coming years. Fourth, the New York Central was making good progress in containerization of freight, a rapidly growing segment of the business. Moreover, at about this time the prospect of a merger between the Pennsylvania Railroad and the New York Central, while still distant, seemed to be getting somewhat more probable, and a basis for the merger which would allocate to New York Central 1.3 shares of the new company's stock for each share held, as compared with one share for Pennsylvania, had been established.

With this background, the firm in question, late in 1962, began by issuing a cautiously worded wire which said in part ". . . if, as may be the case, the overall railroad picture is on the threshold of an important change for the better, we feel that this could more dynamically be reflected in New York Central than in Pennsylvania." The recommendation was to buy New York Central at 15.

The research process continued in detail during ensuing months, during which the price of New York Central stock rose slowly. Interviews were held with financial and operating people of the New York Central and Pennsylvania. Numerous visits to Washington were made to discuss merger prospects with the staffs of the Interstate Commerce Commission (ICC) and of the relevant Congressional committees. Estimates were made of operating ratios, capital needs and net profits under varying economic conditions. Early in August, 1963, the firm issued a "Special Institutional Report" discussing in detail all aspects of New York Central's business and predicting that, "If things work out well, it is entirely possible that the next several years could witness a return of earnings to the $5.00–$6.00 level . . . with additional long-term benefits likely to accrue from the proposed merger with Pennsylvania." At this time the price of the stock was about 24. In September, a shorter report was issued for general distribution which contained the statement, "It does not seem too much to expect that within the next several years New York Central's earnings could come . . . to $5.00–$6.00 per share before Federal income taxes." (Earnings in 1965 were, in fact, reported at $6.06 per share, and a dividend of $2.60 per share was paid.)

On June 2, 1964, with Central at 36, the firm's branch offices were informed by wire: "Presumably weakness in New York Central is predicated on . . . the brief filed by the Justice Department seeking to block the merger [with the Pennsylvania]. We feel that this reaction to the attitude of Justice . . . is wholly unwarranted. We would stress that in a situation of this nature the monopoly aspects of the case are entirely within the province of the Interstate Commerce Commission, and that the Justice Department has no official standing. . . . In our opinion the stock . . . should be purchased on this sell-off."

On December 9, with the stock selling at 48, a research wire was sent out forecasting minimum earnings of $4 per share for New York Central in 1964 and adding, "Next year's results could well top the 1964 estimate by at least $1.00." Again, purchase was recommended.

On March 22, 1965, with the stock at 60, another research wire said in part: "Earnings for the full year are still expected to top last year's $4.06 by a good margin, but . . . the stock seems adequately priced on near and intermediate term earnings prospects"—a "sell" recommendation.

This "sell" recommendation was well timed, since in the next several months the market as a whole had a severe setback and the stock dropped to 41. On June 9, at which point New York Central stock had recovered to 47½, a renewed recommendation to buy was made purely on the basis of price. Subsequently, in early 1966, CN rose to a level just short of 90. However, in this instance the firm was slow to react, and it was not until June 22, 1966, with the stock at 77½, that the following wire was issued: "In line with the uncertainties surrounding the economy for next year . . . we are removing CN from the Master List. . . . Although we expect record first half results from New York Central, and full year consolidated earnings of better than $9.00 per share, we believe that fourth quarter results could be disappointing. . . . We also can envision some delay in . . . the merger with Pennsylvania. On the basis of these conclusions, we believe CN is adequately valued at these levels and recommend switching."

This record presents a clearcut example of security analysis at its best. The major factors shaping a basic change in the affairs of a great and widely known corporation were discerned at an early date. Subsequently an intermediate term trading opportunity appeared and was neatly taken advantage of. Finally, an emphatic sale recommendation was made, which enabled all of those who had bought on earlier advices to withdraw with substantial profits. The analyst drew his information in the main from published sources, but he also had sufficiently close personal contacts with the corporation itself and the regulatory authorities, plus a basic understanding of the economics of his industry, to be able to interpret correctly events as they occurred.

4

How the Bears Operate

By Elizabeth M. Fowler

There are literally hundreds of books which tell investors and speculators how to make money on the stock market by buying stocks which, it is hoped, will go up. But there is only a handful of manuals which discuss how to make money on the stock market by picking stocks which one hopes will go down. Yet any material change in the price of a stock—whether it be on the downside or the upside—constitutes an opportunity for profit. Let us exclude, for the moment, tax considerations and brokerage commissions: on this basis, a trader can make ten points on a transaction by buying a stock at 90 and selling it at 100, or by selling a stock short at 100 and buying it back at 90. Short selling is a fairly common procedure on most organized securities (and, for that matter, commodity) exchanges. Yet even *The Wall Street Journal*, which presumably addresses itself to a financially sophisticated audience, feels called upon to offer a parenthetical explanation every time it refers to selling short. So let us begin with a simple definition.

A short sale is a sale of stock one does not own, stock that has been borrowed and must eventually be returned. It is made in the expectation that the stock will go down and that

Elizabeth M. Fowler is a financial writer on *The New York Times*.

one will in due course buy it at a lower price. The mechanics of the transaction are in essence as follows: the short seller's broker "borrows" the stock (either from one of his customers who holds it in a margin account or from another broker) and delivers it to the buyer. The proceeds of the short sale pass through the seller's account, and the funds are actually deposited by his broker with the lender. The short seller has to pay dividends on the borrowed stock, as they become due. Sooner or later, he must "cover" the short sale by buying the stock and returning it to the lender. The difference between the sale and purchase prices represents his profit or loss. There are certain stock exchange and federal regulations governing the conditions under which a short sale can be made on a national securities exchange. One of them is that a short sale can be effected only on an "up tick"—that is, at a price higher than that of the preceding transaction (or equal to it if the latest price change in the stock was upward). Short selling is the basic tactic—though by no means the only tactic —in the strategy of the bears.

The folklore of Wall Street reminds us that many famous bears have died in bankruptcy. Daniel Drew usually heads the list (and we might add, parenthetically, that his good friend Jay Gould partly tricked him into his downfall). Jacob Little is another bear cited as ending his days in poverty. And the late Bernard Baruch has been widely quoted as saying, "Bears don't live on Park Avenue." (Ironically, Mr. Baruch made a fortune at thirty-one by taking a bear position in a famous "growth stock" of the early 1900s—Amalgamated Copper. But more of that later.) In any event, the argument that the bear travels a harder, riskier and lonelier road than the bull certainly has merit, and we propose to examine it before discussing in further detail how to operate as a bear.

Americans, traditionally, have been optimists about the future of the nation's economy and over the past two centuries they have been right. The population has grown steadily; industrial production has surged; gross national product has grown at a better sustained rate than anywhere else in the world. Consequently, stock prices—though subject to periodic setbacks, some of them extremely drastic—have shown an emphatic historic uptrend. History is on the side of the bulls, and for those able and willing to take a long-term view, the overworked slogan, "Don't sell America short," has much to recommend it.

In recent years, the case for the bulls has received fresh support from the more enthusiastic proponents of the so-called New Economics. The argument, in essence, is that the government is now fully committed to management of the economy and to promoting its growth; and further that, through the flexible and sophisticated use of the instruments of fiscal and monetary policy, the economic planners are able to mitigate and correct the fluctuations of the business cycle. Thus the belief has arisen that major depressions may well be a thing of the past. The validity of this thesis cannot be debated here. If it is correct—and time alone will tell—the periodic downturns in the stock market are less likely to attain calamitous dimensions. Should this be so, it would strengthen the familiar argument that in the long run it is easier to increase one's capital by investing in good-quality issues and riding out market declines than to try to profit by declines by selling out and playing the short side of the market.

There are certain special difficulties involved in operating as a bear. For reasons which we will explain presently, short selling calls for close attention to the day-to-day behavior of the market; a keen sense of timing; a good knowledge of company developments; and an exceptional degree of intestinal fortitude.

In the first place, it is a matter of historical record that stocks are moving up more of the time than they are moving down; declines tend to be sharper and shorter-lived than upward movements. Consequently, the bear is more dependent than the bull on timing. The latter, especially if his holdings are of good quality, need not suffer unduly through a moderate market decline. He is reassured by the belief that eventually the market will turn upward, and meanwhile he is collecting his dividends. In contrast, the bear comes under extremely severe pressure if the stocks he has sold short persist in moving counter to his expectations. Not only are his losses mounting but he is also paying out dividends on borrowed stock, and he is faced with the hideous possibility that he has misjudged the trend and will be forced to cover at a tremendous loss.

In this connection, one of the peculiar hazards of short-selling must be mentioned: the short seller faces, theoretically at least, unlimited liability. The investor who buys 100 shares of stock ABC at 30 knows that under no circumstances can he lose more than $3,000; in fact, at worst, it is extremely unlikely that ABC will decline to zero. On the other hand, the bear who has sold ABC short at 30, may see it go up to 70, 90, 120, or even higher. (Most short sellers protect themselves against a runaway on the upside through the use of a stop order—an order to buy the stock if it reaches a specific price.)

To operate successfully as a bear it is essential to be able to think and act counter to crowd psychology—a quality that few people possess. There is not much profit in being pessimistic when pessimism is prevalent; by that time the negative developments or prospects are usually already reflected in stock prices. The successful bear foresees a decline in the market or in the stock of a particular company, and acts accordingly, at a time when there is still plenty of optimism in the air and prices are high; and he must have the self-confidence to maintain a posture which may not be proved right for some time. In short, the bear, by nature, should be a lone-hander, armored by a strong sense of inner direction against the influences which surround him.

We have indicated why bears are generally a small minority—and a somewhat unpopular one—within the investment community, and why their course is a hard one. (We might add that in periods when bearishness is universal, or nearly so, the market is usually close to a bottom, and it is high time to be bullish.) Let us now examine the reverse of the coin and try to show the opportunities that exist for those willing and able to operate on the bear side of the market.

OPPORTUNITIES FOR THE BEAR

The historical record, which was cited earlier as supporting the bulls from the long-term standpoint, also shows that well-timed pessimism can reap large rewards in the stock market. The National Bureau of Economic Research has made a detailed study of depressions and recessions for the period stretching from 1854 to 1954. It found that these 100 years encompassed 24 business cycles. On the average, the economy expanded nearly 30 months in the typical upward cycle, then contracted for nearly 20 months. Generally, a booming economy brought with it a booming stock market, and the ensuing downturn was usually preceded or accompanied by a decline in stock prices. Thus there were at least 24 periods of some duration in the course of a century of robust growth when it paid to be a bear in the stock market. Turning to the more recent past, we find a list of the significant declines which have taken place in the stock market since 1954 (given in Table 1).

Table 1.
Stock Market Declines Since 1957

Year	Decline in Dow-Jones Industrial Average	Length in months	Recovery in months
1957	19% to 419	3	11
1960	17% to 566	9	5
1962	27% to 535	6	15
1965	10% to 840	1	3
1966	26% to 740	8	

Each of these declines offered ample opportunities for profit on the bear side of the market. How then can an investor try to gauge when the market is nearing a peak, when it is time to put into practice the techniques of the bear?

To answer the question in any degree of detail would carry

us far beyond the scope of this chapter, but some guidelines can be suggested. There are three main areas which should be studied for clues as to whether the market is topping out: (1) the behavior of the national economy; (2) the general level of stock prices in relation to prospective earnings and historical valuations; (3) the technical condition of the stock market. Sources of information about these areas are numerous and readily available; they are listed and discussed in Louis Stone's chapter, "Wall Street's 'Knowledge Industry.' "

The stock market is what is known as a "leading indicator"; it usually starts turning downward at least six months before an economic downturn. Consequently the investor seeking to anticipate market peaks must concern himself with how the economy may be behaving six or nine months in the future. He must look for signs that an economic uptrend is entering the final boom stage, which usually precedes the crest of the business cycle. Industry working at or close to maximum capacity; shortages of skilled labor; rising inflationary pressures; insatiable demands for credit—these are just a few of the signs that the economy is overheated and that a cooling-off period lies ahead. All of these conditions were very much in evidence in the early part of 1966, and in the months which followed, the Dow-Jones Industrial Average declined 26%.

The level of stock prices and the technical condition of the market are continuously analyzed and discussed in brokerage house market letters and in the publications of investment advisory services. The brokerage house letters (with exceptions) tend to have a bullish bias. Periodically they say that "caution is in order"; or they recommend maintaining "cash reserves"; or they urge "a high degree of selectivity." They seldom indulge in outright bearishness except when the market has been declining sharply. The investment advisory services, in the aggregate, also have a pronounced leaning toward what they would call "a constructive attitude." Moreover, those which do express extreme bearishness in many cases have a record of having been persistently bearish at times when pessimism proved utterly wrong. To be sure, some brokerage house letters and investment advisory services have given advance warnings of a major market downturn, but such instances are not common, and for a basic reason which has been alluded to earlier. If everyone is warning that the market will go down, it will almost certainly *not* go down, since the pessimism prompting the warnings will already have been reflected in stock prices. The prospective bear should nevertheless carefully study market analyses and commentaries. They will provide him with no end of information, statistics, historical comparisons and other data on the basis of which he can draw his own conclusions; and they will furnish him with indications as to whether prevailing investor sentiment has become overoptimistic. When the facts tell him that the market is probably too high, and the majority of investors are confident that it is going significantly higher, the time has come to start taking bearish action.

We have so far discussed bear operations largely in terms of over-all market declines. But many of those who favor the bear side of the market are much more concerned with the prospects for individual companies than with the general level of stock prices. Even in rising markets, a considerable number of stocks decline for a variety of reasons: a disappointing earnings report; indications that projected earnings for the year may be below original expectations; failure of new contracts or of acquisitions to materialize; introduction of supposedly superior products by competitors; loss of key figures in management; adverse developments in the industry in which the company is operating; major lawsuits or adverse regulatory decisions or investigations by the federal government; indications that new equity financing may be on the horizon; and so on. The most dynamic of growth stocks and the bluest of blue chips sometimes suffer sharp dips in the face of such developments; and of course general weakness in the market sharply accentuates the decline. Even AT&T—the widow's friend, the epitome of a conservative investment—experienced two major declines in the five-year period

1962–67. The first (a drop of nearly 28%) was attributable to the market collapse of 1962. But the second—which carried the stock down to 49¾ in 1966, a drop of 32% from the 1965 high of 70½—was in part due to a proposed government investigation and in part to rising interest rates, which diminished the stock's attraction on a yield basis and prompted massive liquidation by institutions and other investors who held AT&T largely because of its relatively high dividend return.

THE "IDEAL" SHORT SALE

To sell a stock short in a rising or even a sideways market, one should have a good knowledge of the company's affairs and prospects, and possess information of negative developments which are not yet fully in the public domain. Even in such cases, a caveat is in order. If the stock in question is one strongly favored by institutions and sophisticated investors, a moderate decline may conceivably induce strong buying and bring about a quick recovery in price; and the short seller will soon see his profit evaporate or even wind up with a loss.

The ideal candidate for a short sale might be described, in a general way, as follows. The stock appears overvalued on fundamentals and vulnerable from a technical standpoint. An adverse development of some consequence and not yet generally known is in the offing. The stock is volatile. The company is not one of the strongest in its field, and its management is not highly regarded. The issue is not so thin that holders of the stock, when they see that the short position is large and growing—figures of the short interest are published monthly by the New York and American Stock Exchanges—can create a "squeeze" simply by hanging on to their shares. (In such a situation, as the shorts try to cover, they drive the stock up.) Obviously, to find the ideal short sale calls for a good deal of informed research, and even promising short sales are not discovered without considerable effort.

One major coup on the short side of the market was

chronicled by the late Bernard Baruch in his autobiography, *My Own Story*. In the first decade of this century, a group of businessmen launched a company called Amalgamated Copper without putting up a penny of their own money. They acquired Anaconda Copper and some other properties in exchange for a bank check in the amount of $39 million, which, however, was not to be cashed for a certain period. The organizers of Amalgamated then sold $75 million of securities in the new company at $100 a share—with plenty of fanfare—and their creditors were told they could cash the $39 million check. Then the fireworks began. Prestigious names were induced to become directors or sponsors of Amalgamated, whose objective was to become a trust that would control much of the world's copper supply and keep copper prices high. (At that time trusts were in fashion, and the government, though it had made some attempts to break them up, was not yet a formidable adversary.)

Within a few months of the public offering of Amalgamated, the shares had moved up to 130. At this point Bernard Baruch—who had watched the formation of the company, had noted its obvious overcapitalization, and had also come to the conclusion that the current high prices of copper could not be maintained—sold Amalgamated short. When the news got around Wall Street, Mr. Baruch, then thirty-one, was warned by important friends in the financial world not to antagonize "the big fellows." He was also told "how wicked it was to be short of the market and to tear down a constructive enterprise." "All this is nonsense, of course," he observed in his autobiography. "If the Amalgamated organizers had not overcapitalized and then blown the stock up, it would never have risen to such heights or descended to the depths it afterwards did. What was dropping the copper shares was the irresistible force of economic gravitation seeking its proper level." Amalgamated presently cut its dividend from $8 to $6, and in due course the stock dropped to 60. After covering his short position, Mr. Baruch emerged with a profit of $700,000.

OTHER TACTICS

Short selling, as we noted earlier, is not the only weapon in the bear's arsenal. It is simply one way of translating a bearish outlook into action. We will now consider the other three.

1. An investor can sell out his holdings and put the cash into savings accounts or bonds of various kinds, presumably with the idea of reinvesting it when stock prices have declined to lower levels. The motivation may be essentially defensive—to guard against serious loss—but it could also be aggressive. For there are times when the bond markets offer opportunities for handsome profits. When the economy is booming and stock prices are at unusually high levels in a market dominated by speculative activity, the Federal Reserve Board is liable to try to cool things down by raising the discount rate, which is the rate of interest banks must pay when they borrow from the Federal Reserve System. This tends to raise interest rates all along the line; and when interest rates go up, bond prices go down. Thus, with good timing, it is sometimes possible to switch out of stocks when they are still relatively high and reinvest the proceeds in bonds selling at depressed levels. When interest rates are eventually lowered again, bond prices automatically turn upward. The profits obtainable from a successful switch from stocks into government or municipal bonds can be large if leverage is employed. The margin requirements for Treasuries are 5 to 10% and 25% for municipals, as compared with 70% for common stocks (at the beginning of 1968). Thus an investor with $10,000 can buy on margin $200,000 of government bonds (200 bonds). A one point rise in the price of the bond from, say, 98 to 99 ($980 to $990) will result in a profit of $2000 or 20% on his cash commitment.

2. A second bear tactic is selling short "against the box." Many investors are understandably reluctant—partly for tax reasons—to sell stocks they have bought or perhaps inherited at a very much lower price. Or they may be unwilling to sell out because they own shares of the company for which they work. To protect themselves and yet not liquidate their positions (and perhaps pay stiff capital gains taxes), they can sell short "against the box."

Suppose, for example, that an investor owns 100 shares of General Motors, originally purchased at 40 and currently selling at, let us say, 100. He is worried about the market outlook; indeed, he expects a sharp decline in prices. So he asks his broker to sell 100 shares of GM short. If, as he expects, the market falls, dragging GM to 85, he can buy 100 shares and make delivery to cover his short position. He still owns his original 100 shares, and though they are down to $85, he has made a 15 point profit on his short sale (minus the brokerage expenses involved). If, contrary to his judgment, the market moves up, he would have a profit on his original shares, but a loss on his short position. Either way, he has an "insurance policy" fixing his price at the $100 point, minus expenses.

3. A third way of implementing a bearish outlook is through the use of options called "Puts." The buyer of a Put acquires an option contract entitling him to sell (to the "writer" of the option) 100 shares of a given stock at a specified price at any time within a specified period—30 days (rare), 60 days, 90 days, or 6 months and 10 days. The cost of such options is not fixed; it is determined by supply and demand in a competitive market. The buyer of a Put may be charged between 6% and 15% of the stock's market price, depending on the duration of the option, the volatility of the issue, the market environment, and numerous other factors. The best way to illustrate how Puts work is through a hypothetical example. In order not to complicate matters, brokerage commissions and transfer taxes (although they affect results significantly when the percentage gain or loss is small) have been omitted from the calculations which follow.

Mr. John Jones buys a 90-day Put on stock XYZ (100 shares) at 50 for, say, $350—in the expectation, of course, that XYZ will go down. He need not own the stock; he can buy it to make delivery if and when he decides to exercise the option. His break-even point on the transaction is a price of 46½ ($4650 for 100 shares) for the stock—50 ($5000 for 100 shares) less the cost of the option ($350), which is equivalent to 3½ points per share. If Jones waits until just before the option expires (as many option buyers tend to do) and XYZ is then selling at 52, he will simply do nothing: the option lapses and his loss is $350. If XYZ is selling at 48 ($4800 for 100 shares), he sells the stock at the option price of 50 ($5000 for 100 shares), buying it in if he does not own it, and the arithmetic is as follows: profit on sale—$200 ($5000 less $4800); cost of option—$350; result—loss of $150. However, if XYZ is selling at 40, Jones will make a profit of $650—the proceeds of a 100-share Put at 50 ($5000) less the cost of buying the stock at 40 ($4000) less the cost of the Put ($350)—a gain of 186% on his cash commitment.

A word of caution must be entered here. The tax laws state that the purchase of a Put option acts as a short sale. If you are long on a stock, which you have held less than six months, any gain on the exercise of the Put is a short-term capital gain, whether you use your long stock or buy new stock. If you buy new stock to deliver against the exercise of the Put, your holding period on your original stock starts anew. Moreover, the holding period starts anew even if you let your Put expire. The one exception to this rule is when stock and a Put are bought on the same date, and so identified one against the other.

The opposite of a Put is a Call, an option to buy; and there are several other types of option—a Straddle, a Spread, a Strip and a Strap. All of these options can be used for defensive purposes, but to discuss them in detail would carry us beyond the subject of basic bear tactics.*

---

* The interested reader can get further information from the following publications: *Understanding Put and Call Options* by Herbert Filer (New York: Popular Library, 1966). *90 Days to Fortune* by Elizabeth Fowler. Appendix II, "Put and Call Options" by Paul Sarnoff (New York: Ivan Obolensky, Inc., 1965). *The Nature of Puts & Calls* by Anthony M. Reinach (New York: The Bookmailer, Inc., 1961). *Taxes, Puts and Calls* by John D. Cunnion (Larchmont, New York: Business Reports, Inc., 1962).

Most option business is done in stocks listed on the New York Stock Exchange, some in stocks listed on the American Stock Exchange, and a small part in securities traded over-the-counter. Most brokerage houses will handle option orders. They in turn sell options to and buy them from the members of the Put and Call Brokers and Dealers Association. The financial sections of the leading New York newspapers regularly carry advertisements indicating some of the options available and the prices and premiums involved. All options issued by Put and Call brokers carry the endorsement of the New York Stock Exchange member firm that handles the margin account of the seller of the option; they are, in effect, guaranteed by the seller's broker.

A dramatic instance of the successful use of options by an amateur investor occurred in the great bear market of 1962, when a young man named Jeb Wofford made a small fortune in the stock market while many people were losing large fortunes. A midwesterner best known as a member of the 1952 Olympic equestrian team, Jeb Wofford had no experience on Wall Street. In fact, aside from the rigorous discipline required to train for championship riding, he had few qualifications for business. Late in 1961—believing that the stock market was heading toward serious trouble—he became worried about the handling of his family's money, much of which was held in trust by a large midwestern bank. The bank officers balked at the idea of selling out the leading common-stock holdings, pointing out that the investments were in high quality companies such as American Telephone & Telegraph and International Business Machines. Where could they find sounder investments? And what about the large capital gains taxes that would have to be paid? Such stocks, they insisted, would ride out any economic downturn. Besides, they doubted that any drastic market break would occur.

Faced with this impasse, Mr. Wofford set about investigating ways of protecting his capital in a market downturn. Having carefully studied the basic tactics of the bears and the costs involved, he decided to devote a limited amount of capital, $30,000, to buying Put options, because they offered a combination of defined risk (the cost of the option) and a high degree of leverage.

He began his operations in the early part of 1962, and by April he had made a substantial sum of money. At that time a stockbroker brought Mr. Wofford to the attention of *The New York Times* and an article was written about him which was published in June. By then there was no doubt about it. Jeb Wofford, by dint of determination, disciplined judgment, and hard work, had succeeded as a novice where many more experienced men had failed. He had centered his attention on IBM Puts, owning more than 20 of them at one time; and on each he made a profit. He also bought Puts on Xerox, U.S. Steel, and 14 other issues, and all of these options, with the exception of three, were exercised at a profit. His total gains were estimated by his broker at "several hundred thousands of dollars."

In theory, any investor who expects a severe break in the market can do what Mr. Wofford did; but relatively few people have the determination, the time, and the temperament required to put his approach into practice systematically. However, those who believe there is a place for bear tactics in investment strategy and wish to leave the decision-making to experts can now invest in the so-called hedge funds.

Alfred Winslow Jones has been credited with sparking enthusiasm for this somewhat new approach to investing sizable sums of money. Mr. Jones manages an investment company which operates as a partnership composed of large investors. His strategy differs from the conventional one of mutual funds in that his long position is hedged in varying degrees by selling some stocks short, partly as a protection against a general market decline, partly to profit by the declines which occur in certain stocks even when the over-all trend is up.

The minimum participation in Mr. Jones's fund—and in several others similar to it—is far beyond the means of the average investor. However, the Samson Fund, which is authorized by the SEC to engage in hedging operations, is open to the general public; so, too, is another hedge fund, the

Hubshman Fund, formed toward the end of 1966. If they build a good record, it seems likely that the hedge-fund concept—that of simultaneously maintaining long and short positions—will gain increasing acceptance, and possibly the hedge funds will write a new chapter in the history of Wall Street.

5

"Performance" is the New Name of the Game

By George J. W. Goodman

Justly or not, the most talked about investors on Wall Street in both manic and depressive phases are mutual funds, variously described as "swinging," "go-go," or "maximum capital gains," depending on the gravity of the observer. Speculation as to what "performance funds" are doing is commonplace in board rooms. "Performance" as a philosophy is having an impact on all managed money, including the savings of 100 million Americans. Keith Funston, formerly president of the New York Stock Exchange, has said it is "the most significant change in the marketplace today." To some Wall Streeters, "performance" is a cult with dangerous overtones for orderly markets; to others, it is simply the application of professionalism to a maturing industry.

In one way, "performance" is an inaccurate term, for all funds seek to perform in accordance with their stated objectives, and maximum capital gains are by no means the objective of every fund. But the term has come to mean a kind of investment policy that seeks rapid appreciation, leaving dividends, safety and diversity behind.

To try for the capital gains results, the "performance funds" have concentrated on far fewer stocks than the aver-

George J. W. Goodman is editor of The Institutional Investor.

age mutual fund, and have turned over their portfolios much more rapidly than the average fund. Thus they represent something of a change in the traditional image of mutual funds, which up to now have been identified with long-term investments and a broad, diversified list of stocks. Around the policies of concentration and turnover there has developed a stir of controversy.

In a larger sense, the "performance funds" are a symptom of a gradual but enormous change in investment attitudes. The effect of the change is to downgrade the preservation of capital as a goal and upgrade the search for capital gains. The reasons for this shift are not hard to find: a long bull market which has rewarded capital gains investments, and a constant inflation which has punished those who invested for stability. "Only now, after twenty years," says one partner on Wall Street, "have investment managers realized the permanent political implications of a policy of full employment." Once capital gains are accepted as a criterion, competition leads to comparison, and the race is on to chalk up the best record by any procedure that will do the job. As of mid-1967, there was little doubt that the "performance funds" as a group had indeed performed well. In 1965, their average gain in net asset value was 40.7%. In 1966, while the Dow-Jones Average dropped 19%, and traditional balanced funds dropped 5.8%, the "performance funds" dropped only 1.2%, bettering not only the market but all their competitors, according to figures compiled by Arthur Wiesenberger & Company. The reasons for this may be unusual enough to make dangerous the assumption that this trend will continue; but the 1966 record will certainly do nothing to slow down the trend toward performance or the public hunger for it.

The list of "performance funds" is ill defined because, as Ivest Fund's Robert Doran puts it, "All capital gains funds try to be performance funds. The ones that achieve a record are performance funds. The ones that don't, aren't, and say that wasn't their intention."

The clamor for this kind of "performance" record showed

up in 1966 in the tremendous public demand for Gerald Tsai's Manhattan Fund. But the Manhattan Fund is not unique. "Our dealers tell us that more than half the new accounts that come in insist on a performance fund," says John Bogle, executive vice president of Wellington Management, which runs the Wellington Fund, third largest in the country. Because Wellington was a more conservative, balanced fund, it went out and bought the management company advising a small "performance" fund, Ivest Fund, in order to get the four young managers who ran Ivest, and so that its dealers could have a Wellington "performance" fund to offer prospective clients. If the same percentage holds true for the entire industry as holds true for Wellington, the demand for "performance" funds is now running at a rate greater than $1 billion a year.

But the influence of "performance" goes beyond mutual funds. "We talk to a lot of company officers who are also responsible for the pension funds of their companies," says Richard Jenrette, vice president of the brokerage firm, Donaldson, Lufkin & Jenrette. "Most of these pension plans have been administered by banks, and the long bull market masked lackluster performance—as long as there was some growth, the company officer didn't worry about how much. Now that growth is harder to come by, we see these pension officers paying more attention to it. Some of them are putting a portion of their funds into 'performance funds.' This has an effect not only on the direction of mutual funds, but also on the banks that don't want to lose the business. To compete, the banks may begin to change their policies. Even without a formal change, the bank officer managing funds can be unconsciously influenced by this change in direction. The funds involved are so large that only a small fraction has to change direction to give a whole new tone to the investment scene."

THE ORIGIN OF PERFORMANCE

On Wall Street the funds pioneering performance are considered to be the Dreyfus Fund and two of the funds of Boston's Fidelity Group, Fidelity Capital and Fidelity Trend. Dreyfus was started by Jack Dreyfus, who brought the sensibilities of a superb bridge player to the market place, and built the fund up to $1.5 billion at the beginning of 1967. Dreyfus himself is now less active and the managers of his fund dislike the short-term trading connotations of "performance."

The Fidelity Group is the creation of Edward Johnson, a sprightly, articulate sixty-nine-year-old proper Bostonian lawyer who took over Fidelity when it had $3 million in 1943 and brought the total assets of all the Fidelity funds to $2.25 billion in 1967. Some of the Fidelity portfolio managers went on to run other funds quite successfully—Gerald Tsai being one alumnus—and now there is a certain mystique in the industry about "Mister Johnson," as he is respectfully called. Johnson, who likes to study the mass-emotion currents in the stock market, says he did not consciously pioneer anything except a certain autonomy for his portfolio managers. "In a law firm," he says, "such as the one I came from, each associate or partner is responsible for his own clients, and this carried over to fund management. I think it was traditional among the funds to have investment decisions made by a group, but I believe positive decisions have to be made by an individual. Even with computers and machines, security management is very much an art, the intuitive feel of a single man."

Performance fund managers as a group are young, mostly from the "generation gap" in the investment business; Wall Street did not attract new men during the depression and war years. Consequently those who entered the business about ten years ago found a vacuum ahead of them, and now have positions of responsibility.

But still another reason is that the trend of "performance" has brought tremendous pressure into the business of managing securities. Most of the young managers, since they are employees in a regulated and traditionally reticent industry, insisted they not be identified for this chapter. "You can really feel the pressure," says one. "It's as bitterly competitive as a pro football league with a tight race. Every day, we have our salesmen calling up, saying give us a record to sell, give us performance. Every day, we check the gain or loss of our portfolio against our competitors. When one of my competitors outperforms me, I check: How did he do it? Was his timing better catching the airlines? Why did he sell the textiles before we did, was his information better? It's a business that's going to burn up people pretty rapidly, because the guys who are good in one kind of market aren't good in the next, and the pressure is there all the time, in every kind of market. It's going to be as much of a pressure business as Madison Avenue. My boss was sixty-two, and he couldn't wait to get out and get to a farm in Vermont."

The emphasis on timing brought increased emphasis on the technical aspects of the stock market. A number of performance funds have a "war room" with charts covering the walls, like a small Strategic Air Command base. In them, the chartists hunch over boards, tracking the pattern and volume of stock movements, trying to find the proper points at which to buy and sell.

Pressure for results brought about the greater attention to short-term swings in the market by performance-fund managers. It is this focus that differs so much from the traditional investment approach, and the reason some Wall Streeters feel "performance" means "trading" rather than "investing." All mutual funds are turning over their portfolios more rapidly. In 1955, the average turnover—purchases and sales—of all funds was 16% a year; in 1966, it was 33% a year. But among many of the "performance" funds, the rate was well over 100% a year. In short, there were few stocks owned by a performance fund on December 31 that had been in the portfolio the previous January. "This is evolution, not revolution," says W. Nicholas Thorndike, president of Ivest Fund. "The cycle of appreciation is much faster than it was in the fifties. Then you could make your choice and sit with it three or four years. Now a stock gets where it's going much more quickly, and you have to be more alert."

Turning over the portfolio more rapidly, of course, generates commissions for stockbrokers and may explain the popularity of "performance" funds among brokerage firms, which help to sell the funds. The added commissions are an expense to the shareholders of a fund, but few shareholders seem to care, as long as the results are there. Much of the criticism directed at "performance" funds comes from other investing institutions. The opinion most frequently expressed by older managers is that a fund, an institution, has no business getting involved with short-term fluctuations.

Gerald Tsai, for one, disagrees. "By setting performances as a goal, you may trade more," he says, "but the only real test is how well you perform for your shareholders. Turn the criticism around: these prestigious institutions with their slow turnover, how have they done for their shareholders? The fact is, there are fashion cycles in the market just as there are in women's dresses. Sometimes the market wants growth stocks, sometimes it wants defensive stocks, sometimes it wants money-rate stocks. You have to have maximum attention and a sixth sense to catch the fashion cycle. A time of rapid change demands an adaptable management."

Tsai's comparison of stock market fashions to those of hemlines provoked some controversy, but it is not new. John Maynard Keynes, the most influential economist of this century, took a particular chapter in 1935 when writing his *General Theory* to point out the "fashion" or "game" element in the supposedly rational world of investing:

> . . . the energies and skill of the professional investor and speculator are occupied largely not with making superior long term forecasts of the probable yield of an investment over its whole life, but with foreseeing changes in the conventional basis of valuation a short time ahead of the general public. . . . The actual, private object of the most skilled investment today is "to beat the gun," as the Americans so well express it, to outwit the

crowd, and to pass the bad, or depreciating, half crown to the other fellow.

This battle of wits . . . does not even require gulls amongst the public to feed the maws of the professional; it can be played by the professionals amongst themselves . . . for it is, so to speak, a game of Snap, of Old Maid, of Musical Chairs—a pastime in which he is victor who says Snap neither too soon nor too late, who passes the Old Maid to his neighbor before the game is over, who secures a chair for himself when the music stops.

For many years, Wall Street has gone out of its way to present itself as an extension of Main Street, and there can be no doubt of Main Street's involvement: when Keynes wrote his treatise there were seven million American investors; today there are more than 20 million. Yet with the power of institutional investors increasing, Keynes's words may become as true in the future as they were when he wrote them. Some aspects of professional investing have become a game of beating the gun. Certainly some of the events of 1966 illustrated the Keynes chapter.

1966—TRIAL AND THREAT

For the "performance funds," 1966 was a year of trial, the first major bear market since the concept of "performance" became popular. The attention to maximum capital gains, critics felt, would result in sharp losses if the market turned down drastically, as in 1962. Moreover, concentration and high turnover provoked the criticism among some Wall Streeters that the performance funds were a threat to liquidity— that by ganging up in a few stocks they accentuated swings in price, increased volatility, and destroyed the orderly market for stocks in which they concentrated.

Concentration by performance funds in 1966 was due to a variety of factors. Analysts could see the business cycle topping out, and the Vietnam war produced dislocations and extraordinarily high interest rates, always a dampening factor. The cresting business cycle meant that the stocks of many basic industries—autos, steels, chemicals, and so on—could not be expected to "perform"; the point at which their profits would start dropping could already be seen. Hence the performance funds scouted vigorously for areas in which innovation and growth were so strong that they would supposedly be relatively immune to the business cycle: color television, airlines, and electronic stocks (especially in the semiconductor field) were popular.

To some degree, the stock choices of a performance-fund manager are confirmed by other fund managers if they are still buying. The stock rises and "looks good on the charts." There is nothing collusive about this among the managers. They talk to the same brokerage houses, whose analysts are searching out investment ideas; analysts of the same generation who have been to the same business schools, Harvard and Pennsylvania leading the list. The young portfolio managers also run into each other at popular restaurants: Joseph's and Locke-Ober's in Boston, Oscar's Delmonico and the Lunch Club in New York. Brokers such as Robert Brimberg give informal lunches, where off-the-record opinions on the market and the economy are aired. Thus a manager has a "feel" of what those around him are doing. It is not surprising to find many of the funds in the same stocks or the same groups.

THE BREAK

For several months in 1966, stocks from the "performance" areas mentioned above continued to rise while prices of the more mature companies that make up the Dow-Jones Industrial Average were dropping. But when the 1966 market break really got under way—it was the second worst drop since World War II—the "performance" stocks did not simply drop, they collapsed, some of them as much as 50% in a few weeks, the most precipitous drops since 1929. Fairchild Camera, which had sold at 216½ in February, hit 96½. Motorola dived from 233½ to 89. Xerox, which had sold at 267½ earlier in the year, reached a low of 125¼. Trading in several of the most widely held of performance stocks was suspended at one time or another. What made the drop so surprising to many market observers is that many of the performance stocks—the three named above, for example—were to show higher profits in 1966 than in 1965, and barring some calamity they were expected to show higher profits again in 1967. The long-term reasons for their previous popularity were still there, and short-term problems were foreseen by experienced analysts. The fund managers knew this, but they seemed to be following another axiom of Lord Keynes: "All I know about the long run is that we are all dead." No fund manager wanted to show in his portfolio a stock which had suffered a major drop. Published there, it would be a standing rebuke to his original decision. Hence the original favorites were sold simply because they ceased to perform.

"The funds," said Bradbury K. Thurlow, of Winslow, Cohû & Stetson, "behaved like the worst of small investors, showing speculative exuberance at the top, dire forebodings at the bottom, and steadfast timidity during the recovery." Another broker commented: "When a couple of fund managers want to get out of the same stock at the same time, it's like the Green Bay line hitting a revolving door. There's nothing to do but stay out of the way and hope the door can be repaired."

In the period of steepest decline, the five weeks ending September 30, 1966, trading in the popular performance stocks began to account for a large percentage of stocks traded on the New York Stock Exchange. Twenty performance stocks, even though they amounted to only 1.7% of all the shares listed on the New York Stock Exchange, accounted for 17.6% of the trading. Fairchild Camera provides an interesting case in point.

Fairchild's low in 1965 was 27½; all the way to its 1966 high of 216¾, there was aggressive buying. At the time of the decline, 16 funds held 625,800 shares of Fairchild, 22.1% of the total of 2,836,793 shares. But since anywhere from 10% to 20% was held by the founder, Sherman Fairchild, and other early, low-cost stockholders, and was considered "locked up and put away," the funds held close to a third of the Fairchild "float."

Analysts from both funds and brokerage houses had checked the industry and they expected demand to exceed supply for several years. But Fairchild's price weakened with the market slide, and there were rumors of production problems. Security analysts swarmed to the Fairchild plants, dogging Dr. Robert Noyce, the semiconductor division chief. Noyce assured them that the problems were all short term, and other company officials indicated that even with the problems Fairchild's earnings would be up at least 30%. One New York analyst went out of his way to arrange a tennis game with one of Fairchild's suppliers in order to get a cross-reading on Fairchild's inventories between sets.

But once the avalanche was under way, nothing could stop it. In July, Fairchild sold at 200; in September, at 150, in October, at 100. On November 17, Fairchild traded 562,000 shares—a fifth of all the stock and probably more than a fourth of the supply. One fund, Fidelity Trend, sold 137,000 shares in a single block. Trading in Fairchild was suspended for several hours, and by the time it reopened and then closed for the day the stock had dropped 20 points.

With the stock moving so quickly, even normally quick-footed funds were caught without a chair when the music stopped. "I was out on the Coast talking to dealers," one fund manager reported. "And one of my colleagues called me. The Fairchild earnings were going to be less than the Street expected and our chartist said there wasn't much buying power in evidence. I figured we'd better get out—some of these guys will just throw their Fairchild at the floor—and we can get back in after the smoke clears. But by the time I got the call, Coast time, and gave the order, they'd stopped trading, and the stock was down 20 points. I figured, okay, we'll keep it. But I don't like hanging onto a mistake. You do that too often, you end up with a portfolio full of mistakes."

During the course of 1966, Fairchild traded 14,521,800 shares, more than four times its capitalization. Obviously, funds alone could not have accounted for all of this, and a fund, like an individual, must have the right to change its mind. But there is no question that funds helped to accentuate the swings by selling such big blocks so quickly.

Ironically, the panic to get out of Fairchild was succeeded in less than 90 days by a scramble to get back in. Like many of the volatile "high flyers," Fairchild was up more than 50% from its low by March, 1967. A leading Wall Street firm wired its branches in February that Fairchild had "turned around" (i.e., that its troubles were short term, just as Dr. Noyce had maintained); and the volume of shares traded and the size of the blocks suggested that the buyers were once again institutions.

THE MARKET IMPACT PROBLEM

While the SEC apparently took note of the impact of funds in increasing volatility in stocks, the Commission did not propose any changes on this subject in its 1967 recommendations to Congress. All Chairman Manuel Cohen said was, "Several instances have been reported to us in which institutional selling, done in a manner which exaggerated the market impact of the decision to sell, has triggered rapid movements in the prices of particular securities."

The particular securities, of course, took the brunt of the squalls of selling. But in a nervous stock market, the collapse of one stock seems to cause sympathetic declines in others. Only one stock may drop under heavy selling, but the psychology of the whole market place is affected.

One of the chief criticisms of performance funds is that the manner of their buying and selling destroys the liquidity, or orderliness, of the market. Obviously, when funds were buying stocks to put away, this could not have been a point. Nor is there much danger that the market will be dislocated when the funds are buying and selling stocks with large capitalizations. But when the funds move into stocks with relatively small capitalizations, or when many of them invest heavily in a single company (and in 1967 funds owned more than 20% of 24 companies), there can be problems in the market place. "It is not often reasonable," as Keith Funston has said, "to expect the market to absorb a block of stock of magnitude as smoothly as if the same amount were offered to the market over a period of time."

THE SPECIALIST'S VIEWPOINT

Even stronger in their opinions on fund trading are the specialists. But since they plan to continue doing business with the same people, none of the specialists consulted for this chapter would permit themselves to be identified.

Specialists are of course expected to maintain "orderly markets." The system breaks down when there is an overwhelming influx of orders on one side or the other. While specialist firms have been combined and their capital strengthened, 100,000 shares of a $100 stock is $10 million, and that is a lot for one man or one firm to buy in one afternoon.

When the specialist cannot handle the order, he appeals to a Governor of the Exchange for permission to suspend trading—in Wall Street parlance, "to shut the stock down." There was no way on the afternoon of November 17, 1966, to buy or sell the stock of Fairchild Camera. No specialist likes to shut his stock down; it is a reflection, ordinarily, on his capitalization, on the kind of job he is doing, and on his stature among other specialists. The purpose of shutting the stock down is to gain time to evaluate a situation if there has been some major news development, and/or to find matching orders.

"I hate to shut my stock down," one specialist said. "But what else can you do? Even the broker that executes the order is apologetic—I can tell by his face as he comes across the [Exchange] floor. He asks how is the market, then he says, very softly, he has sixty thousand XYZ to sell. Sixty thousand: That's a couple million dollars right there. I tell him I'll take twenty, off a couple points from the market, if he'll give me time to match the rest. He says okay. Now I have to scramble around to find buyers. I find them, after a lot of frantic work. And you know what? I get back, and now there are three or four other guys around the post, with the same apologetic looks on their faces, waiting to throw more stock at me. The word has gotten around, and some of these funds with their instant research, they figure, let's get out, we'll find out why later. Like sheep! They come thundering through like a bunch of sheep! And six weeks from now, they'll all come thundering through in the other direction! One of these days I'm gonna shut this stock down and it can stay down, or they can find somebody else."

Ganging up on the specialist is no conspiracy; it is a simple matter of nervousness, of "passing the depreciating half-crown," of wanting to have a chair before the music stops. But part of the cloudburst nature of buying and selling also comes from "technical" considerations, performance managers, the "war rooms" and their charts. Not all the sellers in the decline in 1966 were performance funds; in fact, several of the most widely watched performance funds were buyers in the falling market. All funds use some degree of technical work, but at times in 1966 it seemed as though the technical work was leading funds to accentuate the trends, even though for the year as a whole the mutual fund industry acted counter to the main trends.

In the third quarter of 1966, when both the Dow-Jones stocks and the performance stocks were dropping sharply, 67 funds with assets of $15.8 billion, or about half of the industry, were sellers on balance, selling 13.3% more than they bought.

"What we saw in 1966," says Bradbury K. Thurlow, "was a Pavlovian response to chart patterns, bordering on and degenerating into a mania. This is trend-trading carried to absurdity. Trend-trading says a stock is only going up as long as it's going up. If charts are a means of keeping track of what everyone else is doing, it doesn't take much to see that sooner or later all the charts will say the same thing. One crack, the chain reaction starts, the public sees the stock take a big dive, and then the rumor mills start about how badly the company is doing. Next time the smart people will be on the other side."

THE CORPORATE DILEMMA

One effect of the violent ups and downs in prices of performance stocks has been to leave the officers of the companies in question in a state of utter confusion. There is of course no way for them to prevent purchases and sales of their stock. Some of them earlier courted performance funds, thinking that as institutions they would be stable, long-term stockholders. Fund analysts were given budget projections, weekly figures and complete access to management. Then when the institutions sold, the company officers felt personally betrayed, and cooled off on the whole idea of paying close and friendly attention to certain institutions. William F. Rockwell, Jr., president of the Rockwell Standard Corporation, complained that "unskilled" selling on the part of funds had needlessly knocked down his company's stock: Mr. Rockwell said in 1967 he was seriously thinking of delisting his company from the New York Stock Exchange, reasoning that in the over-the-counter market the funds would be less likely to pay attention to it. Rockwell Standard was not a company particularly favored by performance funds, but its president's public statements parallel those made privately by officers of several companies which were performance favorites in 1966. Keith Funston's approach to the problem was one of moral suasion: "For their part, some institutions probably will want to give more thought to the effect their transactions have on the companies in which they invest, and on the rank and file of stockholders. If an institution elects to own a significant portion of the floating supply of stock in a given company, it should acquire or dispose of shares only with due regard to the effect of such transactions on fellow stockholders. No investor, least of all an institution investing indirectly on behalf of large numbers of people, is a law unto itself."

What corporations find most upsetting about violent fluctuations in their stocks is that they can get in the way of day-to-day business. Executive energy can be wasted in dealing with questions about why the stock is bouncing around, and potential customers may go elsewhere because of rumors about financial stability or production capability. Even more serious perhaps, expansion opportunities may be missed. When a prospective merger is based on the recent price of a corporation's stock, the merger partner may pull back if the stock swings away from the price at which the details and ratios were worked out.

"Many companies," says Richard Jenrette, "didn't realize the degree to which the performance-oriented funds had changed. They thought of all funds as pleasant, silver-haired gentlemen who only bought stock and put it away. Now they know it can go both ways. Sophisticated corporations will now go out of their way to avoid such fluctuations. This means cooling off overly optimistic earnings projections from Wall Street; heretofore, they've been in no hurry to correct pessimistic news and they've let the optimistic stuff stand. Even beyond this, some companies will plan their quarterly earnings to show more gradual results, insofar as accounting procedures will permit them to."

THE FUTURE OF "PERFORMANCE"

Whatever the criticisms, there cannot be any doubt that the performance funds over-all have to date achieved a superior record and that performance will be an increasing influence in the market place. Some of the brokerage firms which deal with institutions believe the performance funds will be more wary of stocks with limited markets, and may show a higher degree of responsibility in their buying and selling.

Stephen Lieber, a partner of Vanden Broeck, Lieber & Company, finds that "about half the performance boys have slowed up, and think twice about getting aboard a stock that is moving too fast. They are also willing to forego the maximum gain, the last few points. The other half—well, the other half are sharpening up their reflexes, saying, 'Next time, I'll be faster.' "

Other industry observers believe there will be a swing to a middle-distance point of view. "The short term tactical approach worked very well for Fidelity and the people that pioneered it," says one. "But now too many people are trying it. First the funds were acting on next year's prospects, then next quarter's, then the reaction time was growing so short it concerned weekly inventories and sales figures. The next step will be the reverse: some institutions will buy on bad news."

A strategy of this kind has already been used to some extent by the Dreyfus Fund, according to its president, Howard Stein: "Part of our strategy is to buy in groups of securities that are out of favor, and we don't concentrate on making quarter to quarter gains. We try not to know what our competitors are doing. When you're in an out-of-favor group, there's no trend to help you quarter by quarter, to show immediate performance. You have to look at things on a three to five year basis."

There is also little doubt that performance funds will continue to appeal to mutual fund investors, at the expense of less speculative funds. For their own shareholders, the funds will probably continue to do well, although for the potential buyer deciding which funds are going to be performance funds is like deciding which stocks are going to perform. Unfortunately, "performance" is a hindsight definition. There is no guarantee that any aggressive trading fund will outperform any other kind of fund. Furthermore, there is even no guarantee that a fund which has had a record of performance can continue that record. Funds, like their managers, are sometimes better in one kind of market and one kind of economy than another, and the cycle changes every few years.

In the volatile performance end of the investment spectrum, the implications for the stock market are fairly clear. Since the performance funds will probably continue to be popular, and since they have found that concentration pays, they will concentrate. If the favored stocks have small capitalizations, they will be extremely volatile.

Long-term investors, who buy stocks and put them away for their children's education or for retirement, need have little concern about the advent of the performance concept. But there is a large and growing number of Americans who enjoy the emotional cross-currents of the market place, who watch their stocks, morning and evening, and love to feel a part of the game. Some of them even subscribe to services that tell them what the funds have bought and sold in the previous quarter, and use this as a guide. Any investor who tries to out-trade the funds on a short-term basis is likely to find himself buying what the funds are selling and vice versa. There are indications, for example, that in 1966–67 many performance funds charged right back into the same stocks they had sold a few months previously. An individual trying to follow the funds' movements would have been run over from both directions.

In the investment management business both competition and professionalism are increasing, and performance is likely to be part of the scene for some time, even though its advent has presented the Exchanges and the investment community with some problems. The flow of information from Washington and Wall Street, from industry and from computers has increased vastly in the last several years. In the end, of course, it is not merely the information but the anticipation of how the information will be received by buyers and sellers that governs investment success, "the average opinion of what average opinion will be," as Lord Keynes, himself a successful speculator, put it. All the psychic satisfactions of playing the maximum-gain, maximum-risk course are still there, but the reflex-reaction time is growing still shorter for those who want a chair when the music stops.

Part II

Fields of Investment

6

Investing in Bonds

By James Karanfilian

In the world of investments, common stocks, one might say, are the sports cars and bonds the sedate, chauffeur-driven limousines. Like all generalizations, this comparison is subject to numerous reservations. It is perfectly possible to speculate in bonds, and periodically fortunes are made and lost in the bond markets. It is also perfectly possible to see a portfolio of high-grade bonds decline in value at a time when the majority of common stocks are climbing upward. Nevertheless there is a basic truth to the simile: of the vehicles available to investors, bonds are among the most conservative.

James Karanfilian supervises the bond investment program of Bernstein-Macaulay, Inc., a New York investment management firm.

Common stocks are vastly more familiar than bonds to the investing public; even among Wall Street professionals there are many who know surprisingly little about bonds. Yet bonds play a crucial role in the economy, both in the private and the public sectors. For example, in 1966 the state and local governments came to the bond market to raise over $6 billion while corporations marketed almost $11 billion in net new bonds. In the same year, equity financing by corporations—that is to say, the sale of new common stock—totaled about $1.2 billion, less than 10% of the amount raised through bonds.

THE ANATOMY OF BONDS

A bond is a debt instrument similar to a promissory note: it is a legally enforceable contract that requires the borrower to pay a stipulated rate of interest and to repay the principal on fixed dates. The term "bond" denotes a long-term instrument used to finance long-term capital needs. Investors seeking to put money to work for a few days, weeks, or months find borrowers who need funds for temporary or revolving financing, and special credit instruments to accommodate this type of financing have evolved: U.S. Treasury Bills; Banker's Acceptances; Commercial Paper; Corporate and Municipal Notes, federal funds, etc. In a sense, these interest-bearing instruments are competitive with bonds, but their short duration makes them unsuitable for long-term investment. The dynamic market for short-term funds—it is called the "money market"—is beyond the scope of this chapter.

Bonds have several distinct features that distinguish them from other types of credit instruments.

Denomination. The denomination refers to the principal amount or the face value, which is the same as the value of the bond when it matures. While there are denominations of $500, $100, and even $50, the standard denomination is $1,000. Many new issues have come to the market in $5,000 units, and this denomination appears to be rapidly gaining acceptance.

Coupon. Bonds may be issued in either coupon or registered form. Coupons, which are attached to the bond certificate, are claims for periodic interest and can be clipped and cashed on the specified payment dates. Coupon bonds are negotiable to the bearer, which makes transfer of ownership simple, but necessitates extra care in handling to guard against loss or theft. Interest on most bonds is payable semiannually, and the rate of interest is indicated on the coupon.

Accrued Interest. Whoever owns a bond on the interest date can collect all of the interest due on the bond for the period. If a bond is sold between interest dates, the seller cannot cash part of the coupon. Therefore, in order to make the proper adjustments, the purchaser pays the seller for all the interest that has accrued from the last interest payment date up to the date of delivery. For example, if $20,000 of a 5% bond (with interest payment dates on January 1 and July 1) were sold for delivery on April 1 (exactly three months after the last interest payment), the purchaser would pay the seller $250 accrued interest. On July 1, the purchaser would collect $500, the full interest payment for the six-month period; but having already paid out $250, he would in effect receive interest only for the three months in which he has owned the bonds.

Registered Bonds. A bond that bears the owner's name on the face of the certificate and does not have coupons attached is called a registered bond. Registered bonds are payable to the parties whose names are recorded in the bond register or transfer books kept by the issuer or the transfer agent. Such bonds are transferred only when notation of the change of ownership has been made on the bond register. In most cases, the buyer may request bearer (coupon) or registered bonds. In practice, most municipal and government bonds are kept in bearer form, but there is a growing tendency for corporate bonds to be issued in registered form only.

Measuring Bond Yield. A common measure of investment return is *current yield,* which is simply a ratio of the annual amount of income received from a security to the actual amount paid for it. For example, a 4½% ten-year bond purchased at 90 (i.e., $900—bond prices are expressed in percentages of par value) would yield $45 for each $1,000 par value. Thus the yield on the purchase price, the current yield, is $45/$900 or 5% per annum.

But what about the $100 profit which the holder of this particular bond will receive when the bond matures in ten years? This increment (or loss if the bond had been purchased for more than $1,000) must be taken into account in measuring total return, which is called *yield to maturity*. Here is a crude but simple method for computing the yield to maturity:

$$\frac{\text{Annual interest} + \text{average annual capital gain (or loss)}}{\dfrac{100 + \text{purchase price}}{2}}$$

In the case of the bond mentioned above, the yield to maturity works out as follows:

$$\frac{\dfrac{\$450 + \$100}{10 \text{ years}}}{\dfrac{\$1000 + 900}{2}} = \frac{55}{950} = 5.8\%$$

as compared with a current yield of 5%.

Fortunately, investors seldom need to compute yield to maturity. Elaborate bond yield tables are available which show at a glance rates of yield to maturity for various coupon rates, bond prices and maturity dates.

Yield to maturity is a common denominator which enables the bond investor to compare quickly the investment return of various bonds with different coupons, prices and maturities. In fact, most professional bond dealers and sophisticated investors express bond prices in terms of yield to maturity in order to make one bond comparable to another.

The Call Feature. Some bond issues can be called for redemption—that is, paid off—before maturity. This option is useful to the issuer for several reasons. It makes possible the elimination of bond issues with unfavorable indenture provisions; the refunding of high-interest bonds with low-interest bonds when interest rates decline; and the elimination or realignment of the debt structure. Periodic redemption of a portion of the bond issue may also be a required provision of the bond agreement. A sinking fund with specified appropriations of cash for the purpose of calling bonds for redemption (or making purchases in the open market when the market price is significantly lower than the call price) is also a common feature of many corporate bond issues. The call or redemption price is usually fixed at a small premium over the face value of the bond. The premium ranges from 2% to 10%, depending on the life of the particular bond issue, the original offering price, and the dictates of the market place.

The call feature is a hazard for investors, because it allows the issuer the privilege of terminating a particularly good investment. High coupon bonds, purchased when interest rates were high, can be called away from the investor, leaving him with the problem of reinvesting funds in a less favorable market. Bond investors should be alert to the call feature of each bond issue.

U.S. GOVERNMENT BONDS

Aside from the $52 billion of special nonmarketable direct obligations sold to government agencies and $51 billion of nonmarketable savings-type bonds, there are two active types of U.S. government obligations that make up the government bond market (Table 2): (1) direct marketable debts consisting of Treasury Bills, Treasury Certificates, Treasury Notes, and Treasury Bonds; (2) the obligations of federal agencies (Table 3), which in practice are regarded as part of the government market.

Treasury Bills, though more properly part of the money market, have a very important bearing on the bond market and deserve comment. They usually have maturities of 91 days, but there are also issues of 180 days, six months, and one year. Bills have no coupons. They are sold at a discount from par (redemption value) and the difference between the purchase price and par is considered interest income. Treasury Bills are a favorite vehicle for investing temporary funds with virtually no risk of loss.

Certificates of Indebtedness, which compete with Bills, are interest-bearing short-term obligations with maturities not exceeding one year.

Treasury Notes are similar to Certificates but are of intermediate maturities of one to five years. *Treasury Bonds* are long-term obligations with original maturities of over five years. They are limited by law to a maximum coupon of 4¼%. This restriction does not apply to other Treasury obligations and coupons of 5⅜% and 5⅝% for Notes have been used in recent years. The Treasury could sell Bonds at a discount to yield more than the 4¼% limit, but has not considered it appropriate to circumvent the 4¼% ceiling in this way.

Table 2.
Marketable U.S. Government Debt, December, 1966
(in billions)

Total	Bills	Certificates	Notes	Bonds
$218	$65	$6	$48	$99

Agencies. Several agencies and instrumentalities, created by the federal government, are authorized to sell debt to the public. While such bonds are not direct obligations of the government, they have been accorded a quality classification next to that of U.S. government securities. Listed in order of size, the most important agencies are: (1) Federal Home Loan Bank, organized to extend credit to home mortgage lending institutions, mostly Savings & Loan Associations. (2) Federal Land banks, a system of twelve regional banks that make long-term farm mortgage loans through farm associations. (3) Federal National Mortgage Associations (FNMA), whose principal function is to provide a secondary market for first mortgages on homes that have been insured by the FHA or guaranteed by the Veterans Administration. (In recent years the FNMA has sold participation certificates representing an interest in its mortgage portfolios to the public. The Attorney General, in an opinion dated September 30, 1966, stated that the participation certificates are in fact a "general obligation of the United States backed by its full faith and credit.") (4) Federal Intermediate Credit Banks, created for the purpose of discounting agricultural loan paper. (5) Banks for Cooperatives, also created as part of the agriculture aid program and to provide loans for agricultural cooperatives and associations.

Financial Quality. U.S. government obligations enjoy the highest quality ratings, despite the fact that there is no specific security behind government bonds and that the bondholders have no legal right to sue the government. The excellent credit standing of government obligations is founded on the ability and the willingness of the federal government to meet its promise to pay its debts. Because of the vast wealth, political stability and taxing power of this country, a detailed analysis of our government's ability to pay is hardly necessary. In contrast, the appraisal of many foreign government obligations requires careful analysis of the issuer's credit record, present economic situation and political problems. Political changes resulting in the deferment or repudiation of government debts have been a not uncommon occurrence.

The Government Market. New issues of Treasury Bills can be purchased each week by submitting bids to the Treasury (usually through commercial banks). Bids may be competitive, with the issues being purchased by the most favorable bidder; or noncompetitive, in which case the bidder agrees to accept Bills at the average price of the accepted competitive bids. Thus the discount price set by competition in the market determines the yield for Treasury Bills.

Table 3.
Federal Agency Marketable Obligations Outstanding,
December, 1966 (in billions)

Agency	Amount
Federal Home Loan Bank	$6.8
Federal Land Bank	4.4
Federal National Mortgage Assn.	2.9
Federal National Mortgage Assn. Participation Certificates	2.1
Federal Intermediate Credit Banks	2.8
Banks for Cooperatives	1.1

Source: Federal Reserve Bulletin.

The Treasury markets new bond issues by selling directly to the public. There is no underwriter, but dealers in government securities sometimes serve that function by taking large positions. After announcing terms, the Treasury opens cash offerings for subscriptions, reserving the right to make allocations in the event an issue is oversubscribed. While cash offerings are most common, the Treasury may offer to exchange a new issue for maturing issues, or even to refund outstanding issues in advance. Since most Treasury Bonds are noncallable or have long-call protection, refunding and exchange offers give the Treasury a means of exercising control over its maturity schedule.

New issues of Agency securities are offered for cash through dealer groups composed of investment bankers and commercial banks. Although Treasuries are listed on the New York Stock Exchange, almost all trading in them takes place in a highly sophisticated over-the-counter market maintained by several dealer firms and a few large commercial banks. These dealers and banks quote prices on a net basis (no commission added) and act as principals dealing directly with large investors, or with other brokers and local banks, who add on a small commission when they reoffer the securities to their customers. Certificates, notes and bonds are quoted in thirty-seconds of a point. For example, on May 23, 1966, the price for U. S. Treasury 4⅛ % due 5/15/94 was 93–16 bid—

94 asked to yield 4.51% to maturity on the asking price. Dealer quotes refer to "round" lots of $100,000 (par value), with slightly higher quotes for smaller lots. Settlement for U.S. Treasury securities is usually made the day after the trade date. Most dealers in Treasuries also make a market in Agency obligations. Trading practices are very similar to those in U.S. goverment markets, but volume and activity are considerably smaller.

CORPORATE BONDS

Unlike government and municipal issuers of bonds, corporations have other classes of securities—preferred and common stock. Summarized below are the features which distinguish corporate bonds from other types of corporate securities

(1) Bondholders, in common with other creditors, have a *prior* claim on the company's assets and this claim must be satisfied before stockholders can receive any kind of payment. (2) Bondholders have a claim for a fixed amount of interest and principal which must be met in full at the specified time if the company is to avoid insolvency. This claim is based upon a contract with the bondholder which is irrevocable and binding regardless of earnings or financial conditions. In contrast, dividends to stockholders are paid when the board of directors deems that they are warranted by earnings. (3) Bonds have a maturity when the principal must be paid, while equities, theoretically, have an infinite life. (4) As long as the corporation meets its contractual obligations to the bondholders, they have no voting power or voice in management.

There are many types of corporate bonds, issued under a great variety of terms. The contract under which corporate bonds are issued, called an indenture, is not made directly with the bondholders. A third party, the trustee, makes the agreement on behalf of the bondholders and acts for the bondholders in enforcing the many covenants and pledges contained in the trust indenture. The trustee, normally a bank, must see to it that the company keeps its pledges and observes the restrictions set forth in the terms of the indenture.

There are two major classes of corporate bonds: unsecured bonds that depend on the general credit of the issuer, and bonds issued under an indenture granting the bondholders a lien on certain property that can be sold in the event of a default. The secured form is used by the corporation to make the bonds more attractive to investors. Secured bonds are further classified by the type of asset pledged.

The most popular type is the *mortgage bond,* which involves a pledge of the land, buildings and equipment of a corporation. Bonds issued under a first mortgage lien have priority in the distribution of proceeds from any necessary sale of property. The mortgage may cover all the real estate and equipment of a company, or a stipulated portion of the property, but usually bonds are issued to the extent of only 50% to 60% of the estimated value. A closed mortgage arrangement prohibits further use of the pledged property as security for additional bonds. But additional bonds may be issued under junior liens.

A more flexible method is the use of an open mortgage with an *after-acquired clause,* which subjects to the mortgage all property acquired after the bond has been issued. In this way a growing company can issue additional bonds under an existing mortgage as the value of its property increases. The existing bondholders can be protected by provisions requiring property value and earnings to reach stipulated levels before additional bonds can be issued.

Railroads finance the purchase of new rolling stock by selling *trust certificates.* Under this arrangement, a trustee buys the equipment from the car manufacturer, using funds obtained from the sale to investors of certificates of beneficial interest in the trust. The railroad leases the equipment with an initial payment of 15% to 25% and additional payments designed to retire the certificates in 10 to 20 years. The railroad usually guarantees the principal and interest of the certificates, although title to the equipment is held by the trustee

for the benefit of the certificate holders until the debt is retired. If the railroad fails to make rental payments, the trustee has full title and can sell the equipment.

In the case of a company whose assets consist principally
of securities of other companies, these assets may be pledged
to issue *collateral trust* bonds. Title to the assets is transferred
to the trustee (until the debt has been paid) under conditions
outlined in the trust indenture.

Debentures are unsecured bonds with no special claim on
particular assets of the corporation. In the case of default, debentures have the same claim as general creditors, which includes all assets not specifically pledged. Security for debentures is obtained by including in the indenture provisions designed to strengthen the company's ability to meet its credit
obligations. Such provisions include maintenance of adequate
working capital and restrictions on dividends and on the issue
of additional bonds.

The *subordinated debenture* is an unsecured obligation that
is specifically made junior to other designed credit claims,
such as bank loans or private loans extended by financial institutions. In the event of bankruptcy or liquidation, all debt
senior to the subordinated debentures must be paid in full before the junior bondholders are considered.

Income bonds may be debentures or may have their principal secured by a mortgage, but such obligations stipulate that
interest will be paid only if it is earned. Income bonds are
usually issued under reorganization plans, or for the promo-
tion of new enterprises.

Convertible bonds are usually subordinate debentures that
can be converted at the option of the holder into common
stock of the issuing corporation. Thus the convertible bond
has investment features of both a conventional bond and a
common stock. As a bond, it offers a fixed rate of return,
senior position, legal recourse and the return of principal at
maturity; and through the conversion privilege, the investor
gains price appreciation potential similar to that of a common stock. Conversion terms are set when the bond is issued,

but these terms often change during the life of the bond and may be adjusted when stock dividends are declared.

The two important things to know about a convertible bond are its value when converted into common stock; and its value as a straight bond without reference to the conversion feature. If a bond is convertible into common stock at the rate of $25 principal amount of debenture per share, it means that each $1,000 bond is convertible into 40 shares of common stock. The *conversion value* of a bond is the market price of the common stock multiplied by the number of shares into which each bond can be converted. For example, if the common stock of the above bond were selling at 30, the conversion value of the bond would be 120 ($1,200). If the stock dropped to 20, the conversion value of the bond would be 80. But the market price of a bond and the conversion value may not be the same. If the current price of the stock is 25, and the price of the bond is 115, the bond would be selling at a 15% premium over conversion value. On the other hand, if the stock sells down to 15 (making the conversion value only 60) and the market price of the bond remains at 85, the convertible is obviously reflecting its investment value as a straight bond.

The best kind of convertible bond to buy is one which is selling very near its conversion value and its investment value. Under these ideal conditions, the bond would immediately reflect any increase in the market value of the common stock; and should the price of the common fall, the price of the bond would be held up by its investment value. The advantages offered by convertibles are well recognized by investors. Thus the key question usually is: How much is the premium over conversion value and how much is the premium over investment value?

Financial Quality. Corporate bonds offer the widest range of quality and therefore require more analysis of the financial risk than do government or municipal obligations. Broadly speaking, investors judge the financial quality of a bond by the strength of the indenture obligating the bond issuer, and the funds available to a corporation for payment of interest and principal. If such funds are ample, the contractual rights of the bondholder need not be tested. The first and most important criterion is the ability of the corporation to pay—in other words, the quality and size of a company's earning power and financial resources in relation to its obligations.

The most widely used measure of quantitative financial adequacy is the ratio of earnings to interest coverage. There are many methods of calculating this ratio, but probably the most accepted is the "over-all" or total deduction method. Using this method, all fixed charges (including the interest on all classes of bonds, bank debt, etc.) are lumped together and divided into the income available for interest payments. Since interest is a pretax expense, it is more realistic to use income before taxes have been deducted. The total deduction method results in one ratio for all the bonds of any company, and it therefore understates the coverage for senior issues. It is a prudent approach, however, since insolvency resulting from default of a junior issue is extremely detrimental to even prior mortgage or senior bondholders. This method enables the investor to gauge quickly the financial strength of a company, but a thorough analysis requires detailed examination of each particular bond issue.

How many times should the interest be covered? Adequate coverage depends upon "the quality" of earnings. If a company has a favorable earnings trend and a long record of earnings stability, the quality of its earnings is considered high. This means that industries and companies which have demonstrated their ability to withstand economic adversity need less coverage than companies in industries characterized by large fluctuations in earnings. For this reason many bond analysts use average earnings over a period of seven to ten years, or they use earnings of a very poor year, as a test of quality.

Experience also suggests that the size of an enterprise can be a useful, if somewhat arbitrary, criterion of financial reliability. In a study of industrial bond offerings from 1900 to 1943 that went into default before 1944, W. B. Hickman discovered a correlation with size which emerges from Table 4.

The particular terms of an issue that designate the security pledged and the restrictions designed to safeguard bondholders have an important bearing on the quality of a bond. But the corporation's ability to pay is the paramount criterion of safety—even in the case of secured bonds, where the value of the pledged property will theoretically compensate the bond-

Table 4.
Industrial Bond Offerings Defaulted, 1900–1943

Asset Size of Issuer	Percent of Offerings Defaulted
Under $5 million	38.0
$5-99 million	25.3
$100–$199 million	17.2
$200 million and over	3.4

Source: W. B. Hickman, Corporate Bond Quality and Investor Experience (Princeton University Press, 1958).

holder in the event of default. For in practice, the property of a bankrupt company often loses much of its value. Moreover, taking possession of the property is often a slow and frustrating procedure.

THE MARKET FOR CORPORATE BONDS

Although more than 1,000 bond issues are listed on the New York Stock Exchange, the bulk of corporate bond trading is executed in the over-the-counter market. This market is dominated by the large investment banking firms, which supply the market with bonds they underwrite. Despite the fact that investors tend to "put away" bonds purchased for investment, the larger issues ($50 million or more) generally enjoy good secondary markets. The focus of attention, however, is on the new-issue market. The reception of a new issue serves as a test of the market and a benchmark by which bond traders gauge their own bids and offerings.

Trading activity in the over-the-counter market is a private affair. There is nothing corresponding to the stock ticker or the listing of prices in the press and no reporting of transactions to the public. Business is conducted over the telephone, with traders from different firms competing with each other and buyers negotiating for the best price.

Institutions such as insurance companies, corporate pension funds, state and local retirement funds, and so on account for 85% to 90% of the demand for corporate bonds. In 1965, approximately $7.9 billion of the $13.5 billion corporate bonds sold were privately placed with institutions without ever being offered for sale to the public. The advantage to the corporate borrower is that a private deal can be consummated in a few weeks, and it eliminates the red tape and the legal expenses of an SEC registration. For the buyer, a private placement can mean a little extra yield, or additional benefits such as warrants to purchase common stock of the issuing corporation.

MUNICIPAL BONDS

Bonds issued by local governmental units such as states, counties, towns, special political subdivisions and authorities are known as municipal bonds. The most important distinction for investors about municipal bonds is their tax-exempt status, which has made them a very popular investment for wealthy individuals and taxpaying institutions.

There are more different issuers of municipal bonds than all other types of bonds combined, but most municipals can be classified into two basic categories: *general obligation* and *revenue* bonds. General obligations—the larger category and the customary form used by most cities and states—are secured by the issuer's pledge of its "full faith and credit." There is no pledge of property, revenues or particular taxes, but the issuer undertakes to levy and collect the taxes necessary to service its debts. While some communities may pledge their "full faith and credit," their pledge is subject to the limits imposed on their taxing power by state or local legislation. In such cases, their obligations are known as *limited tax bonds*.

Revenue bonds are payable from specific revenues, usually derived from facilities constructed with proceeds of the bond issue. They are often used to circumvent municipal debt limits and to avoid increasing general taxes. They also have the virtue of allowing the beneficiaries of a facility to pay for the facility as they use it. A municipal revenue bond is an obligation of the community, but the obligation extends only to the payment of the bond from a special source of revenue. In situations where a facility extends beyond the geographical limits of a given community or even a state, revenue bonds issued by agencies or authorities provide an avenue for financing a cooperative effort, such as bridges, tunnels, irrigation.

Not every municipal bond falls neatly into the general obligation or revenue classification. Some issues combine the two forms. They provide for turning to the taxing power of the municipality should the specified revenues prove deficient. A particularly interesting type of municipal is the Public Housing Authority bond. Federal legislation provides for the building and operating of low-rent housing by local government with aid from federal funds. The bonds used to finance such construction are secured by a pledge of annual contributions from the Public Housing Authority. In effect, the government guarantees interest and principal. Investors consider PHAs to be among the highest quality municipal bonds.

Municipal bonds are authorized for issue by the constitutions, statutes and ordinances of the various issuers. To assure investors that a bond issue is legal, the issuer or bond dealer retains an independent law firm to render an opinion as to its validity. This legal opinion accompanies bond certificates when they are transferred and is a necessary condition for a good sale or purchase.

Financial Quality. When bond analysts and investors evaluate the credit quality of a municipality, the first factor considered is the community's record of debt management. Relatively few municipal issuers have defaulted, and only U.S. government obligations have a better credit standing with investors.

Analysts of municipal bonds examine statistics about the population trend of the community, its sources of economic wealth and the quality of local government. Within this framework, they then consider the purely financial aspects of the issue, which are related to the adequacy of the resources subject to tax and the effectiveness of the tax-collection effort. To measure this, bond analysts assemble such data as average income per capita, value of the real property in the community, debt service, taxes per capita, etc., and seek to project these over the relevant period of time. These data are used to determine the relationship of the debt service (interest plus scheduled debt retirement) to the total revenue of the municipality.

Appraising the quality of revenue bonds requires a different approach, since they are usually dependent on a single source of income. If the revenue source is an operating facility such as a toll road or a power project, the facility is analyzed in much the same way as a business enterprise. It should be economically sound and protected against competition, and its prospective revenues should be sufficient to cover debt service and provide a margin of safety against unforeseen contingencies.

THE MARKET FOR MUNICIPALS

The market for municipals is characterized by thousands of different issues, representing almost every state, county, city, town, and school district, not to mention all the revenue issues for toll roads, bridges and airports. These issues range in size from over $100 million to very small issues of under $1 million. Trading is conducted in the over-the-counter market by investment banking firms, the bond departments of brokerage houses, some of the large commercial banks and many small municipal bond dealers.

The large number of issues and the difficulty of being familiar with so many makes it hard for traders to make a good secondary market for every municipal issue. The problem of bringing buyers and sellers together is alleviated by a booklet called the *Blue List,* which contains bond offerings by dealers arranged alphabetically and classified by state. The *Blue List,* often more than 100 pages in length, is published every weekday. Prices are quoted on a yield to maturity basis. However, revenue bonds with a sizable issue outstanding are quoted in dollar prices.

WHAT DETERMINES BOND PRICES?

Interest—the price paid for the use of money—is subject to the laws of supply and demand that apply to the pricing of all goods and services. When interest rates rise, the rates on new bond issues must also be higher in order to find buyers in the market place. Since the rates fixed by the coupon on bonds already outstanding cannot be changed, adjustment to the new rates takes place through a change in bond prices—a decline in price raises the yield. Thus the prices of outstanding bonds tend to decline when interest rates go up, and bond prices rise when interest rates go down. The movements are always in the opposite direction.

The effect on bond prices of changes in the interest rate is frequently called the *interest rate risk;* it is the most important problem facing the bond investor. The other kind of risk that bond investors must contend with is the *financial risk*— the risk that the borrower will not be able to meet his obligations for financial reasons. The investor can guard against it by selecting only the highest-quality bonds. The interest rate risk is more difficult to contend with, and the effects of poor judgment can be as devastating on a bond portfolio as a sprinkling of defaulted issues. The magnitude of changes resulting from fluctuations in interest rates is at times considerable. For example, in 1967 the financially impeccable U.S. government 3% due 2/15/95 dropped to 73¾, a decline of about ten points for the year, and a 26% decrease in market value since the bond was issued at par 12 years earlier.

The effect of a change in interest rates on a particular

bond depends on two factors: the maturity date and the degree to which financial risk is a factor in the price of the bond. An equal increase in interest rates for bonds of all maturities will cause the price of long-term bonds to drop much more than the price of a short-term issue. This relationship between length of maturity and degree of interest rate risk is determined by the arithmetic of bond yields. For example, a 4% $1,000-bond due in two years and purchased at par yields 4.00% to maturity. If rates suddenly rise to 6% (a 50% increase), the market value of this bond will drop to $962.80 in order to adjust to the 6% yield. (The $40 annual interest plus the $37.20 discount—equivalent to an annual increment of $18.60—makes a total annual yield of $58.60, which works out to a 6.00% yield on the average value of the bond over its life.)

However, a 4% bond due in 20 years and purchased at par would fall to $768.90 if rates increased to 6%. A discount of $231.10, equivalent to an annual addition to interest of $11.555, is required to raise the yield to maturity up to the 6% level.

From the foregoing illustration it is easy to see that the longer the maturity of a bond, the greater is the exposure to interest rate risk. By the same token, if interest rates drop, long-term issues will appreciate more in value than short-term bonds.

Since there is very little chance that a high-quality "money rate" bond will fail to meet its interest or principal payments because of internal financial conditions, such bonds closely reflect movements in basic interest rates. Lower quality bonds that carry a higher degree of financial risk are subject to market appraisal of changes in the financial condition of the issuer, and to changes in investors' evaluation of the premium required for financial risk in a particular economic climate.

Supply and Demand for Credit. Investing in bonds calls for a thorough understanding of how changes in the supply and demand for credit affect bond prices. A useful approach to this problem is to catalogue the main types of fluctuations in bond prices and to examine the forces that generate these changes.

Any examination of bond prices over an extended period reveals three principal types of fluctuation: (1) long-term secular trends, which encompass at least two business cycles; (2) cyclical movements lasting from one to four years; (3) short-term movements lasting a few weeks or months.

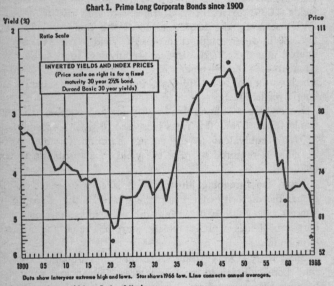

Chart 1. Prime Long Corporate Bonds since 1900

Dots show interyear extreme high and lows. Star shows 1966 low. Line connects annual averages.

Source: Courtesy of Salomon Brothers & Hutzler.

Secular Trends. Any trend that persists for an extended period must be powerful enough to dominate other cyclical and seasonal forces influencing changes in interest rates. Chart 1, which dates back to 1900, clearly shows a series of trends toward higher or lower bond yields, each lasting for ten years or more. It is evident that interest rates increased (and bond prices fell) from 1900 to 1920, moved sharply in the opposite direction from 1920 to 1946, and from that point on increased, challenging the high levels reached in the 1920s. The great sweep of secular trends in interest rates makes short-range cyclical movements seem like ripples on a great wave.

A further examination of the statistics back to 1900 reveals an interesting correlation. Almost all the great periods of rising rates have been related to wars and an accompanying inflationary trend. An exception to this pattern was evident during World War II, when the government kept interest rates low by creating a vast supply of credit and deliberately fixing interest rates on government bonds at a low level. The bear bond market of 1966 was also an exception, and was probably due to an extremely powerful cyclical movement coinciding with the direction of the secular trend.

The range of rates revealed by the secular pattern of bond prices gives a rough indication of when rates are either extremely high or extremely low by historical standards. In principle, long-term bond purchases should be avoided when interest rates are extremely low and should be favored when rates are high, despite the pressure of immediate needs.

Cyclical Trends. A close inspection of bond prices over the years reveals cycles of rising and falling prices lasting from one to three or four years. These cycles, which resemble saw-teeth on the secular trendline, are widely attributed to the influence of the business cycle on the demand for credit. It is certainly reasonable to expect the acceleration phase of the business cycle to exert an upward pressure on interest rates, since increases in business activity call for additional credit. Conversely, during a recessionary phase of the business cycle, the demand for credit ebbs and interest rates should fall. This process appears so logical that many investors believe that low interest rates in recessions, and high rates during booms, are an automatic occurrence. Several recent studies indicate that this correlation *does* hold good at the top of a boom or the bottom of a recession. At other times, however, the bond market may be dominated by the secular trend, or influenced by external events or by the competitive imperfections of the economy. This was demonstrated in 1950, 1952, 1955, 1962, 1964 and the early part of

1965, when a business uptrend did not lead to significantly large rises in interest rates.

Even though the correlation between interest rates and the business cycle is imperfect, bond investors should at all times have a working hypothesis about the course of the economy. Such a framework is a prerequisite for responsible assumptions about the probable supply and demand for credit and the probable course of monetary and fiscal policy. The bond investor should also study a breakdown of credit demand (mortgages, corporate bonds, municipal issues, etc.) and of the sources of credit supply. Such studies show, among other things, which sources of credit are expanding or contracting, and they can be a valuable guide as to which sectors of the bond market (corporate, government or municipal) present the best relative opportunities in any given period.

Changes in economic conditions that affect the supply and demand for credit must be viewed against the background of government monetary and fiscal policy. Nowadays, the government uses the price and availability of credit as a lever to influence the economy, and the bond market is extremely sensitive to policy changes. These are several avenues of credit control open to governmental authorities. The most influential is the Federal Reserve System, which controls the commercial banking system through its power over the volume of commercial bank cash assets and the supply of credit that a given level of cash reserves can support. The Federal Reserve Board can also influence the entire structure of interest rates through changes in the discount rate, the rate that banks must pay to borrow from the Federal Reserve. An even more powerful tool is the Fed's open-market operations, which also influence bank reserves through the purchase or sale of government securities. The effect of such transactions is to raise or lower bank reserves and their ability to extend credit in the economy. The government can also influence the economy through the regulation of lending policy for banks and savings institutions, through budgetary measures and through tax policy.

Short-term Movements. The forces behind the short-term moves in bond prices are often identical to those that influence cyclical and secular moves. In addition to reflecting real (if temporary) changes in the credit situation, short swings are caused by investor expectations. These expectations are tested in short-run price adjustments, which evolve into major moves only when confirmed over a period of time by substantive developments.

While short-term price changes are difficult to foresee accurately, there are a number of indicators which furnish possible clues to the direction of the market. The most reliable is the calendar of scheduled bond financing. A light calendar means that few bonds will be coming to market and therefore buying pressure is likely to be concentrated on available issues. A big calendar and heavy inventories in the hands of dealers spell lower prices until the excess supply can be worked off.

TIMING BOND PURCHASES

Timing in the bond market refers not only to when a purchase should be made but also to the selection of maturities. The purchase of a long-term bond means assurance of a specific return for the life of the bond, but it also means exposure to price fluctuations that result from changes in the interest rate. If a long-term bond is purchased during a period when interest rates are low, the investor is stuck with a small income and a bond that will decline in value if rates should rise again. A short-term bond, however, will not depreciate much in value as a result of changes in the interest rate and one can expect to get the full principal on maturity in just a few years.

Given the disadvantages of long-term bonds, why should anyone buy them? Why not simply keep rolling over short maturities? One important reason is that, despite the relative stability of principal, short-term rates are more sensitive to cyclical forces and the yield on short maturities fluctuates more widely than the yield on long-term bonds (Chart 2).

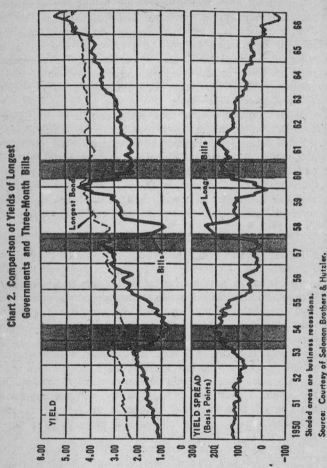

Chart 2. Comparison of Yields of Longest
Governments and Three-Month Bills

Shaded areas are business recessions.

Source: Courtesy of Salomon Brothers & Hutzler.

Consequently, a portfolio consisting exclusively of short-
term maturities would be subject to radical changes in income from year to year. Thus investors who require stability
of principal will favor short maturities, while those who seek

to minimize fluctuations in income will find long-term bonds more suitable. A skillful investor, however, will so structure the maturity of his portfolio that he can take advantage of changes in the relationship of yields and maturities.

The ideal procedure is to buy long-term bonds when rates are high and stay with short-term issues when rates are low. However, to catch the major moves in the market involves waiting for the periods that occur every 20 or 30 years when rates reach secular high points, and very few investors can be expected to do this. A more workable program is to increase holdings of short-term bonds as interest rates decline. For example, in the case of corporate bonds, a policy based on the experience of the past 50 years would suggest restraint in the purchase of long-term bonds when rates (as measured by high-grade bonds) fall below 3½%; a modest increase in purchases as rates rise above 4%; and a strong commitment when rates exceed 5½%.

The relationship of short- and long-term rates during cyclical fluctuations (and indeed for longer periods) can also help in timing the purchase of long-term bonds. Chart 2 indicates that long-term bonds are better buys when the spread between short- and long-term bonds is narrow. Despite the fact that bond prices generally declined during the period from 1950 to 1966, the investor who purchased long-term bonds only during the peak periods for short-term rates would have done considerably better than average.

RISKS VS. RETURN

Most investors depend on the quality ratings and analyses prepared by independent financial services: Moody's, Standard and Poor's, and Dun & Bradstreet. Both Standard & Poor's and Moody's use an alphabetical rating system that is widely accepted by the investment community. For example, bonds rated AAA by Standard & Poor's are described as the highest-quality obligations. They possess the ultimate degree of protection as to principal and interest. Marketwise they move with interest rates and hence provide the maximum safety on all counts. Bonds rated B (five ratings lower) are categorized as "speculative" because "payment of interest cannot be assured under difficult economic conditions."

The extent to which quality is stressed in a bond portfolio should be a function of the investment requirements. Banks, pension funds and other fiduciary-type investors guard at all costs against the risk of default. A miscalculation about the direction of interest rates can be costly, but the investor will still receive the specified interest and the full amount of principal on maturity.

There are, however, many investors who are in a position to take a reasonable risk provided it is justified by the extra return. One of the best historical studies of investor experience with corporate bonds from 1900 through 1943 was that made by W. B. Hickman for the National Bureau of Economic Research, *Corporate Bond Quality and Investor Experience*. It showed a direct correlation between quality (as indicated by ratings at the time of issue) and the frequency of defaults. For the period covered, only 6% of the bonds in the first two grades were ever in default. On the other hand, 19.1% of the bonds in the fourth grade and 42.4% of the bonds below the fourth rating defaulted. Even allowing for the fact that defaults for lower-grade issues were seven times more frequent than for high-grade bonds, Hickman's study found that on the average investors obtained a better return on low-grade bonds.

There are many opportunities to make judicious investments in bonds that do not measure up to the exacting standards of the highest grade. The Moody's Aa and A ratings, and the comparable Standard & Poor's designations, represent good-grade bonds with many favorable investment attributes. The weighing of return vs. risk can become an endless game. The decisive consideration is that the investor should not be seduced by unusually high return, for to take large risks in bonds is a poor utilization of this investment medium. An examination of the behavior of the various grades of bonds under conditions of economic stress points up the vulnerability of lower-grade issues. For the six-year period 1925–30, bond averages compiled by Moody's indicate that, on the average, bonds rated Baa sold to yield about 145 basis points (1.45%) more than comparable Aaa issues. At the very bottom of the depression in 1932 the differential had increased to 475 basis points. Expressed in a different way, a typical 25-year Aaa bond that sold at par to yield about 4.55% in 1930 would have declined 15 points by 1932; a comparable Baa issue would have fallen 44 points, almost three times as much. By 1934, the Aaa issue had recovered to seven points above par, whereas the Baa bond was still down four points.

In his authoritative work, *Security Analysis*, Benjamin Graham calls bond selection a "negative art" that involves a process of exclusion and rejection rather than search and acceptance. This sharply contrasts with the process of selecting common stocks, where the rejection of a particular issue can be as damaging as the choice of one that turns out to be a mistake. The investor can refuse any number of excellent bonds without ill effect so long as he finally makes a sound choice.

BONDS FOR CAPITAL GAINS

There are three methods of using bonds aggressively when the objective is capital gains: (1) purchase of low-grade and/or defaulted issues in the hope that they will make a financial recovery; (2) use of leverage; (3) purchase of convertible bonds. The first method calls for specialized knowledge of the situation in question and keen analytical powers. The key to most bond speculation is leverage—the use of borrowed funds to purchase a large amount of bonds. How this works can be illustrated by the experience of a university professor who turned speculator in September, 1966. During that month, the professor purchased 125 U.S. Treasury bonds (3½% due 2/15/90) at 80 for $100,000, using $10,000 of his own capital and the $90,000 borrowed from the bank. In December, 1966, he sold the bonds at 86¼ for a gross profit of $7,812—more than 75% on his investment. Of course, leverage works both ways. Had the U.S. Treasury bonds declined 6¼ points, the professor would have suffered a very severe loss.

Convertible bonds are ideally suited for the pursuit of capital gains, when the conversion privilege can be combined with low margin requirements. This combination makes it possible to reap spectacular profits. For example, a speculator who purchased $100,000 Scientific Data 5½% convertible debentures at the issue price of 100 on November 4, 1966, could have sold these same bonds five months later for a $90,000 profit—3.6 times his capital investment (assuming he used the then available 25% margin). While this would have been an extraordinary coup, substantial capital gains could have been made in at least 50 other issues during the same period.

Practically all convertibles sell at premiums over their investment value, and every convertible with any speculative promise also sells at a substantial premium over its conversion value. The attractiveness of a convertible and its downside vulnerability are largely determined by the level of these premiums. When the premium over investment and/or conversion value becomes excessive, a simultaneous decline in the bond and stock market can be brutal to convertibles. This combination of circumstances in the period from November, 1965, to September, 1966, resulted in a decline for many convertibles that was almost equal to the drop in the stock market.

The floor for a convertible is a function of the investment value of the bond component, but this does not mean a convertible will not fall below this level. Investment value reflects current prices in the bond market. A 4% coupon on a convertible will provide little protection against a decline in the price of the common at a time when straight bonds are yielding well over 6%.

It is difficult to set forth rules as to when convertibles should be purchased, but there are two key considerations:

(1) Buy only those convertibles that appear to have some definite advantage (yield or downside protection) over the common. (2) Avoid convertibles unless the common stock looks attractive.

7

Investing in Mutual Funds

By Richard E. Blodgett

One of Wall Street's greatest success stories of the past quarter century is not about a young man who moved east from Peoria and made a bundle in the market; it is about the industry that was born in Boston in the early 1920s, was snubbed for years by the Street, suddenly blossomed after World War II, and is now a mover and shaker in the securities business.

The story is seasoned with intrigue, including chapters on "Hanky panky before the 1940 Act" and "What are they going to do to the market today?" And among the dramatis personae are such renowned individuals as the Chinese gentleman, the barefoot boy in Battery Park, and the cigar-smoking Presidential press secretary.

The industry is, of course, the mutual fund business—one of the most profitable and fastest-growing segments of the securities industry. And the "renowned individuals" referred to above are Gerald Tsai, Jr., the Shanghai-born founder of the Manhattan Fund; Jack Dreyfus, Jr., the man behind the Dreyfus Fund, who used to spend occasional hours shoeless in Manhattan's Battery Park; and Pierre Salinger, President John F. Kennedy's press secretary and an organizer of a Bahamas-based fund that is sold abroad.

Richard E. Blodgett, a financial writer, is a former editor of *Business Week.*

Wall Street had long pondered a multi-million dollar problem: how to bring the small investor into the stock market and make money on the deal. And the answer it came up with was mutual funds. Today they are one of the most important forces, if not the most important, in the market. Their heavy buying and selling sometimes drives the prices of individual stocks up or down 10% or 20% in a matter of weeks and occasionally days. And they have come under increasing government criticism in recent years on a variety of counts.

Although the industry made its start in the early 1920s, by 1940 it held less than $500 million on behalf of shareholders —a tiny portion of total private investments. In that year, however, the industry underwent a far-reaching change, one that still is protested by a few old-time fund executives but which, most others acknowledge, helped build a foundation for its spectacular postwar growth. That change was the Investment Company Act of 1940, which established a long list of industry standards and, as some fund men put it, thus "inspired public confidence" in the integrity of mutual funds. Since then, the growth in public confidence has been such that at the beginning of 1967, the number of mutual funds had risen to around 350 and their aggregate net assets were in the area of $35 billion.

The basic idea behind a mutual fund is both simple and sound: A group of people get together, pool their money and hire a professional to manage it. In this way they can raise enough cash to by a diversified portfolio and, it is hoped, get some top-flight investment management besides. A mutual fund thus appeals mainly to individuals of moderate means who don't have the time or the know-how to follow the stock market themselves.

Of course, these individuals don't exactly "get together." The impetus comes from the fund itself, which sets up shop and then tries to sell its shares to the public. Mutual funds are sometimes called "open-end" investment companies, becase they continuously offer additional shares to investors rather than having a limited sale period. Likewise, the funds undertake to buy their shares back at any time from any holder who wants the cash.

A "closed-end" investment company, in contrast, has a fixed number of shares outstanding and generally doesn't sell additional ones or buy back those already in the public's hands. Because of this limited capitalization, the size of the closed-end industry has tended to remain static in recent years.

The mutual fund concept, though, has caught on in the biggest of ways. More than 3.2 million American investors—a respectable 16% of the United States investing public—owned *only* mutual fund shares in 1965, according to a study made by the New York Stock Exchange. And this doesn't include the countless others who owned mutual funds in addition to other types of securities. The 3.2 million total was up 48% from 1962, the study went on to show, making funds the fastest-growing vehicle for investment. The number of Americans owning shares listed on the New York Stock Exchange itself rose 12.8% during the three-year period to about 12.4 million.

The Investment Company Institute, the funds' own trade group, puts out monthly figures on the industry's size, and these, too, tell a tale of rapid growth. At the end of 1966, the Institute found, the funds had a record $35 billion in assets, up from $25 billion three years earlier and $17 billion four years before that.

Their power in the stock market is even greater nowadays than their assets indicate. This is because the funds—traditionally conservative, long-term investors—started becoming more speculative in the early 1960s. Mutual funds increased the annual turnover rate of their investments from 16% of their portfolio in 1955 to 21% in 1965 and 33% in the first half of 1966. This 33% annual turnover rate compared to only 18% for all investors on the New York Stock Exchange in the first half of 1966.

This heavy involvement in short-term trading has resulted mainly from the funds' growing concern with "performance" —their eagerness to outperform each other and thus to attract new shareholders. It was encouraged by the success of the Dreyfus Fund and the Fidelity group of funds in short-term trading—a success not duplicated by a number of their imitators. One "performance" fund, for instance, tried to make a quick purchase of Xerox at $250 a share and drove it up to $280 in the process—hardly an example of well-managed, professional buying. Another drove Motorola down from $184 to $175 by unloading a big block of shares.

The public's enthusiastic response to mutual funds would seem to indicate that most of them do a good job of investing for their shareholders. Actually, mutual funds are just like anything else—their performances range all the way from outstanding to mediocre to ineptly bad, depending on the fund.

During 1965, for instance, one fund—Security Equity Fund, a small Topeka, Kansas, outfit—provided its shareholders a whopping 77% gain. In contrast, the 30-stock Dow-Jones Industrial Average, which many investors use as a guide to how well stock prices are doing, rose a bit less than 11%. The Fidelity group of funds in Boston, which have been performing well for years, also turned in some nifty price gains in 1965: 55% for Fidelity Trend Fund, 49% for Fidelity Capital Fund and 17% for Fidelity Fund. (The Fidelity group, early in 1966, lost one of its chief strategists, young Gerry Tsai, who set out on his own and founded the Manhattan Fund. His reputation was such that, at its first public offering, the Manhattan Fund sold $270 million worth of its shares to investors eager for Mr. Tsai's investment management. A year later, the Fund's net assets were up to $457 million.)

At the other end of the scale in 1965 was American Pacific

Fund, a Honolulu-based fund whose price slid about 10%; American Pacific invests mainly in insurance stocks, which had a bad year, thus accounting for the fund's poor showing. But at least a dozen other mutual funds also suffered price losses in 1965, despite the over-all advance of the market, as measured by the Dow-Jones Industrial Average.

A number of concerns regularly publish comprehensive tables on the funds' performance, including Arthur Wiesenberger & Co., and *Forbes* magazine in New York, and *Fund-Scope* magazine in Los Angeles. It would be unfair, of course, to match all funds against the Industrial Average. Some are not even trying to outperform "the Dow"; their formally expressed objective is to invest in a balanced portfolio of stocks and bonds which, they hope, will give their shareholders relative safety of principal together with good dividend yield. Nonetheless, the wide variations in the performance of those funds that are out to do better than the popular averages point squarely to a wide range of management ability within the industry. The Wiesenberger reports give an idea of just how varied the performance is in these funds. In the five-year period, 1962 through 1966, American Investors Fund topped the list with a 145.3% price gain, followed by Ivest Fund with a 111.2% rise and Fidelity Trend Fund with a 103.4% gain. Peoples Securities Corporation, which seeks maximum capital gains, ended the five years with a 0.8% capital loss; and Fund of America was up only 4.2%. The Dow rose 7.5% during the five years.

In the ten years through 1966, the Wiesenberger tables show, the performance of capital gains funds ranged from a 217% increase by the Value Line Special Situations Fund down to a 50.1% rise by Group Securities' Aerospace-Science Fund, which despite its mediocre ten-year performance was one of the outstanding funds in 1965 with a 56.9% gain. During this ten-year period, the Dow rose about 60% and several indices of growth stocks registered much larger gains.

However well they do their job, the fund managers—and

their salesmen—are handsomely compensated. Most management companies (the management company usually is a separate corporation from the fund itself) are paid annually up to one-half of 1% of the fund's assets. Although this may look small in percentage terms, it builds up to a large sum when the fund is a big one. Investors Mutual, the biggest of all, paid $10.4 million in 1965 to its manager, Investors Diversified Services (IDS). (In addition, IDS collected $20.3 million in sales fees from investors who bought shares of Investors Mutual.)

In return for such fees, mutual fund shareholders get their investments planned and watched over by a team of securities analysts—anywhere from one to several dozen of them, depending on the size and policy of the fund and its manager. The fund also performs certain administrative services, such as the safekeeping of the stock certificates owned by the fund and the passing along of dividends. (Under federal law, any fund that turns at least 90% of its dividend income and capital gains over to shareholders each year generally is not taxed on the money. This benefit is designed to avoid an extra layer of taxation so long as the moneys filter down from the fund to the actual investors, the fund shareholders.)

The size of the management fees has at times come under bitter attack, both in and out of court. Court actions were brought against most of the major funds in the late 1950s and early 1960s by disgruntled shareholders who claimed their fund was being milked by its manager. While the funds stoutly denied the charges, they nevertheless gave ground and reduced their management fees a bit.

Perhaps the most blistering attack on the size of management fees came, however, from the University of Pennsylvania's Wharton School of Finance and Commerce. The school was commissioned by the Securities and Exchange Commission to make a thorough study of the fund business. What it found would make almost any fund manager turn red—either from anger or blushing.

For one thing, the 1962 Wharton report charged, the 0.5% management fees were "excessive" because they ate up as much as 40% of a fund's investment income. The study also raised doubts about the effectiveness of the funds, contending that many an investor would do better in the market on his own. And as if that wasn't enough, the report also lashed out at the industry's sales practices, charging that many salesmen were merely out to make a quick buck rather than being interested in the financial needs of their clients.

The Wharton report was followed in December, 1966, by the SEC's own report on the fund industry. The SEC study agreed that management fees were too high and asked Congress to pass a law requiring that the fees be "reasonable." The proposed law would further provide that any lawyer, or the SEC itself, may go to court to try to get a fund's fee reduced if it does not appear "reasonable." Joseph E. Welch, president of the Wellington Fund, pretty much summed up the industry's reaction to this proposal when he told a conference at the University of Pennsylvania in February, 1967: "I am strongly opposed to having management fees controlled directly or indirectly by a government agency. . . . The matter should be left to the natural forces of competition, which will in time cure any ills that exist."

Robert M. Loeffler, vice president of Investors Diversified Services, agreed with Welch at the conference. He reported that the annual management fees on IDS's three biggest funds declined to 0.34% of their net assets in 1966 from 0.58% in 1956. "Competition is there," Mr. Loeffler said, "and it is coming into play."

The 1962 Wharton report may have been unduly harsh in some respects, but there's little doubt that it spurred some much-needed reforms within the industry, especially in sales practices. The part-time salesman, who used to sell fund shares whenever he was able to get away from his regular job, appears to be headed for oblivion. He has been increasingly replaced by full-time professionals. Also, many funds have been stepping up their training programs—not always successfully—in the hope of assuring that informed and competent men will be selling their shares.

The salesmen generally do well for themselves. The sales fees on most mutual funds are as large as 8½% of the purchase price, and the salesman keeps a good part of this. On a transaction of $5,000, a mutual fund sales fee could be nearly ten times as large as the average commission for stocks listed on the New York Stock Exchange—namely $425 vs. perhaps $45. That is one reason why some brokers are particularly anxious to sell fund shares.

Insofar as sales methods are concerned, there are basically two types of funds: the "direct sellers," which hire their own sales forces, and the "indirect sellers," which market their shares through stockbrokers. Investors Diversified Services, the biggest fund manager, is a direct seller. Dreyfus Fund, the largest of the Wall Street-based funds and the fifth largest in the industry, relies on brokers.

Many brokerage firms, lured by the big commissions earned from selling funds, have in recent years set up special departments to push mutual fund sales. (One house has even gone so far as to offer its salesmen Green Stamps, occasionally, as an incentive for selling fund shares.)

It was the high sales fees and commissions, mentioned above, that drew the biggest blast in the SEC's 1966 report. The report asserted that there was an "unjustified disparity" between mutual fund sales fees and sales charges for other securities, and it requested Congress to reduce the maximum sales "load" on mutual funds to 5%. The SEC charged that competition has actually driven sales fees up instead of down, because the funds have competed to get brokers to sell their shares by offering them increasingly large rewards.

The 5% proposal was the most bitter of the SEC's suggestions, from the standpoint of the mutual fund industry. Many funds were worried that brokers would have second thoughts about selling fund shares if the load were reduced to 5%. "It would be disastrous," said Leon Levy, president of the highly successful Oppenheimer Fund. Many other fund executives expressed fears that the industry's spectacular growth might come to an end if the maximum sales fee were reduced to 5%. Such a reduction would probably slow down the industry's rate of expansion, but it certainly wouldn't bring it to a halt. Many large brokerage firms would almost certainly continue to sell fund shares; the main effect of the change would be to drive small, low-profit brokerage houses out of mutual fund sales.

The New York Stock Exchange appears to view the whole matter with a certain disdain, preferring that its members sell listed stocks instead. In 1954, in fact, the Exchange set up a special program of its own aimed at recapturing some of the ground it was losing to the funds. This program is called the Monthly Investment Plan (MIP) and is designed to allow an investor to make regular purchases of a listed stock at relatively low commissions. The plan has done poorly, however, in comparison to the growth of mutual funds; there were 210,000 MIP accounts in operation at the end of 1966, compared with well over six million mutual fund accounts. The only major brokerage house to do much to promote MIP has been Merrill Lynch, Pierce, Fenner & Smith, which incidentally, is also one of the very few large houses that still resist selling fund shares. Merrill Lynch contends that its customers can do better investing for themselves than letting a fund manage their portfolios. But Merrill Lynch—by far the largest of the U.S. brokerage houses—is one of the few that can afford to take such a stand and bypass the profits available from selling mutual funds.

The New York Stock Exchange, though it has shown no enthusiasm for mutual funds, has actually benefited from their growth. For the money invested in mutual funds in due course reaches the floor of the Exchange. At the end of 1966 the funds owned $24 billion of Big Board stocks, and much of this sum would probably never have been invested in the market had not a fund sold someone in Ames, Iowa, or Shreveport, Louisiana, on the idea of owning stocks.

There are all types of mutual funds: income funds, growth funds, balanced funds, speculative funds, hedge funds (which simultaneously maintain long and short positions), and international funds. There are specialized funds for those who wish to invest only in a particular industry, for example, electronics. There is even a fund which concentrates only on companies located in southern Florida. Then, too, there are funds whose investment decisions are based on a particular approach to the market, notably the Dow Theory Investment Fund. These funds are spread out all over the country: Boston, Chicago, Dallas, Los Angeles, Minneapolis, New York, Omaha, Philadelphia, Tacoma and elsewhere.

The hedge funds, a fairly recent innovation, have been particularly popular with affluent, sophisticated investors. The hedge funds use part of their assets to buy stocks and the rest to sell other stocks short. They thus are hedged against either a rise in prices or a decline. Like the "performance" funds, they tend to do a good deal of short-term trading and consequently are often the cause of sharp, short-lived price movements in a particular stock. Hedge funds are usually partnerships rather than corporations. As such they sell their shares only to a limited number of people and are therefore not required to register with the SEC, as most publicly owned funds must do. Thus there is little information about them in the public domain, although their tactics and growing impact on the market are much discussed, and sometimes criticized, on Wall Street.

Other recent twists given to the mutual fund concept include "exchange" funds and "dual" funds. Until early 1967, investors were allowed to exchange, tax free, individual stocks in which they might have large profits for shares in a so-called "swap" fund, thus obtaining diversification without paying a capital gains tax. But the Internal Revenue Service has put an end to further tax-free swaps. Dual funds, pioneered at about the time that exchange funds were on the way out, offer two classes of stock: growth shares and income shares. An equal amount of each class is sold. The holders of the growth shares receive all the capital gains and absorb all the capital losses from the combined pool; and the holders of the income shares get all the income from dividends and interest.

The wide variety in objectives, management quality and performance should make any prospective investor careful to take a good look at a fund's character and record before committing his money to it. Unfortunately, few investors do this. Mutual funds, in the lingo of the trade, are "sold rather than bought." In other words, most purchases are generated by a persuasive salesman rather than by spontaneous action on the part of an interested investor. Once he gets his foot through the door an aggressive salesman can be hard to get rid of. Nevertheless, investors should firmly resist being railroaded into a hasty and perhaps quite inappropriate commitment. The best policy is to ask a stockbroker for the prospectuses of some of the better funds, study them, and then decide which appears to be most suited to one's situation and objectives.

Investors should not neglect to look into those funds which do not have a sales force and do not market their shares through brokers, but rely on newspaper advertisements and word-of-mouth to sell their shares. These are known as "no load" funds because the buyer does not pay a sales charge. Many of them are managed by investment counseling concerns, such as Boston's big and prestigious Scudder, Stevens and Clark. While the no-loads represent about 50 of the nation's 350 funds, they account for a far smaller proportion of the industry's assets. At first sight they would appear to offer better value than the funds with an 8½% sales fee. However, the "load" funds argue that the service and management which they provide cannot be matched by the no-loads for the simple reason that the latter do not make enough money to afford it. The no-loads, of course, disagree. Statistics—the great impartial arbiter—indicate that in the long run a top-flight no-load performs about the same as a top-flight load fund, and that there are both load and no-load funds whose records range from poor to indifferent.

The mutual fund industry has done so well, and its prospects have appeared so rosy, that a growing number of outsiders have been elbowing their way into it. Since 1960, a rather startling list of industrial and other concerns have either bought into existing mutual fund management companies, or have announced plans to set up their own. Among these are Kansas City Southern Industries (owner of Kansas City Southern Railway); Gates Rubber Co.; Sears, Roebuck & Co.; International Telephone & Telegraph Co.; and First National City Bank of New York.

The public, too, has been buying into the management side of the mutual fund business. Nearly twenty companies that manage funds are publicly owned. Perhaps the best known is Dreyfus Corp., which first offered shares to the public in October, 1965. The sale grossed $41.8 million (taxable at the 15% capital gains rate) for the company's former owners, the partners in Dreyfus & Co., a New York brokerage house. Dreyfus Corp. manages the Dreyfus Fund, which rode to success on the investment acumen of a team headed by dapper, soft-spoken Jack Dreyfus, Jr., powerfully reinforced by a national television and newspaper advertising campaign featuring "the Dreyfus lion."

Some of the outsiders who have been entering the mutual fund business have more in mind than just marketing fund shares. What they have been doing is selling mutual funds and life insurance in a single package. The trend toward such packaging has been particularly evident among the industry's direct sellers, who can train their personnel in the arts of selling both funds and insurance. ("If a prospective client doesn't want one, at least we might be able to sell him the other," argues one fund official.)

This move has drawn a flood of protests from conservatives in both the fund and insurance industries, mainly on the ground that the salesmen are not qualified to operate knowledgeably in both these fields. The New York Stock Exchange has barred the salesmen of member firms from marketing insurance. But the trend is nonetheless gaining ground. In many cases, the salesman induces the investor to agree to regular purchases of a fund's shares and at the same time to buy "term" life insurance. As the value of the fund investment builds up, the insurance is gradually reduced. In this way, advocates of the plan contend, the investor is able to establish immediately, through the term insurance, an estate of a specified value (say, $50,000) and then gradually replace the insurance in his estate with fund shares. Many insurance executives argue, however, that the investor would be better off purchasing a straight $50,000 life policy in the first place and then hanging onto it.

Frequently, when selling funds and insurance in combination, the salesman makes a special effort to market the fund shares in the form of a "contractual plan." In signing such a contract, an investor generally obligates himself to invest a specified dollar amount each month or so in a fund's shares. The contract usually runs for ten years. Contractual plan advocates—and there are many—contend the programs are especially good for a long-term investor, because they set up a regular investment program for him.

But contractual plans have been coming increasingly under fire, both from government regulators and from some fund executives. The SEC, in its 1966 report, in effect recommended that such plans be banned. What these critics find objectionable is that most of the sales fees on a contractual plan come out of the investor's first-year payments; usually about 50% of these first-year outlays go to the salesman and his firm. Consequently, if for any reason the investor is forced to cancel the contract in its early stages, he gets only part of his money back. One of the more significant developments in the contractual plan controversy occurred in 1965, when Investors Diversified Services offered its first contractual program. IDS's innovation was to reduce the first-year sales fee to 20% of the payments and to spread the rest of the fees over the life of the contract. Thus an investor buying an IDS contract would lose significantly less than he would on other funds' plans if he decided to bow out in the early stages of the contract. What effect this will have on other contractual plans remains to be seen.

Probably the best advice for anyone interested in buying a contractual plan is not to do it unless you fully understand what you are getting into and are sure you will be able to meet all the payments for the next ten years. (It would be ridiculous, for instance, for someone planning to retire in three years on reduced income to buy a ten-year contractual plan.) If in doubt, remember that you can always buy the shares on your own without a contract.

IDS, in addition to its role in the contractual plan controversy, is involved in another industry dispute, one whose repercussions are being felt by the entire financial community. In 1965, Waddell & Reed, Inc., of Kansas City, manager of United Funds, announced it was purchasing a membership on the Pacific Coast Stock Exchange, and IDS promptly followed suit. Both are big direct sellers who do not rely on brokers to market their shares. Thus they have nothing to lose and much to gain if they handle their own brokerage business, bypassing the brokerage houses and the New York Stock Exchange. The move signals the growing independence of the funds from Wall Street, and their growing power in the securities industry.

The funds already have helped to pump new life into the nation's "regional" stock exchanges—that is to say, those outside New York—but the funds' aid may prove temporary. Most of the regional exchanges, such as those in Boston and Detroit, allow their members to share commissions with non-members, whereas the New York Stock Exchange bans such commission-splitting between members and nonmembers for transactions executed on its floor. The funds find it convenient and economical to compensate brokers for research work and for selling fund shares by giving them brokerage business. But a problem arises when the broker in line for compensation is not a member of a major stock exchange and is therefore unable to handle the funds' orders. In such cases, the funds give the business to a brokerage house with the necessary exchange membership and they direct that house to execute the orders on a regional exchange and to "give up" part of the commission to the nonmember broker. *If the orders were executed on the New York Stock Exchange, such "give-up" to nonmembers would not be permitted.* The result of this situation has been a gradual siphoning off of some trading from the New York Stock Exchange to the regional exchanges, although the Big Board continues to maintain by far the dominant position. The SEC has been threatening to ban the give-up system. Such a ban would undoubtedly put a damper on the regional exchanges' new-found glory.

The funds would seem to be fully justified in handing out "reciprocal" business—brokerage orders given in return for services rendered—when the services are for investment research. For such research, it is hoped, improves the fund's performance and so directly benefits its shareholders. But when reciprocal business is simply a reward for selling the fund's shares, the situation is entirely different. The question has been raised as to whether, in such cases, the fund is not violating its fiduciary responsibility to its shareholders. For the sale of additional shares benefits the salesman and not the fund's shareholders. And yet it is the shareholders' money which is being used to pay brokerage commissions handed out as a reward for good salesmanship.

The various criticisms leveled at the mutual fund industry should not be allowed to obscure the fact that it rests on solid foundations and meets a genuine need. By providing investors of moderate means with diversification and professional management, mutual funds have enabled millions of

Americans to reap the long-term benefits of share ownership in an expanding economy. The well-managed funds—and there are many of them—have a long-term record which the average investor would find it hard to match.

8

Investing for Growth

By Dan W. Lufkin

To distinguish "investing for growth" from "investing for income" misses the point. One invests in common stocks for growth in earning power and subsequent stock appreciation and dividend payout. If one invests on the basis of income (dividend payout) alone, and does not pay sufficient attention to earning power in support of income, obviously "income" is fleeting. In part these distinctions are enlarged by our archaic tax codes which distinguish income and capital gain via tax rates. In many instances the investor has let the politician set the framework of investment thinking for him. In investing one should be concerned primarily with growing earning power, and whether that is represented in the dividend or retained earnings account makes no difference. Barring peculiar legal definitions of "income" such as in trusts, income is a dollar bill, whether it comes in the form of a dividend check or appreciation and subsequent sale of all or a portion of a common stock holding. Hence when any thoughtful investor invests in common stock, he must invest for "growth."

There are two main areas of "growth" as we are defining it here: market growth and company growth. Market growth

Dan W. Lufkin is chairman of the board of directors of Donaldson, Lufkin & Jenrette, Inc.

can be achieved through investing in "names and numbers" per se. By names, I mean the fashions of the time—those general areas endowed with "romance" at any given moment in the market place. Over the last five years we have witnessed a number of such "name" cycles—boating and recreation, electronics, transistors, publishing, educational services, to name a few. By numbers, I refer to the general "underpriced" areas which are statistically cheap relative to the market or to their industry or to any generally accepted measuring standard or norm. Much work has been done on Wall Street within the past few years in measuring relative values —relative price, earnings, yield and price/earnings ratio—to pinpoint areas for market growth in stock values.

Company growth, and it is here that the word "investing" is more applicable, is a different subject. Company growth takes two forms—growth in the company's revenues, assets, net worth, markets and so on; and appreciation in the company's stock market price as a result of such company growth. In this chapter, we will devote ourselves primarily to these two areas of company growth—"internal" company growth, growth of the company itself; and "external" company growth, growth in the market price of the company shares and successful investing in these shares.

Fundamental to investing for growth is the recognition that there is no such thing as a "growth" company; there is only that company so *managed* and *structured* and *positioned* as to take advantage of one-shot and continuing opportunities for growth. What then are the key ingredients for such growth?

The first is inherent in the statement above. That is *management* ability—imagination, creativity and organization. Although it can occur, rarely is a company positioned to take continuing advantage of opportunity—either internally generated or through good fortune—without careful forethought and planning by people. Other things being equal, it is the dedication and the foresight and the will of people that create growth. Carrying this a step further, it is usually an individual or a few people who set the stage for growth, and they set this stage with a concept, even a definition of their enterprise, that is daring in its innovation, broad in its scope and lasting in its execution.

Think of the great growth companies of the last few decades. Minnesota Mining & Manufacturing began with as lackluster a product line in its time as any of hundreds of smaller companies we are all familiar with today—natural abrasives serving a declining market. Yet, to oversimplify, the company defined its business not as abrasives but as surface coatings, and from this definition have come products as wide-ranging as pressure-sensitive tape, roofing granules, carbonless copy paper, infrared image transfer, indeed over 30,000 such diverse products.

IBM began in the office equipment field, when it could barely be called a market. The company saw its market as tools and systems for the handling of information, not as paper or hardware as such. Such a definition later allowed the company to pioneer systems plus computer technology and, when threatened by the earlier introduction of a competitor's computer, to recognize the interrelation of the two and build the great service system which in 1967 had given the company over 75% of the computer market. Xerox began with a rather narrow technology and, with some good fortune, developed the Xerographic method of copy reproduction, still the leading technology in this area. Yet the company does not view itself as an office copy machine manufacturer, but rather as a leader in graphic communications in information handling. In part because of this definition, it is a good bet that this great growth company, with present sales and earnings keyed to xerographic reproduction, will be in business and moving forward long after today's workhorse, the 914 office copier, has become obsolete.

Theodore Levitt, writing in the July-August, 1960, *Harvard Business Review*, aptly defined the importance of the individual to company growth:

No organization can achieve greatness without a vigorous leader who is driven onward by his own pulsating will to succeed. He has to have a vision of grandeur, a vision that can produce eager followers in vast numbers. . . . Management must think of itself not as producing products but as providing customer-creating value satisfactions. . . . And the chief executive himself has the inescapable responsibility for creating this environment, this viewpoint, this attitude, this aspiration. He himself must set the company's style, its direction, and its goals. This means he has to know precisely where he himself wants to go, and to make sure the whole organization is enthusiastically aware of where that is. This is a first requisite of leadership.

The key role of the individual in investing for growth is at once the opportunity and the danger. At the risk of oversimplifying, there are three types of people needed at various stages in company development: first, the innovator-promoter; second, the builder-entrepreneur; and third, the professional manager. Rarely can one man fit more than one classification and even more rarely can a man change classifications during his lifetime. Yet the successful growth company has a need, at various stages of development, for all three such men. It is probably this single fact above all else which keeps the ranks of great growth companies thin indeed.

Analysts have chosen to qualify a great number of "outside" variables as ingredients for growth companies; a few might be maturity of industry, position in and types of markets served, company size in relation to market and so forth. Again, a number of analysts have concentrated on "inside" variables—management attitudes, type and quality of sales organization, labor and personnel policies, executive relations and depth of management, accounting and cost controls, effectiveness of Research and Development and so forth. To be sure, some or all of these characteristics are probably part of growth companies. But for that matter, they are a part of a good many companies that are not growth companies. They are not the cause, but in many instances are the effect, of the outstanding management leadership described earlier.

This leads me to my second point—the *structure* for growth of the organization. The key here is the recognition by management of just exactly what is the main line of the business; in part it is the definition by management of the business. Avon Products is really not in the cosmetics business; it is in the business of managing one of the most effective, and frustrating, door-to-door sales organizations known to man. Over 200,000 sales representatives handle the product line, a line which stimulates growth because of its excellent inherent qualities for door-to-door distribution. Yet it is the creative management of this sales monster which is the main line of Avon's business. Certainly here as in many companies, advertising, effective product creation, accounting and cost controls, and so forth are important. But the main line of the business is the achievement of growth in, motivation of, and control over one of the greatest specialized merchandising-distribution systems the world has ever known.

Dun & Bradstreet is not in the printing-publishing business. In fact, in 1966 the company completed the sale of its last major printing facilities. The main line of the business is effective information organization and dissemination, at the heart of which lies the D & B reporter who regularly calls on well over three million businesses for credit information. The organization of this information to serve a myriad different markets—some as yet not defined—is the challenge and the opportunity. Properly handled, and by that I mean properly structured and defined, Dun & Bradstreet has greater opportunities for growth today than at any time in its long and illustrious history. IBM, as is the case in a number of industries, has more than one main line to its business. Yet one above others stands out in my mind. It is the total servicing ability of IBM, rather than unusual product superiority, that has gained for the company its dominant market position. The main line of the business is serving its customers' needs in information handling. The superior tool is interesting, but it is the recognition of the need to set up a system to handle this tool that has put IBM way out in front and should keep it there. Clearly IBM does not think of itself as creating computers, but rather as "providing customer-creating value satisfactions." Sperry Rand had a wrong concept of its business when it was satisfied to see itself as the producer of the first and best computer, which proved a Pyrrhic victory at best.

Peter Drucker, in his book *Managing for Results*, pinpoints one "main line" for any business which would create lasting growth—"the ability to envisage as a system what to others are unrelated, separate elements." To the exent that management can so order its thinking to envision this main line, be it in the blast furnace or the baking business, it is well on the way to becoming a true growth company.

The third ingredient for growth is the *position* of the company in its industry and the industry itself. All other things being equal, the good fisherman is going to catch more fish in the well-stocked than in the poorly stocked stream. It's that simple. It's easier to grow in a growing market than in a declining market; it's less disruptive to competition to take a market share in an expanding market than in a static market.

However, the size and growth of the market are somewhat difficult to gauge for a true growth company. The problem has its roots in the definition itself of the market. What is Avon's market? Is it the present total market for cosmetics or is it the female, and perhaps the male, population in developed and developing countries? Do you measure Xerox's market against total office copiers in use or against the needs —known and unknown—for graphic communication in a range of applications throughout the world? What is the market for Syntex, the company that developed the ingredients for the birth-control pill? Is it the total present market for reproductive physiology or is it a range of applications from the company's steroid technology, which is unsurpassed in medicine today? Suffice it to say that the size and growth of the market, even narrowly defined, for the growth company within the growth industry have an important bearing on results.

The position of a growth company is not as important if one accepts a more restricted view of true growth. The key differential here as to company position has been best expressed by Peter Bernstein writing in the September-October, 1965, *Harvard Business Review:* "True growth is organic and comes from within . . . the ability to create its own market is the strategic, the dominating and the single most distinguishing characteristic of a true growth company." Mr. Bernstein would probably define Polaroid as such a true growth company. Narrowing the field of true growth, I would add to this the condition that the market created should carry a high degree of difficulty to enter. This degree of difficulty need not, in fact it should not, depend merely on artificial or temporal restraints such as quotas or patents, but rather on a definition of business which either through tangible assets, intangible assets or "understanding"—i.e., the system vs. unrelated parts —place severe obstacles in the path of would-be imitators.

Investing for growth has as its ultimate test the return in the market place. One might say that market growth logically follows company growth, and this is true. Just look at the index of market growth of IBM, Xerox, Avon, and other true growth companies, and with benefit of 20–20 hindsight see how much one dollar invested has grown over the past 20 years! But how many investors have participated in this full range of growth? Not very many. And the reason is confusion and fuzzy thinking over *when to buy* and *when to sell*.

There is really no one proper time to invest for growth. A review of any of a range of investing periodicals over the past 20 years will disclose no end of comment and analysis as to why IBM is "too high priced now." In fact, IBM has always been "too high priced." There really has never been one time when the market, the company and the economy were all in tune and the share prices of IBM were "reasonable." Thus if one did not own IBM, it seemed probably best to wait a while and buy when prices were "more nearly normal"; if one owned IBM, it seemed probably best to "sell a bit and buy back later" when the company was "more in line with the market." Given intelligent judgment of the factors discussed regarding company growth, there is no more devastating single barrier to successful investing for growth than fuzzy thinking about buying and selling growth company stocks.

Starting with the fact that there is never a "right" time to buy growth company stocks, I have arrived at two tenets which have been helpful for me.

The first is to buy on a regular basis, not all at once. The psychology of this is appealing—and "psychology" is the right word, for this is a matter of emotion as much as of logic. If one buys a 25% position and the stock goes off, there is comfort in the fact that after all the next purchase will deliver you more shares for the same price; and if your long-term judgment of the company is sound, this is indeed a most favorable turn of events. If the stock goes up to "unreasonable prices," your next purchase, when averaged with your first purchase, gives you an average net cost below the then current market and provides the much needed courage to buy more stock at prices that appear to be "too high."

The second tenet is more difficult in that logic must overcome an emotional market psychology. It consists in making purchases when company performance is outwardly disappointing. For any number of reasons, a growth company can show lackluster earnings performance for a period of time, as a result of new plant expansion, new product introduction, sales force expansion, basic research costs rising as the goal of a "breakthrough" draws near, and so forth. Just when investors should be gaining increasing confidence for the longer term future, the market may be reflecting concern about the next quarterly report. Such concern often provides unique opportunities to buy growth company shares.

In conclusion, perhaps the most succinct comment on

when to sell a growth company stock comes from Philip Fisher in his brilliant book, *Common Stocks and Uncommon Profits:* "If the job has been correctly done when a common stock is purchased, the time to sell it is—almost never."

9

Investing in Science and Technology

By Richard L. Geiger

One of the most memorable advertisements in recent years shows two seagulls perched on a wooden pylon during a storm-tossed night, and one bird is saying to the other: "Only the men are flying." This is an extraordinary tribute to the science and technology of the twentieth century. A catalogue of the century's discoveries includes these breathtaking achievements: quantum theory, relativity, nuclear fission and fusion, superconductivity, semiconductor theory, crystal theory, radio carbon dating, chemical synthesis of complex organic molecules (like chlorophyll, insulin, and penicillin), genetic theory, cosmological discoveries like quasars, the synthesis of new elements and isotopes, lasers, masers, radar and sonar.

The application of these scientific discoveries—what we call technology—has resulted in atomic power and atomic bombs, jets, rockets and satellites, radio reception and television transmission around the globe, discovery of hidden ores and oil deposits tens of thousands of feet below the earth's surface and on the continental shelf, hybrid corn, RNA and DNA, heart pacers, structural concrete, wonder metals, plastics and drugs, to name but a few. Indeed, since 1940 science

Richard L. Geiger is an independent financial consultant with a background in engineering.

has brought about a revolution in technology comparable to that spanning the previous 25 millennia in which metals were first smelted, tools first manufactured and the wheel invented. Granted this gigantic achievement, technology, in terms of modern time-concepts, has had trouble converting scientific discoveries into useful products. It has taken 25 years to arrive at the economic use of atomic energy. The transistor has already had a stupendous effect on communications, but it was nearly a generation before its inventors used it for the purpose for which it had been designed. The use of lasers for communication and industrial purposes in other than experimental areas is somewhere in the future. The industrial use of super-conductivity and the technological fruits of the space program are probably further off.

Basic research—the pursuit of knowledge of the physical world—is the soil from which technology springs. Until World War II, it was in university laboratories or in a half dozen great industrial laboratories that many of the scientific discoveries were made. World War II produced the great national laboratories, and government has since become the principal sponsor of basic research, whose cost has risen so astronomically that it is now largely dependent on government spending. For 1968, the National Science Foundation estimated that research and development expenditures in the United States would probably equal $25 billion. Basic research totaled about $3.5 billion in 1967, a larger sum than that spent by all other nations combined (excluding the U.S.S.R.).

Technical development, designed to produce useful objects, can be conducted on many levels by many differently qualified researchers. Hence, although a major portion of the government's research funds are spent on technical research in the National Aviation and Space Agency, the Atomic Energy Commission, the Department of Agriculture and the National Bureau of Research, we find industry-sponsored technical research ranging from Bell Laboratories, with its 10,000 or more scientists and technicians, down to industrial laboratories with one chemist and an assistant. We also find industry-sponsored technical research being done in universities and by private research organizations such as Battelle Memorial Institute or the Franklin Institute.

The subject of this chapter is investing in science and technology. Its purposes are: (1) to survey some of the current and prospective developments in science and technology which appear most relevant from the standpoint of investors; (2) to set up criteria for the selection and evaluation of science and technology stocks.

Many people, when they think of this field, tend to think only of electronics. But it also embraces chemistry, drugs and medicine, petroleum derivatives, chemurgy, metallurgy and oceanography. The intense interest of investors in the scientific and technological sectors is certainly warranted, but it is in danger of being misdirected. Whereas the period from 1849 to 1920 might be called the Age of Chemistry, and the period from 1920 to 1960 the Age of Physics, *the sciences of most significance for men today are biophysics and biochemistry*. New discoveries of earth-shattering importance will be made over the next 20 years in these fields: the synthesis and control of the molecules of life; the conquest of cancer and virus diseases; the improvement of agriculture and ocean farming; the generation of new sources of energy from fossil and living life; and the growth of giant molecules for computer use. Nuclear physics and geophysics will also unfold hidden resources of great importance. Investors should become familiar with the researches of the chemical, pharmaceutical and petrochemical industries, and not concentrate solely on the much publicized but now potentially less dynamic electronic industries. Modern technology is a synthesis of numerous powerful techniques. For example, the replacement of the propeller-driven engine by the jet, which caused a revolution in transportation, involved aerodynamics, metallurgy, chemistry and many branches of engineering.

During the 1950s the electonics industry—the industry which deals with the use, characteristics and properties of electrons, especially in gas-filled or vacuum tubes—captured the imagination of the investing public. It might almost be said that the less analysts and investors understood electronic products and processes the brighter were the potentialities attributed to them. And so the shares of electronic companies rocketed upward only to fall to earth in 1962. Following the collapse of this speculative boom—in which all but the most sophisticated investors failed to take into account the crucial profit-making factor, managerial ability—the electronics industry settled down to a period of retrenchment and consolidation, from which it appears to have emerged.

The future of this industry—which includes the instrument, computer, automation, communication and entertainment sectors—is convincingly bright. There are three compelling reasons for this statement.

In the first place, despite world-wide population growth, the supply of trained labor will not keep pace with demand; hence electronic technology will be urgently needed to increase productivity. Second, there is an unceasing drive in the United States to improve standards of living. Third, there are the crucial exigencies of national defense and the huge requirements of the aerospace program.

This chapter will discuss some of the main areas of science and technology which appear to be of particular interest to long-term investors.

THE COMPUTER INDUSTRY

The computer industry serves all markets. Only a handful of companies have the technical know-how and marketing ability to make and sell computers. There are two general types of computers. A digital computer translates information received into discrete pulses of electricity with which it performs simple arithmetical processes. An analog computer translates information received into varying voltages proportional to the input information and can perform algebraic analysis and calculus as well as arithmetic.

Analog and digital computers may be programed to do the same thing. However, in practice analog computers are confined almost exclusively to the scientific and engineering fields because results, while serviceably accurate, are not exact. The digital computer serves scientific, engineering, industrial production and office purposes. Until very recently it was much faster and could handle much more data (including memory) than analog computers. There has been progress in devising combination analog-digital computers, which combine the best features of both. Eventually this may lead to a computer that learns from experience.

Any computer requires input equipment, computation equipment, including memory capacity, control equipment and output equipment. The manufacture of these subsystems or components is an exacting task. Reliability and speed are the two essentials. Because of the length of time required to test this equipment, the cost of manufacture and the engineering skills needed, it has become increasingly difficult for smaller companies to enter the field. The rate of scientific progress has flattened out. The memory cells of a digital computer are now so fast and accurate that both input and output equipment have failed to utilize the memory capacity of the computer. Information (bits) can be flashed in and out of the "brain" in a billionth of a second. The speed of light has become the only limiting factor in the computational part of a computer. Present-day models calculate a million to ten million times as fast as a man.

Peripheral equipment is limited in speed to the fastest of the input or output methods—punched card, punched tape, optical scanning, or magnetic tape or card. To a certain extent, asynchronous computers have overcome some of this problem by being programed to work on a dozen problems at the same time. These are called "real-time" computers.

While, on the one hand, computers have been designed for industry, which demands a certain amount of economy of space, the military has required even smaller and faster special-purpose computers, which have been used in airborne, navigational, fire control, radar, and sonar work. These so-phisticated analog and digital computers have not yet been adapted for industry, but they probably will be when industry (particularly process-control industry) is ready for them. Meanwhile, the general-purpose computers have, with some exceptions, fulfilled all demands made on them.

The Business and Defense Services Administration esti-mates that on a retail basis, factory shipments have been ris-ing at an average annual rate of 9% per annum over the past few years and reached $4.2 billion in 1967. The installed value of U.S. computer systems by 1967 year-end exceeded $4.7 billion.

Some 51,000 computers were in use in 1967, many in the service of the federal government, which is the industry's largest customer. The government spent some $276 million for new computers in 1965 and $206 million on rentals. Where are all these computers used? How big can the indus-try get? And who will benefit?

The computers are used to replace or supplement clerical labor. They handle small or vast amounts (bits) of informa-tion, and since their memories are relatively faultless, they can compare, audit and recompute data at electronic speeds. Computers can play an important role in areas ranging from census taking to insurance payments to process control to ad-vanced logic.

Actually they are capable only of low-grade moron work. Hence the programing of computers is all-important. Each step in a program must be carefully integrated with all the others. These programs are quite valuable auxiliary items and companies with worked-out programs for a variety of needs are far better off than new companies. Standard program lan-guages have facilitated the writing of programs and will ex-tend the use of computers into interdisciplinary fields.

Thus the future of the industry is tied to complete com-puter systems to a greater extent than it used to be. Bread-and-butter items, such as punch-card processors, are still profitable, but sales growth will continue to come elsewhere in the computer field. While this growth will be the most rapid of any major industry, sales growth does not always imply growth in profits. When the airline companies were off and running in 1946, their revenue growth was amazing but their earnings were poor.

In the computer field, there have been a series of major technological changes in recent years. With the introduction of the IBM 360, the Sigma Seven, and similar advanced building-block types, the only major change to be looked for is the expanded use of integrated circuits (as they come down in price) and of large-scale integrated systems.

Thus purchasers of today's machines do not face the rapid obsolescence of the period 1955–64. There will therefore be an increased tendency on the part of large companies to purchase equipment rather than to lease it. However, shortage of money makes computer leasing most attractive for medium- and smaller-sized companies. Additional reasons for leasing are: (1) capital is released for other purposes; (2) the ever present fear of obsolescence is thrust off on the lessor; (3) maintenance problems are avoided; (4) lease payments are ordinary expenses and therefore serve to reduce taxes; (5) the lessor has better access to credit; and (6) in the case of a severe recession or depression a company that leases a computer may find itself able to re-lease it to others, thus reducing expenses.

Some 27 companies have attempted to enter the computer field and have withdrawn after suffering aggregate losses exceeding $200 million. These include companies such as Addressograph-Multigraph, Autonetics (a division of North American Rockwell), Bendix, Clary, General Mills, IT&T, Packard-Bell, Philco, SCM and Underwood. Six companies, which have spent over $600 million, are still in the field *and still in the red or barely breaking even.*

Despite slackening in the rate of technological progress, it is more difficult than ever now for a new company to enter the computer field because of the strong sales forces and services and software facilities built up by established companies. World-wide, this industry could well end up—like the automobile industry—with a handful of U.S. companies, and perhaps one national company in each of the developed countries, sustained by governmental sales. Some smaller companies may subsist on the fringes of the industry, furnishing input or output devices, or specialized military or space computers, or special forms. But the computer industry requires such large capital expenditures as to eliminate all but the largest companies as potential competitors.

This leaves only six companies with nearly 98% of the U.S. industrial and commercial market, surely the market where the most profit can be made. Clearly the giant is IBM. Since 1954 it has dominated the field, and until recently has earned at least 15% per year on invested capital, has increased sales at a comparable rate, and has built such a marketing and servicing lead as to make all other competitors acknowledge that they were fighting for second place, with no idea of dislodging the leader. As a long-term investment IBM has had no industrial equal in recent history. Over the next five to ten years, its growth will be slower, but in 1968 it still remained the prime investment in the computer industry, though smaller and much more speculative companies offered the possibility of more spectacular gains.

ATOMIC POWER

Atomic power is increasingly competitive with power based upon natural resources. One kilogram (2.2 pounds) of matter, if converted entirely into energy, would give 25 billion kilowatt-hours of energy. In contrast, burning a kilogram of coal produces 8.5 kilowatt-hours. By 1975, the Federal Power Commission expects nuclear power in use to be equivalent to 100 million tons of coal, or nearly half the coal used for electric power in 1960. This may be too optimistic. There are too many prejudices still to be overcome to count on such rapid domestic growth, but a figure equivalent to 75 million tons seems attainable. Outside the United States those developed countries which are poor in oil and natural gas and lack hydroelectric possibilities will have a strong incentive to build nuclear power plants.

The principal beneficiaries of the expected growth of nuclear power will be manufacturers of electrical equipment, such as General Electric and Westinghouse in this country. However, since they are already the principal beneficiaries of growth in the use of electrical energy irrespective of how it is produced, the development of nuclear power does not dramatically enhance their prospects. Other beneficiaries of the growth of nuclear power will be the companies that furnish the raw material of atomic energy—uranium. As a result of recent breakthroughs in the economic production of atomic power in large utility-type power generators, a new look at uranium is warranted.

In *Natural Resources for U.S. Growth,* H. H. Landsberg states: "U.S. uranium reserves, in terms of U_3O_8, are currently estimated at some 25,000 short tons. This quantity, at present levels of technology, may have an energy equivalent to slightly more than total U.S. energy consumption in 1966. Currently estimated reserves . . . would be sufficient for the next forty years only if improvements in efficiency raise energy production per unit of uranium three or four times above current levels." At the moment, reserves in Canada and the United States are sufficient, but a step-up in nuclear power plant construction would call for renewed exploration in both countries within the next five years. Meanwhile, Anaconda, Kerr-McGee, Rio Algom and Denison are the principal sources of natural uranium in North America.

The increasing use of nuclear energy will reinforce the existing growth in the use of copper and aluminum for the distribution of electrical energy; and beryllium will come into greater prominence as the metal in its pure form is required for reactors.

WATER TECHNOLOGY

Drought conditions in the Midwest have reached such proportions that only a wet era lasting many years could restore the level of the Great Lakes, the Mississippi River and the water table. Scientists are considering the creation of a huge, 350-mile lake, into which the surplus rainfall in western Canada can be directed. This multi-billion dollar undertaking—a perfectly feasible engineering project—would assure ample water for the midcontinental region, and additional electrical energy would be made available in Alberta, Montana, and other areas. From the investment standpoint, the principal beneficiaries would be construction companies, pipe companies, cement companies and metering companies.

Of more immediate interest is the ever increasing need for pure water for drinking and for industrial purposes. As the water table drops, water becomes more polluted with unwanted chemicals. The future, therefore, looks brighter for companies that treat water to make it potable or usable. There are companies, such as General Electric and Westinghouse, that make stills for this purpose. Semipermeable membranes, another device developed to desalt brackish water and make it potable, are produced by Ionics, among others. Companies such as Culligan sell water-softening equipment for home purification. Others in this field are Water Treatment Corporation, Ritter Pfaudler, Calgon and Nalco Chemical. It has been estimated that 85% of the market for home water-softeners is still untapped.

SHALE OIL

World oil production in 1967 was some 34 million barrels of oil a day, up 4.5% over 1966. The United States alone produced 9.5 million barrels a day. U.S. demand is about 12 million barrels per day. While world supply still exceeds demand, the world's oil industry ended 1967 nearer a balance than it has for many years. Proven oil reserves—estimated at 400 billion barrels—would last less than 35 years at current rates of consumption. Unproven reserves may be as large as or larger than proven ones, but to prove up reserves costs money, particularly offshore. Only 7% of the world's continental shelves have been economically surveyed. Already 15% of total Free World oil production is offshore oil.

Just as the discovery of natural gas in the North Sea will profoundly affect the economy of Great Britain and the Netherlands, so would the utilization of oil shale affect the U.S. central region. For there exist in western Colorado and eastern Utah vast deposits of a marlstone known as oil shale. This shale contains a substance (Kerogen) which, when heated to around 800°, turns into a crude oil. The U.S. government estimates that these oil-shale lands contain the equivalent of one and one-half trillion barrels of oil—more than the entire known reserves of oil throughout the world. The government has worked out room-and-pillar methods for mining and crushing the shale that appear to be quite inexpensive. But of the more than 2,500 patents filed on methods of retorting shale—cooking the crushed rock to produce shale oil—none has proved economical in terms of U.S. oil prices. Shale oil has merely set an upper limit for the price of ordinary oil, and has never been used in this country.

Now, however, as a result of separate technical progress made by the U.S. government, Union Oil of California, the Oil Shale Corporation and others, it appears that methods have been developed—including the possible use of atomic bombs—to produce a pipeline grade of shale oil that could eventually become competitive in price with domestic oil. (Foreign oil remains cheaper.) What is more, certain oil companies that are refiners on balance have undertaken to bring the production of shale oil out of the testing stage and into production. Within the next five to ten years, one or more of these methods will enable these firms to produce from 50,000 to 150,000 barrels of shale oil a day. This addition to U.S. production will not be of significance, except that it might enable the United States to bargain with Middle East rulers on a stronger basis. Ultimately we expect perhaps one million barrels a day to be produced from U.S. oil shale fields. The limitation on production is probably only the amount of water available in the parched West to meet the needs of the people needed to bring in this bonanza. Canada has a similar opportunity in the Athabasca tar sands, and Brazil also has rich oil shales.

AGRICULTURE

Investors aware of developments in biochemistry and biophysics tend to think of the drug industry as the only related area of investment. In fact, agriculture has been a principal beneficiary of these two sciences, and we will examine it first.

Hybrid corn is the prime example of the great achievement of genetics in increasing the food supply and preventing it from being outdistanced by world population, the fate that Malthus so darkly predicted. It has brought about a two-thirds increase in the yield-per-acre of the U.S. corn crop with no increase in labor. According to Watson Davis in *The Century of Science*, the increased yield of hybrid corn produced during the war years, 1942–44, was valued at $2 billion—equivalent to the cost of developing the atom bomb.

Science and technology can be applied to the agricultural problems of the world in a large variety of ways. These include irrigation, soil conservation, chemical fertilizers, balanced nutrition, mechanization, chemical and enzyme treatments, insecticides, better food preservation, quality control, packaging developments and shipping improvements. It is not possible in this chapter to point out the opportunities in each area. We will therefore concentrate on two of them.

Protein is the principal need in world nutrition. In the United States, two-thirds of our protein is of animal or fish origin. Protein is composed of 22 amino acids, of which eight cannot be made by man's body chemistry but must be eaten. The conversion of animal feed into animal protein is a measure of agricultural efficiency. Thus it takes 3.9 pounds of protein feed to produce a pound of milk, but it takes 12.5 pounds of feed to produce a pound of lamb. Soybeans are one of the world's fastest-expanding crops because of their high protein content (40%). Agricultural research produced the knowledge, and biochemical research produced the results. With the prospect of world hunger before us, and the rapid dwindling of our agricultural surpluses, major agricultural companies are cooperating with the U.S. Department of Agriculture to meet the challenges ahead. Those companies that specialize in soybean processing and in fish-meal processing have bright futures.

Similarly, when it is realized that without herbicides, fungicides and insecticides our agricultural production would be but a fraction of what it actually is, it is clear that chemical companies will have expanded markets for the new chemicals constantly needed as resistance to existing chemicals increases.

Agricultural chemicals have produced results that border on the miraculous. With the use of propanel, rice yield has been increased from 325 to 5,380 pounds per acre. Naphthaline acetic acid in extraordinarily small amounts (one teaspoon per acre) keeps apples from dropping off too early, and has doubled the apple crop. Gibberillic acid increases the size and quality of grapes. Ethylene Dibromid controls nematodes, a particularly pernicious animal form that heretofore could be held in check only by crop rotation. Chemical weeding has increased the productivity of wheat, oats, and barley land by 10% to 20%, and chemical attractants are used to eradicate the gypsy moth. In fact, fungicides thus have become a significant dollar-earning export, rising nearly 25% per annum. The companies with a major stake in this area of dynamic growth are the leading chemical and drug companies.

Another area with assured prospects of long-term expansion is the fertilizer industry. Along about 1940, fertilizer costs suddenly declined in relation to crop prices received, and the use of fertilizer and lime soared. It has quadrupled since 1940. The U.S. Department of Agriculture estimates that public spending for agricultural research from 1910 to 1960 totaled $3 billion. If agricultural technology had remained at the 1910 level, the cost of U.S. agricultural production in 1960 would have been $230 billion more than it was.

The importance of science and technology to agriculture can hardly be exaggerated. Clearly, the companies best equipped to benefit from this situation offer attractive possibilities to the patient, long-term investor.

THE DRUG INDUSTRY

The U.S. drug industry is divided into two segments: ethical and proprietary. Ethical products are obtainable on prescription only, and are advertised generally only in professional publications. Success in the ethical drug field is dependent upon five factors: the extent and quality of research, the particular specialty of the company, the excellence of the management, the size and aggressiveness of the sales force, and population growth. All ethical drug companies have a built-in growth bias because of population growth, Medicare and the stimulation of increased government expenditures.

In the drug industry, profitability rises with improved production methods and more efficient manufacturing facilities, and also with larger sales volume (because in a process industry such as this, cost of sales does not rise in step with sales increases). Most profits in the drug industry have been realized from the sudden success of a patented new product, be it sulfanilamide, penicillin, Salk vaccine, tranquilizers, steroids, oral antidiabetics, or Asian Flu vaccine. In the absence of such a discovery, profitability is most marked in companies that specialize in pediatric or geriatric drugs—drugs for the very young or the very old, groups which are steadily increasing as a percentage of the total population.

In addition to technological considerations, important factors in the evaluation of drug companies are: (1) foreign sales—a strong position in the export market is a great asset in this business; (2) a strong financial position; (3) an imaginative and capable management, combined with an aggressive sales force and effective advertising.

In the proprietary drug business, investors should look for a combination of superior research with outstanding marketing and distributing ability. It would be very difficult for a new company to compete in this field, but some ethical drug companies may be expected to continue to expand into the proprietary area, particularly if their marketing divisions are strong. The ethical and proprietary drug industries are gradually amalgamating. Some companies, such as American Home Products, already combine both aspects, plus unrelated fields, such as food.

The demand for both ethical and proprietary drugs has been in a well-defined uptrend, which can be expected to accelerate as a result of Medicare and the growing emphasis on private health insurance. In 1966 over 8.1% of the total expenditures of wage-earning families went into health as compared with 7.4% in 1965.

Threats to the continued growth of the industry have come from government action, much of it incorporated in the Drug Amendments Act of 1962. The severest effects of the government's new requirements have been the delays and extra expenses incurred by drug manufacturers in developing acceptable new drugs. Under the old law, a manufacturer had to prove that the drug was not harmful. Under the new law, the manufacturer must prove that the drug is beneficial. The result of this legislation was that new drug applications fell from 282 in 1962 to 136 in 1965. However, by mid-1967 there were indications that a number of new drugs would be released by the Food and Drug Administration (FDA) in the ensuing year or two. A number of drugs have been tested and used in foreign countries, where even the long arm of the FDA cannot reach. The results of these tests shorten the domestic test requirements. Another potent threat is from the possibility of the use of generic instead of brand-name ethical drugs by public institutions and, perhaps, private practitioners. The arguments are persuasive on both sides and some compromise that will allow ethical drug manufacturers to continue to benefit from the fruits of their research is likely to be forthcoming.

Large contributions to profits have already been made by the antibiotics and the tranquilizers. However, the typical profit cycle in the drug industry appears to have run its course in both fields. For example, in 1947 penicillin sold for $1 per million units. It now sells for around 3 cents per million units. It is my belief that those companies concentrating their research on the following fields will prove to be the best investments: (1) cancer research, (2) cardiovascular disease, (3) food supplements, (4) cold prophylactics, (5) sterility and fertility drugs, (6) old-age preventives.

In an industry that spends up to 8% of its income on research, these considerations are particularly important: (1) introduction of new products, (2) lowering of production costs, (3) increasing useful life of products, (4) decreasing maintenance costs, (5) expanding markets for products by improving quality, utility, appearance and other factors in consumer acceptance, (6) utilizing or upgrading by-products. Successful research can be decisive from a profit point of view. For example, more than 50% of Merck's sales are derived from products introduced from research in the past ten years. Occasionally, a whole new nondrug field may be opened up as a by-product of research.

Sales growth in the drug industry approximates 10% per year. Most of the increase in sales will continue to go to the larger companies. Occasionally a small company may break the pattern and come up with an important new product. By and large, however, the probability is that investment in the larger companies will produce better results and involve fewer risks.

INVESTMENT CRITERIA

Companies whose basis is science and technology are by their very nature strongly oriented toward the future. It would hardly be an exaggeration to say that they must grow or perish. Consequently, they plow back an unusually high proportion of their earnings into research and development, and they generally try to keep the payout of cash dividends to a minimum. Thus by and large an investment in science and technology is not suited to those whose primary concern is current yield; it is, par excellence, an investment whose objective is long-term capital appreciation.

Science-based companies can be divided into three broad categories. The first is comprised of great companies, with institutional characteristics, which are fully recognized by investors as having a dominant position in their industry. They have behind them a long (or fairly long) record of sustained earnings growth and of successful innovation. Their capabilities in the spheres of management, research and development, and marketing are of a very high order, and their finances are extremely strong. In short, these companies are the giants who have proved their ability to surmount the challenges of competition, to keep one jump ahead of technological change, and to sustain a high rate of profitability. A partial list would include IBM, Xerox, Eastman Kodak, General Electric, Polaroid, Hewlitt-Packard, Boeing and Merck.

The second category of science-based companies might be described as "enterprises"—that is to say, though they are fairly large and successful, they are still in the entrepreneurial stage. They have varying degrees of managerial talent, sophisticated capabilities in their field, and an impressive growth record. But they have not become as securely entrenched as the giants in the first category; there is a greater degree of uncertainty as to how successful they will be in sustaining growth and profitability in the face of possible loss of government business, new challenges from competition and the hazards implicit in the rapid tempo of technological change. Such companies, if they continue to prosper and grow, eventually move into the first category; if they do not, they become candidates for takeover and in due course are absorbed by a stronger company, or at least one whose management has so far been more skillful or more fortunate. A list of outstanding science-based companies in this category (in 1967) might have included the following: Litton Industries, Texas Instruments, Control Data, McDonnell-Douglas, Burroughs, Syntex.

My third category consists of companies in the venture

stage. These cover a wide range. At one end are infant companies seeking to exploit new, perhaps revolutionary, products or processes whose commercial possibilities are as yet more or less uncharted. At the other end are companies with a good record of perhaps several years' duration and sales of $50 to $100 million. The mortality rate in this large and diverse category is obviously very high. The more successful venture companies gradually achieve the status of enterprises, and a very small number of them eventually grow to institutional stature.

A commitment in the venture type of company is self-evidently a speculation. The rewards of success in this field in the fullness of time can be truly gigantic, but the odds against success are large, and for reasons which few investors fully appreciate. Science-based venture companies are sometimes formed by men who are long on scientific talent but short on business experience. Sometimes such companies have the necessary business capabilities to make a brilliant start, but management gets out of its depth as the business expands. Invariably, growth brings with it a succession of challenges and perhaps crises, for at various sales levels—say, $1 million, $5 million, $15 million—changes are usually required in production, organizational and marketing techniques. The company has to reorient itself to a larger scale of operations, and in the process management finds itself confronted with a multitude of unfamiliar problems. These problems can be particularly acute when a company has expanded as the result of an acquisition, which has led it into less familiar territory. Then, too, the financing of rapid expansion—whether done by issuing additional stock or by incurring debt—can pose difficulties and create hazards. In short, management has to be highly adaptable and evolutionary, and this is rare. The moral for investors is simple (and seldom heeded): When studying a venture company, do not become so mesmerized by its exciting products or processes that you fail to look carefully into the caliber of management. A second counsel might be proffered: If you have invested in a venture company which gives evidence of being on its way to becoming an enterprise, stay with it. To reap in full the huge rewards of having discovered a genuine growth company in its early stages requires, above all, infinite patience compounded with a great deal of fortitude. Thousands of investors who bought Xerox, Polaroid or Syntex in their infancy were happy to get out with a respectable profit—and thereby deprived themselves of a fortune.

The stocks of science-based companies in the first category, the institutional giants, usually command extremely high price/earnings ratios and are subject to violent fluctuations. (For example, the range for Xerox in 1966 was: High—268; Low—125.) One avenue open to the investor is to duck the problem of timing by "dollar averaging," that is, by investing the same sum in the stock or stocks of his choice at regular intervals—say, on the first of every month. The second method is to try to buy the stock when—because of market conditions, or disappointing earnings, or reports of potential problems in the offing—it has experienced a severe reaction. This approach needs to be systematized. One might decide, for example, to make a partial commitment in the stock on a dip of 20% or 25% from the previous high, and to buy additional units on any further dips of, say, 5% or 10%. To act in this manner calls for exceptional self-discipline and adequate cash reserves (unless one is willing to switch out of other stocks which may also be unduly depressed). But investors who have schooled themselves to buy the leading science and technology stocks in bear markets, or in the wake of bad news, have in the long run fared brilliantly.

Subject to one crucial reservation, the identical tactics can be applied to investment in science and technology stocks in my second category, which also tend to command rather high multiples and to be subject to sharp fluctuations. The reservation is this: Dollar averaging and purchases made on sharp reactions are based on the assumption that the long-term growth of the company in question is relatively assured. Even in the case of the established giants, this assumption is only a working hypothesis, based in part on an extraordinary track record; and it has a somewhat lesser validity when applied to companies in the enterprise category. The chances are higher in this category that when bad news triggers a severe price reaction, it may conceivably signal a more than temporary setback—possibly a basic deterioration in the company's prospects because of competition or for some other reason. What I am suggesting, in effect, is that the investor who buys science and technology stocks when they appear to be "on the bargain counter" should look carefully into the fundamentals, or get his stockbroker's research specialists to do it for him.

To pass, now, from generalities to specifics, I propose to describe a systematic approach to the evaluation of growth stocks in general and therefore to science and technology stocks in particular.

The value of a corporation may be stated to be its net worth, plus the present worth of the future stream of earnings over a foreseeable period, discounted to the present at some interest rate that takes the extent of risk into account. The higher the estimated risk, the greater will be the interest rate at which future earnings are discounted. One way to evaluate a growth stock is to ascertain the number of years it would take for the aggregate projected earnings of the company to equal the present price of the stock. Another way, based on the assumption that a stock is worth its book value, is to calculate the number of years required for projected earnings, added to present book value, to equal the current market price of the stock. Still another method is to calculate how many years it would take for earnings growth (at a given projected rate) to reduce the present market price of the stock to a 15 times earnings ratio, which is typical for a high quality issue with an *average* growth rate (5% to 6%).

What these methods attempt to do is to reduce all so-called growth stocks to a common denominator. If Xerox is selling at 40 times earnings and its earnings are growing at 20% per annum, it will take 12.1 years for aggregate earnings to equal the current price of the stock. If Litton is selling at 30 times earnings and its earnings are growing at 15% per year, it will take 12.2 years for aggregate earnings to equal the current price of the stock. Thus we have a common ground—the number of years required to achieve return of principal. This same figure has also been called the price-future earnings ratio, for the figure indicates the number of years of future earnings included in the current market price.

A further refinement is to make the above calculations not on the basis of reported after-tax earnings but of pre-tax, pre-depreciation earnings, since these reflect the actual operations of the company and exclude the effect of changes in the tax rate and in depreciation guidelines. While this is a more accurate approach, as investors we are more concerned with what other investors think than with what they ought to think. And since the majority think in terms of reported earnings, it makes sense to work with the latter. If, however, we keep an eye on operating earnings, we can occasionally learn something of significance before it filters through to the mass of investors.

Table 5 consists of an arrangement devised by Mr. W. Edward Bell in June, 1958. On it any growth stock can be compared with any other growth stock, as well as with the Dow-Jones Industrial Average, to which we would assign a projected annual growth rate on the order of 5%.

How do we arrive at projections of the annual growth rate of earnings per share? The past, of course, is an important guide; if per-share earnings over a period of years are plotted on semilog paper, the slope of the line that best fits the trend of earnings shows the growth rate. But this growth rate cannot simply be projected into the future. A large variety of factors must be taken into account: the long-term outlook for the economy and for the industry in which the company is operating; the size of the company; the strength of competition; the possible effects of technological change; and so on. An analysis of all the factors may indicate that a company which has grown at a rate of 20% per annum over the past decade will probably slow down to a 15% growth rate in the decade ahead; or that a company where earnings in recent years have been compounding 10% annually is about to enter a phase of accelerated growth. The projection of growth rates is still a distinctly fallible undertaking, since there are imponderables in the picture. Subjective factors, too, play a part in the analyst's appraisal, and it is not uncommon for leading authorities on a given company to hold quite divergent views about its growth prospects in the years ahead.

Some analysts and portfolio managers use a supplementary approach to the evaluation of growth stocks, which consists essentially in quantifying a number of qualitative judgments. My own version of this approach rates companies on a scale of one to five on the basis of nine yardsticks, each of which is assigned a multiplier of one, two, or three in order to give due weight to its relative importance. The nine yardsticks or factors are listed below. The figures in parentheses indicate the lowest and highest rating assignable to a company for each factor (1 to 5 adjusted by the multiplier).

1. Past profitability, profit margins and financial strength. The multiplier is two because profitability and financial resources are important determinants of a company's future. (2-10)

2. Growth rate of earnings per share. This is probably the most important single factor influencing stock prices; consequently it is assigned a multiplier of three. (3-15)

3. Research capabilities and expenditures. These are vital elements in growth and therefore rate a multiplier of two (2-10)

4. Area of competence—corporate concept. Here we are judging the present importance of a company in its particular field and management's concept of its corporate identity. There is some overlapping with factor 8, but the latter is concerned with the future rather than with the past. Multiplier of one. (1-5)

5. Managerial strength. This has already been discussed and needs no further comment. Multiplier of two. (2-10)

6. Competitive situation. This factor is assigned a multiplier of one because for well-established growth companies competition, while it is certainly a major fact of life, is not any more crucial than it is for other types of company.

Table 5.
Price–Future Earnings Ratios

The conventional "price/earnings ratio" can be regarded as the number of years' earnings at the recent or current rate for which the investor must pay at the current market price. Where there is a basis for projecting the rate of growth of earnings per share, the "price–future earnings ratio" indicates the number of years of future earnings included in the current market price. This table presents the corresponding price/earnings and price–future earnings ratios for various assumed constant annual rates of growth.

Price/earnings ratio	Estimated annual growth rate of earnings per share													
	1%	2%	3%	4%	5%	6%	7%	8%	9%	10%	12%	15%	20%	25%
6	5.9	5.7	5.6	5.5	5.4	5.3	5.2	5.1	5.0					
7	6.8	6.6	6.4	6.3	6.2	6.0	5.9	5.8	5.7	5.6	5.4			
8	7.7	7.5	7.3	7.1	6.9	6.7	6.6	6.4	6.3	6.2	5.9	5.6		
9	8.7	8.4	8.1	7.8	7.6	7.4	7.2	7.0	6.9	6.7	6.5	6.1	5.6	
10	9.6	9.2	8.9	8.6	8.3	8.1	7.8	7.6	7.4	7.3	7.0	6.6	6.0	5.6
11	10.5	10.0	9.6	9.3	9.0	8.7	8.4	8.2	8.0	7.8	7.4	7.0	6.4	5.9
12	11.4	10.9	10.4	10.0	9.6	9.3	9.0	8.7	8.5	8.3	7.9	7.4	6.7	6.2
13	12.3	11.7	11.1	10.7	10.3	9.9	9.6	9.3	9.0	8.7	8.3	7.7	7.0	6.5
14	13.2	12.5	11.9	11.3	10.9	10.5	10.1	9.8	9.5	9.2	8.7	8.1	7.3	6.7
15	14.1	13.2	12.6	12.0	11.5	11.0	10.6	10.2	9.9	9.6	9.1	8.4	7.6	7.0
16	14.9	14.0	13.1	12.6	12.0	11.5	11.1	10.7	10.3	10.0	9.5	8.8	7.9	7.2
17	15.8	14.8	13.9	13.2	12.6	12.1	11.6	11.2	10.8	10.4	9.8	9.1	8.1	7.4
18	16.6	15.5	14.6	13.8	13.2	12.6	12.1	11.6	11.2	10.8	10.2	9.4	8.4	7.6
19	17.5	16.3	15.3	14.4	13.7	13.1	12.5	12.0	11.6	11.2	10.5	9.6	8.6	7.8
20	18.3	17.0	15.9	15.0	14.2	13.5	12.9	12.4	11.9	11.5	10.8	9.9	8.8	8.0
22	20.0	18.4	17.1	16.1	15.2	14.4	13.8	13.2	12.7	12.2	11.4	10.4	9.2	8.4
24		19.8	18.3	17.2	16.2	15.3	14.6	13.9	13.3	12.8	12.0	10.9	9.6	8.7
26			19.5	18.2	17.1	16.1	15.3	14.6	14.0	13.4	12.5	11.4	10.0	9.0
28				19.2	17.9	16.9	16.0	15.3	14.6	14.0	13.0	11.8	10.4	9.3
30					18.8	17.7	16.7	15.9	15.2	14.5	13.5	12.2	10.7	9.6
32					19.6	18.4	17.4	16.5	15.7	15.1	13.9	12.6	11.0	9.8
34						19.1	18.0	17.1	16.3	15.5	14.3	12.9	11.3	10.1
36						19.7	18.6	17.6	16.8	16.0	14.7	13.3	11.5	10.3
38							19.2	18.1	17.2	16.5	15.1	13.6	11.8	10.5
40							19.7	18.6	17.7	16.9	15.5	13.9	12.1	10.7
45								19.8	18.8	17.9	16.4	14.7	12.6	11.2
50									19.8	18.8	17.2	15.3	13.2	11.7
75										22.5	20.3	17.9	15.2	13.4

Technical Note: If x is the price/earnings ratio, n the price–future earnings ratio, and i the assumed constant annual rate of growth of earnings per share, then

$$x = \frac{(1 + i)^n - 1}{i} \text{ and } n = \frac{\log (ix + 1)}{\log (1 + i)}$$

(This is also the formula for the amount of an annuity of i for n periods at i interest.)
Source: W. Edward Bell.

(When venture companies are being considered, a multiplier of two might be placed on the factor of competition.) (1–5)

7. *Marketing strength.* We consider it not more or less important for growth companies than for other companies and therefore assign it a multiplier of one. (1–5)

8. *Outlook for the industry, or segment of the industry, in which the company is operating.* This clearly has special importance for growth companies. For example, in 1966 the market for radio tubes no longer offered growth possibilities whereas sales of digital computers appeared likely to expand 20% per annum for the foreseeable future. Multiplier of two. (2–10)

9. *Regulatory outlook.* Regulatory restrictions are assigned a multiplier of one, because they are not, in our view, a more significant force in the high growth areas of industry than in industry as a whole. (1–5)

Under the system described above, the ideal company would achieve a score of 75. We have found that a score of 45 is about average; 50 to 65 is good to excellent; above 65 is outstanding. The procedure is open to the criticism that it is cumbersome and that the ratings, unless they are made by specialists, are apt to be somewhat arbitrary. Its value, in our view, is that it forces the analyst and the investor to do some hard thinking about each of the factors that affect a company's future. In addition, by quantifying qualitative judgments, it removes to some extent the comparative evaluation of companies from the domain of fuzzy impressionism.

It should be emphasized, in conclusion, that the methods of growth-stock evaluation which we have outlined are applicable only from the long-term standpoint. At any given point in time, a growth stock that is fundamentally overvalued may continue to rise for weeks or even months, and an undervalued issue may continue to decline to levels so depressing that an investor may well wonder whether he has not totally misjudged the future of the company in question. For those whose interest in growth stocks is confined to short-term trading, or even to performance over the intermediate term, the kind of systematic analysis which seeks to project growth trends and to arrive at comparative evaluations is usually not of much help. The messages given by the tape and the charts are more to the point—but of course they, too, require study and effort. In any event, the richest rewards of investing in growth stocks are reaped only by the exceptionally steadfast, long-term investor.

10

Investing Abroad

By Kurt I. Lewin

Investment abroad is one of the expressions of entrepreneurship in the world of finance. Economic growth varies from area to area and from country to country. Thus the enterprising investor will, at times, commit capital in foreign markets, anticipating appreciation or yield substantially higher than he can realize in his own country. The rewards for the investor who is able to recognize areas of future economic growth are great, provided his investment media are judiciously selected.

Investment abroad is also a function of international trade and payments. Thus the expansion and liberalization of international trade, accompanied by full convertibility of currencies, create a favorable climate for movements of capital.

Stock market history records dramatic rises in Dutch, German, English, Italian, Japanese and other equities. However, these gains were realized only by those who possessed an intimate knowledge of local economic, political and social conditions. Others have suffered equally dramatic losses in the same equities because of trying to evaluate foreign shares with only quantitative yardsticks such as cash flow and

Kurt I. Lewin is vice president and manager of the Foreign Institutional Department at Bache & Co.

price/earnings ratios, without regard for the local environment and its problems.

Investments in Dutch, German and Japanese equities made in 1953 showed a considerable increase in value by 1960 (Table 6).

Investments in the same securities made in 1961 resulted in a substantial loss (Table 7).

While the investor operating in foreign markets today is greatly aided by modern means of communication and transportation, the complexities which confront him have increased enormously. Investment abroad is certainly not an undertaking for amateurs, and even to the most experienced professionals it poses formidable problems.

Table 6.
Foreign Investments, 1953–1960

Securities	1953 High–Low		1960 High–Low	
Farbenfabriken Bayer (DM)[1]	58	50	537	327
N.V. Philips Gloeilampenfabrieken (FL)	20½	15	254	124
Sony Corp. (yen)[2]			1,450	560

Source: Eurosyndicat Investment Research Bureau.
[1] Dusseldorf Stock Exchange. Not adjusted for the issue of convertible bonds.
[2] Trading started August, 1955. High–Low, 1955: 208–128.

Table 7.
Foreign Investments, 1961–1965

Securities	1961 High–Low		1965 High–Low	
Farbenfabriken Bayer (DM)[1]	496	376	409	332
N.V. Philips Gloeilampenfabrieken (FL)	235	185	150	110
Sony Corp. (yen)	1,325	590	485	251

Source: Eurosyndicat Investment Research Bureau.
[1] Dusseldorf Stock Exchange. Not adjusted for the issue of convertible bonds.

BACKGROUND

The internationalization of investments, in a modern sense, followed the industrial expansion of the eighteenth and nineteenth centuries. As capital formation grew rapidly in Western Europe, a part of it sought out investments abroad. The entrepreneur located raw materials, cheap labor and potential markets for his output in foreign countries. These factors, combined with venture capital and imported technical know-how, produced returns which justified the greater risks involved. Thus during the nineteenth century, the enterprising European developed industry in Russia, railroads in the United States and Canada, and mining ventures in Africa. This activity, which reached its peak at the end of the nineteenth century and the first decade of the twentieth century, led to the sale of securities of these enterprises on a large and organized scale. The 1914—18 war interrupted this activity and the foreign investor found his holdings in some areas frozen, nationalized or confiscated.

The period following World War I brought a resurgence of interest in international investments. At the same time, political turmoil, as well as galloping inflation in Germany and other countries, prompted the financial community on the Continent to seek investment opportunities outside of Europe. Thus interest developed in English securities, while the more sophisticated investor purchased shares in African mining ventures and was eventually prompted to try his luck in New York.

Simultaneously, the American investor displayed an interest in European and other equity investment. The bulk of his foreign investments was concentrated in various German bonds used to finance the reconstruction of that country after World War I, and in Latin America. This investment activity reached its peak in 1928. However, the collapse of the American securities market and the great slump of the early Thirties wiped out investors' fortunes both here and abroad and stopped the internationalization of investment activity. The prevailing conditions were further aggravated by limited means of communication and inadequate information, preventing correct evaluation of the situation. The subsequent economic convulsions of the 1930s introduced restrictions freezing international trade and payments. Finally, the outbreak of

World War II once again brought investment activity to a standstill.

The reconstruction after 1945 was accompanied by a renewal of the internationalization of investments. This time, however, uncertainties were caused by the cold war and internal political difficulties which prompted European individuals and financial institutions to look for shelter in more stable markets. Investment in strong and fully convertible currencies was of prime importance to those remembering the inflation which followed the first World War. Thus, the flow of capital to the United States and Canada accelerated, to be placed in the securities markets of New York and Toronto or Montreal.

Table 8.
Highs and Lows, 1955–1962
(in Dutch guilders)

| Years | Securities | | |
	Royal Dutch High–Low	Unilever High–Low	N.V. Philips Gloeilampenfabrieken High-Low
1955	97–75	51–34	65–38
1956	127–89	54–37	61–36
1957	166–103	59–35	53–37
1958	148–103	62–37	80–38
1959	141–113	122–65	147–79
1960	133–91	154–103	254–124
1961	120–89	152–106	235–185
1962	131–100	143–86	208–103

Source: Eurosyndicat Investment Research Bureau, Moody's Industrial Manual, June, 1965.

As the reconstruction of Europe progressed, interest resumed in other securities markets. Recognition of opportunities in the Common Market countries started an intra-European flow of investments primarily channeled through Swiss banks and the City of London. Simultaneously, the spectacular economic growth in Europe attracted the attention of the American investor. Wall Street became interested in foreign securities in the mid-1950s. Selected foreign shares were then successfully introduced, producing spectacular capital appreciation in a relatively short time, as illustrated in Table 8.

These and other shares were introduced through the over-the-counter market and were purchased by investors familiar with foreign investments. Subsequently, the publicity given to the dynamic economic growth of Western Europe broadened the interest in foreign markets. The excellent results encouraged brokers who were active abroad to expand their investigation of European securities. Thus interest spread from Holland and the United Kingdom to German, French and eventually Italian shares. The number of actively traded foreign securities in the United States broadened to include, among others, those in Table 9.

The U.S. securities in fashion at that time on Wall Street greatly influenced the direction of interest in foreign equities. The popularity of U.S. oil shares contributed to the "discovery" of Royal Dutch, British Petroleum and Compagnie Française des Petroles. Wall Street's new cult of growth stocks sparked a search for their German, Italian and French counterparts. The electronics boom brought to New York shares of Machines Bull, Elliot Automation and Siemens & Halske. Olivetti became fashionable following the rise of office equipment equities in our markets.

It should be noted that this discussion of international portfolio investments concentrates on equities rather than on fixed interest securities, despite the fact that before the enactment of the Interest Equalization Tax, the dollar volume of transactions in foreign bonds was greater than that in equities. Prior to 1963, governments and corporations in Scandinavia, Australia, Japan, Austria, Mexico and other countries were attracted to the U.S. capital market because it is larger than their own markets. On the other hand, such bonds generated considerable interest here so long as they were denominated, serviced and retired in American dollars and offered suitable guarantees, since they competed favorably with U.S. fixed-interest securities on a yield basis. Some experiments were made in bonds denominated in other currencies such as the Deutsche mark and the so-called units of account.* However, their marketability was, at times, in doubt. Thus transactions in foreign fixed-interest securities were not truly representative of portfolio investments abroad because the motivation of neither the borrower nor the purchaser was primarily international investment.

The Treaty of Rome of 1957 further fired the imagination of the investment community. Newspapers and magazines created the impression that economic and political integration in the European Economic Community was around the corner. This publicity, coupled with extensive research studies of foreign companies (prepared by some New York brokers, Eurofinance, Eurosyndicat and Eurounion), broadened individual and institutional interest in European equities. These reports compared foreign companies with their counterparts in the United States, pointing out that on the basis of price/earnings ratios and cash flow veritable bargains were available abroad. However, these studies often paid insufficient attention to the many differences of accounting and reporting methods between United States and foreign companies and to the frequent absence of even the most basic comparative data.

This international investment activity was further stimulated by foreign banks active in U.S. securities markets, who took the position that they would deal with those New York brokers who were able to provide reciprocal business in foreign markets. Thus brokerage firms active abroad had a vested interest in expanding sales of foreign securities in the United States and they also engaged in arbitrage and trading activities for their own account. The combined buying pressure produced in this fashion sent the prices of foreign equities to spectacular but also unrealistic levels. To be sure, the resurgence of local interest in equities in European countries contributed in large measure to the price increases. But the

* One Unit of Account is based on a standard of 0.88867088 grams (1/35 ounce troy) of gold (thus equivalent to $1 U.S.).

Table 9.

European Securities Actively Traded in the U.S., 1955–1962

Securities	1955 High–Low	1957 High–Low	1958 High–Low	1959 High–Low	1960 High–Low	1961 High–Low	1962 High–Low
Farbenfabriken Bayer (DM) [1,2]	136–99	110–89	189–111	341–188	537–327	496–376	410–245
Hoesch Werke (DM) [1]	181–135	151–126	156–124	285–139	309–253	279–202	221–130
Badische Aniline (DM) [2,3]	161–122	134–109	228–127	387–226	595–357	579–388	403–273
Saint Gobain (FF)	84–50	177–104	178–113	303–178	408–264	453–353	368–251
Pechiney (FF)	118–77	248–153	198–157	304–202	365–251	380–279	320–210
Rhone Poulenc (FF)	90–69	166–129	224–152	373–203	433–333	649–429	508–347
Fiat (Lire)	1,279–840	1,198–1,054	1,434–1,053	2,477–1,377	3,852–1,176	3,328–2,640	3,135–2,429
La Rinascente (Lire)	47–23	63–46	95–58	213–89	375–171	533–282	493–335

Source: Eurosyndicat Investment Bureau
[1] Dusseldorf.
[2] Not adjusted for issue of Convertible bonds.
[3] Frankfurt.

runaway advances resulted from U.S. institutional buying of foreign securities in quantities astronomical for the local markets. In the case of most stocks traded in the Continental European markets, the number of shares available and over-all market value are very small by U.S. yardsticks. Thus large orders must be executed over a longer period of time than would be required in New York or even London. The impact of U.S. institutional buying was primarily felt in the more prominent foreign securities, such as Philips Gloeilampenfabrieken and German chemicals. The disruption, however, was even more pronounced in stocks with a limited number of shares outstanding and a thin market.

The correction in foreign markets which began in 1962, followed by adverse economic and political news, chilled U.S. enthusiasm for foreign investments; and the Interest Equalization Tax, introduced in 1963 and still in force in 1968, brought American investment activity in foreign markets to a virtual standstill, which was likely to continue until such time as the tax on foreign investments was repealed.

PROBLEMS AND BARRIERS

The Interest Equalization Tax was not the only reason for the virtual collapse of U.S. interest in foreign investments. The bulk of U.S. private and institutional investments were made when prices had been driven to their historical highs. The correction of 1962 and the subsequent market performance of foreign shares caused a disenchantment with investments abroad, and there ensued a wholesale elimination of foreign equities from institutional portfolios. This, in turn, put the prices of these shares under continuous pressure, as the local markets were unable to absorb such large supplies over a relatively short span of time. Thus the same institutions which helped to drive the price of foreign shares to high levels contributed with equal force to their decline.

When this book was published, a renewal of U.S. investment abroad was still not in sight for the following reasons:

1. Political and economic nationalism had once again emerged in Western Europe.

2. There had been a general slowdown of various economies abroad, accompanied by lower corporate profit margins resulting from higher costs of production and excessive wage increases.

3. The market performance of foreign equities since 1962 had been most disappointing.

4. U.S. balance-of-payments problems, which led to the enactment of the Interest Equalization Tax and the introduction of foreign-investment guidelines, made institutions reluctant to embark on new commitments abroad.

5. Experience had shown that foreign securities markets are, at times, manipulated and that those dealing in such markets are liable to encounter discouraging technical difficulties.

Conditions in investment markets are never static. In the future, dynamic opportunities are certain to develop, attracting capital abroad regardless of restrictions and risk. What has experience taught us? What criteria can be established for investing abroad?

ANALYSIS OF FOREIGN SECURITIES

The requirements for analysis of foreign securities are the same as for the analysis of domestic ones and, when possible, the same data and methods are used. However, the information divulged by corporations abroad is at best a fraction of that made public by, or otherwise obtainable from, U.S. corporations. In addition, the closer interrelationship of political, social and economic factors abroad requires that the analyst base his conclusions more on qualitative than on quantitative data. The analytic process is further complicated by the rapid structural changes taking place abroad, changes which render historical analysis meaningless. Therefore, the three steps which the analyst must follow are, in order of importance:

(1) A study of the advantages and disadvantages of alter-

native geographic investment areas. (2) Selection of companies which have not only a promising outlook, but also a large and well-distributed number of shares outstanding, making investments in them practical. (3) Timing of commitments, taking into consideration not only market conditions but economic trends and international political conditions.

The process of developing an investment policy in foreign equities calls for much greater study of general economic problems and political conditions than is required at home. An unusual degree of flexibility and versatility is required of the investor as he might have to evaluate, for example, the impact of the Vatican on the Italian political situation, the future growth of Soka Gakkai * and the direction of its political and economic program in Japan, or the question of the reunification of Germany. The nature of relations between the United States and the Soviet Union, between Western Europe and the United States or between Soviet Russia and China, for example, must be watched and continuously evaluated as they point to structural changes in the economic and political picture.

The primary problem in evaluation and interpretation of economic and political developments abroad is to reduce the maze of news and commentary to manageable proportions. Therefore, some broad guidelines must be developed in order to be able to recognize the fundamental problems.

Political stability is a primary concern, since it is a prerequisite for the safety of the invested capital. We cannot expect a duplication of our political structure in foreign countries. Nevertheless, the key requirement is a history of orderly transition from government to government and a political mechanism ensuring continuity.

A degree of political stability must be accompanied by the tacit understanding that the obligations undertaken by former

* A religious (Buddhist) and political organization which at present claims more than 15 million members throughout Japan, as well as its own political party known as Komei-to.

administrations toward foreign capital will be honored. This is particularly critical in the case of foreign governments, muncipalities or corporations borrowing capital on a medium- or long-term basis. For example, Austria, Finland and Japan equitably settled all external debt following World War II. On the other hand, some countries have invited foreign investment and then expropriated it directly through nationalization or indirectly through induced inflation or devaluation of the currency. For example, the foreign lender incurred substantial losses in Latin America in the 1920s; investments were frozen by the German government in the 1930s; and $6 million in Greek treasury notes, in default since 1936, were still subject to final settlement in 1967, although continuous negotiations had been carried on for some time.

An investor must also examine the laws regarding the tax treatment of foreign capital. These regulations, which are highly complex and vary from country to country, can have serious repercussions on portfolio investments. Specific questions should be referred to an accounting firm or a bank specializing in these matters.

As of December 31, 1965, Income Tax Treaties were in effect between the United States and twenty-three countries * and the territories of the United Kingdom. These countries impose a withholding tax on interest and dividend payments earned by nonresident investors ranging from 0 to 30%. The amount withheld usually covers all tax liability of the foreign investor in that country. Where such treaties exist, the taxes paid abroad are deductible from federal income tax returns in the United States. The size and treatment of these withholding taxes are often an indication of the climate for acceptance of foreign capital in a given country.

* Australia, Austria, Belgium, Canada, Denmark, Finland, France, Germany, Greece, Honduras, Ireland, Italy, Japan, Luxembourg, Netherlands, Netherlands Antilles, New Zealand, Norway, Pakistan, South Africa, Sweden, Switzerland, United Kingdom (*Information Guide for U.S. Corporations Doing Business Abroad*, Price Waterhouse & Co., U.S.A., December, 1965, Appendix II, p. 34).

The balance of payments and of trade are two of the more important conditions which should be examined in conjunction with the gross national product, cost of living index, wholesale price index and other yardsticks of economic analysis. Familiarity with these economic indicators will make it feasible, at times, to forecast monetary and fiscal policies.

Obviously, the political balance of power and all aspects of the labor situation need to be carefully studied and well understood. A striking example of the interrelationship between party politics, economics and stock prices is Italy's experience following the "opening to the left" (*apertura a sinistra*)—the political alliance between the Christian Democrats and the Socialists formulated in 1961 and 1962. The monetary and fiscal policies resulting from this alliance contributed to a slowdown of economic growth and caused a steep and prolonged decline in the Italian stock market.

A study of labor relations provides an excellent point of departure for the examination of political situations. The composition of wages, fringe benefits, retirement programs and the structure of trade agreements affect the cost of production. At the same time, the character of labor relations, the policies of trade unions, and the existence or absence of collective bargaining will point to currents and cross-currents in the political and economic situation. In addition, this is a study which lends itself to examination by an outsider, whereas the activities of political parties and the programs presented by leaders in foreign countries are less easy to analyze. The problem of labor relations is one which can be studied and even measured. Most importantly, comparisons may be made between labor conditions, costs and policies in various countries.

The nature and degree of economic planning is another important area for study. Objective conditions in some countries, historical reasons in others, have produced various degrees of planning. Japan's economy is carefully planned and guided in order to avoid the confusion which might otherwise arise from unlimited competition. Italy has had a high percentage of public ownership and government control over most segments of its economy since Mussolini introduced *corporativismo* in 1932. The French economy is planned and stabilized by the government. While economic planning obviously reduces the degree of free enterprise, the equities of certain corporations operating under these conditions may nevertheless be attractive for investment.

These broad guidelines will serve to eliminate investment areas where even the minimum requirements for relative safety of capital are not met and will direct individual American investors to a limited number of foreign countries. (This approach does not apply to banks, whose fund commitments are of a short-term nature, or to corporations, which must assume a greater degree of risk in their investments and operations abroad. Moreover, they are less vulnerable than the individuals investing in foreign securities.)

The study of political and economic trends also makes possible early recognition of either emerging dangers or emerging opportunities, and is therefore crucial to the proper timing of investments and disinvestments.

This general investment analysis must then be supported by specific analysis of particular industries and corporations. Aggregate statistical data describing conditions in industries are becoming increasingly available, although they still leave a great deal to be desired as to consistency and accuracy. They are published by the research departments of Central Banks, international research organizations, international management consulting firms and commercial banks. The major difficulty encountered is that different methods of reporting and compiling information in foreign countries make comparative studies more difficult than is often apparent or supposed. Thus, after selecting the sources of information and assembling the data from various countries, considerable effort is required to reconcile and interpret them.

Difficulties will also be encountered in the analysis of specific foreign companies. Such critical factors as sales and earnings projections will, at best, be based on sketchy data, due in part to the reluctance of foreign corporations to release adequate information. This reluctance stems from a traditional tendency toward secretiveness, reinforced by fear of competition. In addition, attempts at tax avoidance often render published balance sheets and income statements difficult to interpret. Frequently, foreign corporations make a deliberate effort to obscure real conditions in order to confuse stockholders or union leaders. This obstacle can be partially overcome through personal contacts with management and widely developed banking connections. At the same time, attempts to broaden capital markets have already contributed to a certain liberalization in the disclosure of information by foreign corporations. In some countries, notably Germany and France, legislation has been introduced to make compulsory the disclosure of prescribed information to stockholders. Societies of security analysts have also been formed abroad which are contributing to the standardization of published data.

The following considerations require special attention as they are frequently overlooked in the selection of investment media:

1. Foreign companies are in many instances still controlled by either a family interest or by a very small group. Thus the division between ownership of a corporation and its management is not as well defined as it is in the United States. In some instances, this factor limits the freedom of action of the management and complicates financing arrangements.

2. The existing shortage of capital abroad and relative inflexibility of markets will often affect the capital structure of a foreign company. Frequent capitalization changes, customary in some foreign countries, such as Japan and Germany, dilute the equity of stockholders and therefore have a considerable impact on the market prices of their securities. Knowledge of a company's banking connections and its customary channels of financing is extremely useful in assessing future financing programs.

3. In foreign companies, examination of the structure of

the management must be carried out in much greater depth than is necessary in the United States. Modern management practices long customary in this country are only now being introduced in foreign companies. In some instances, excellent top-level corporate management is not able to carry out its policies because the middle level of management is not sufficiently developed. Other companies, with excellent middle and lower management, are headed by unimaginative and ineffective chief executives.

4. The degree and rate of change in economic and political conditions are more rapid and at times more drastic abroad. Thus the student of foreign investments should be especially alert to the following: (a) the ability of foreign companies to adapt and take advantage of these changes; (b) the relative position of a company in its domestic market as contrasted with its activities abroad; of particular interest is the degree of existing protection for its products in the domestic market which might diminish or disappear in the future, and the dependence of the company on this protection; (c) changes in competitive conditions and the impact of American direct investment, which sooner or later may well induce mergers and amalgamations; study of probable developments in this direction might be especially rewarding.

In the past, many unsuccessful investment decisions were caused primarily by a misguided attempt to analyze foreign companies by comparing them with their American counterparts while ignoring, in most instances, the specific problems of environment. Elaborate studies were made by U.S. analysts and consultants, comparing Machines Bull with International Business Machines, Siemens & Halske with General Electric, and Thyssen-Hutte with Bethlehem Steel Corporation. Considerable progress has since been made in the understanding of conditions abroad and it is now recognized that the appraisal of foreign companies poses problems requiring a specialized approach. A sophisticated understanding of foreign investment can now be found in those brokerage houses with a long record of activity in foreign markets, in some of the large commercial banks, and in investment trusts specializing in foreign securities. (The Japan Fund, the Eurofund and the Nelson Fund are examples).

TECHNICAL PROBLEMS

Though one may achieve successful mastery of the rather complex problem of appraisal of foreign securities through a balanced combination of qualitative and quantitative analysis, one still has to overcome the technical problems connected with dealing in exchanges abroad. The Roman proverb "buyer beware" should also include "seller beware" with respect to foreign transactions. Securities markets abroad are influenced by pressure groups and in some instances are openly manipulated, thus posing another obstacle for the outsider.

The American investor takes for granted the developed markets and wealth of information available in the United States as well as the legal safeguards and tends to assume that a similar investment environment exists in foreign countries. The effectiveness of the maze of existing legislation and regulations in foreign countries pertaining to transactions in securities cannot be compared to that of the Securities Act of 1933, the Securities Exchange Act of 1934, and subsequent regulations, except perhaps in the case of Japan. Most of the securities exchanges abroad, with the exception of London and possibly Paris, resemble the operation of the over-the-counter market in the United States, but without similar legislative safeguards.

The volume in most foreign markets, in terms of number of shares traded and their dollar value is, with few exceptions, relatively small as compared with trading volume in U.S. markets. An investor may well find that the accumulation of a sizable position in the stock of a foreign corporation is not possible within a reasonable time span because the shares are still under control of a very small group and rarely appear on the market. A broad distribution of equities and a keen public interest in investments similar to that in the United States exist only in England and Japan. However, a gradual reorganization of the markets abroad is taking place, owing to the international shortage of capital, which makes it necessary to attract investment funds from foreign countries. There are tentative signs of what could become a trend away from strictly national securities markets to simultaneous listing and trading of securities on exchanges abroad. Nevertheless, maneuverability in foreign markets will remain limited for the foreseeable future. The investor who insists on executing market orders carrying a time limit—as is customary, for example, in New York—will be seriously penalized.

FOREIGN MARKETS

Several studies * are available which describe in detail the structure of foreign markets, existing regulations and procedures. The following comments are restricted to selected markets in which an American might do business.

England. The London Stock Exchange is undoubtedly the most important securities market outside New York—the best organized and the broadest. It claims a larger number of listed securities, although the value of shares traded is only about 30% of those traded in New York. Dealing in the British market poses no special technical problems for the American investor.

In 1968, the continuing problems of the pound sterling as well as the structural difficulties of the U.K. economy made British securities appear unattractive for some time to come. Nevertheless, the British market could prove rewarding for the patient foreign investor taking the long-range view.

France. The Paris Bourse, reorganized in 1962, is a fairly thin but lively market. Operations are carried out on cash and forward markets and there is also an active options mar-

* See Gerald Krefetz and Ruth Marossi, *Investing Abroad, A Guide to Financial Europe* (New York: Harper & Row, 1965), for introduction and bibliography.

ket. Through an *agent de change* or bank, individual investors may deposit shares with a semigovernmental agency known as SICOVAM † where transactions are debited and credited to one's account, obviating the necessity of shares changing hands physically. This clearing house may also be designated to collect dividends and handle other related details.

The banks in France are very important factors in Bourse transactions, and there are several private banks which specialize in portfolio management, acting as research consultants and brokers. However, the *banques d'affaires* or investment banks are perhaps the most influential with regard to the securities market. These banks finance most corporate investment programs in France and in return often take on a large block of the company's stock. At a later date, the bank can offer the stock on the Bourse, usually at a much higher price than was paid. These and related activities, though quite legal, concentrate a great deal of power with regard to the securities markets and the management of corporate affairs in the hands of the banking community. The combination of this type of manipulation and the thinness of the securities markets creates technical difficulties for all but the most sophisticated foreign investor wishing to deal in French securities.

Holland. The Amsterdam Stock Exchange is one of the oldest and best established on the European continent. It can be broken down into three main segments: (1) The shares of so-called international corporations such as Philips Gloeilampenfabrieken, Unilever and Royal Dutch, which have broad and orderly markets in Amsterdam and are also actively traded in a large volume in New York and London. (2) The shares of companies like Zwanenberg Organon, Heineken and Albert Heijn, which are traded regularly, but in much smaller volume. (3) A whole array of extremely well-man-

† *Société Interprofessionelle pour la Compensation des Valeurs Mobilières.*

aged and successful smaller Dutch companies, whose shares are traded only infrequently.

Transactions in shares of the first group pose no problems. In the second group, the accumulation of fairly large positions requires considerable time. The third group is out of the reach of an American investor, except through Dutch mutual funds specializing in the accumulation of these securities.

Germany. Trading in equities in Germany is conducted in a diffused market, with transactions in the same security taking place in Frankfurt, Dusseldorf, Munich, Berlin, Bremen and Hamburg. Roughly 90% of the transactions are conducted outside of the securities exchanges by the banks which dominate, if not fully control, the investment market. The key banks in Germany operate as commercial banks, investment bankers, stockbrokers, and mutual funds, as was the case in the United States prior to 1933. They are also holders of large blocks of shares of various corporations and at times have a controlling interest in a number of companies. In a situation such as this, the banks obviously cannot maintain the standard of objectivity which is expected of them in the United States. A number of smaller private banking institutions are also engaged in the brokerage business, occasionally providing competition for the larger banks by offering at times more efficient service and more favorable execution of orders. However, they are too small to change or even influence the well-established pattern. These factors make German securities attractive only for the very patient, long-term investor. Even so, as long as the German economy remains strong, their securities offer good value despite the complexities of dealing in them.

Sweden. Trading in the Swedish securities market is somewhat difficult for the foreigner by reason of two restrictions. In the first place, in order to ensure that control of Swedish companies remains within the country, corporations limit, in varying degrees, the number of their shares which may be owned by foreigners. A pool of these foreign-owned Swedish securities does exist. However, *de facto,* such shares can be

viate strains on economies and on the inte
mechanism resulting from prolonged e
omplicated by the resurgence of econom
nalism.

rrent phase of consolidation abroad, t
nomy is growing at a satisfactory rat
sses of rapid expansion and of a changii
e have had a profound effect in Weste
. Massive capital investments in these tv
d the world's industrial production. Inte
n has been accelerated because the expa
r manufactured goods has not kept pa
trial capacity. Finally, efforts to reduce t
yments deficit have compelled Americ
ok for capital in international marke
n for funds in Europe will tend to ma
t high levels, partly delaying any furth
Common Market economies.

created by the difficulties of the inter
tem—aggravated by the persistent pr
terling and deficits in the U.S. balance
in restrictions on the flow of capital, a
ught activity in international securi
andstill. The economies of the free wo
nd the expansion of international por
be arrested until these uncertainties

nges which will renew the trend tow
f investment markets are:

just the international monetary me
improve international liquidity.

patterns of trade and payments as a
gration such as the European Com
(EFTA), and others. Setbacks in
y and it is reasonable to assume tha
resumed.

mpact of massive U.S. corporate in

bought only by one foreigner from another. As a result, premiums develop in a narrow market which operates for the exclusive benefit of foreign investors. Nevertheless, there are a number of companies which have very generous quotas of securities available to foreigners, making premiums in these cases nominal or nonexistent.

In the second place, present Swedish law forbids a foreigner to buy any security in that country with foreign or even Swedish currency, unless he is using the proceeds from the sale of other Swedish securities. However, he may buy Swedish securities abroad for the purpose of selling them in Sweden. Premiums paid in the latter form of transaction were, at one time, in excess of 20%, but at the beginning of 1968 they were quite nominal. With due allowance for these technical problems—which can, with care, be resolved—the Swedish market remains an extremely interesting one. The unusual strength of those Swedish corporations which are internationally competitive, and the limited supply of their shares, make them very attractive for long-term investment.

Japan. The Japanese securities market provides a dramatic challenge. Tokyo is a major center of investment activity, and a large number of shares of Japanese corporations are actively traded by the public. Japan's economy, stabilized at times by rather unorthodox measures, has displayed generally impressive growth and vitality.

The brokerage industry, following the continuous decline of security prices in the period 1962–65, was confronted with the possible bankruptcy of leading brokerage houses and indeed the threat of a complete collapse. The Bank of Japan, recognizing the gravity of the situation, provided funds eventually amounting to the equivalent of $1.25 billion for the purpose of acquiring equities to support the market. This unique and massive intervention provided timely support for the market, which subsequently recovered at a fairly satisfactory rate. However, the Bank's action indirectly concentrated in its hands a gigantic portfolio of equities which is gradually being liquidated. This situation, which created an unusual technical position in the Japanese market, should not detract from the basic soundness of the economy and the willingness and ability of the government to cope with its problems. Over the long term, the Japanese securities market promises to offer outstanding opportunities for the knowledgeable foreign investor.

The Swiss and Other Markets. Some interest is occasionally displayed in Swiss securities, primarily those of Nestlé and the large chemical companies. Swiss securities are divided into two categories: those reserved for the Swiss and those available to foreign investors. The latter carry a sizable premium which, combined with a lack of reliable information and markets manipulated by the banks, makes them relatively unattractive.

The securities market in Spain remains an enigma, while others, like the Mexican, are in an experimental stage.

Investors can avoid many of the difficulties which have been described by investing in foreign securities through the purchase of American Depository Receipts (ADRs) in the U.S. over-the-counter market. These are basically substitution certificates for foreign bearer shares. They are issued by American banks or trust companies, and are currently available for the shares of approximately 200 foreign companies. The banks in the United States issue these negotiable receipts simply as a substitute for the shares deposited abroad. Once issued, ADRs are as easy to negotiate as any domestic stock certificate. However, there is often a considerable spread between the price of an ADR and that of the foreign security in its home market. Thus for the convenience of dealing in foreign securities in the over-the-counter market, a penalty is paid at the time of purchase and at the time of sale.

The management problems of portfolios of foreign securities, such as withholding taxes, collection of dividends and rights issues resulting from capital increases, can sometimes be overcome by a custody arrangement with an experienced American or foreign bank. Nevertheless, maneuverability in foreign markets will remain limited in the foreseeable future.

The investor who i
a time limit, as is
will be seriously pe

LOOKING AHEA

At the beginnin
vestment was clou
by lack of confide
national monetary
of capital introdu
nomic problems f
adjustments whic
problems of reha
quidity and the
Fund at the Br
time, the found
monetary mecha
U.S. dollar, link
tem outperform
ertheless, for se
ing increasingly
and adapt it to

To understa
briefly postwar
three major ph

1. The first
tation of the e
heavy damage
States and the
peacetime acti

2. The cre
dominated th
companied b
of living and
dustrial natio

3. The thi

an attempt to all
national monetar
pansion, further
and political natic
During the cr
United States ec
However, the str
industrial structur
Europe and Japar
areas have enlarg
national competiti
sion of markets f
with growing indu
U.S. balance-of-p
corporations to l
Thus the competit
tain interest rates
improvement of the

The uncertaintie
tional monetary sy
lems of the pound
payments—resulted
in recent years b
markets to a near s
are at a crossroads
lio investments will
alleviated.

The structural ch
internationalization

1. Action to rea
nism and eventually

2. Realignment o
sult of regional inte
Market, Outer Seve
activity are tempora
time, progress will be

3. The increasing

ment in foreign countries, which continues to introduce capital abroad, advanced technology, and modern management and marketing techniques. This, on the one hand, creates competition for foreign corporations; however, it also serves to stimulate growth and strengthen the various economies.

4. Progressive resumption of trade between Western Europe and Eastern Europe as a result of the political evolution that is taking place in Soviet Russia and the satellite countries.

Ability to cope with the problems confronting us will determine how fast expansion abroad will proceed after the current period of consolidation. When this consolidation phase is over, an improvement can be expected in the price of foreign securities—an improvement which could be spectacular because of the limited number of available investment opportunities and the relative thinness of the markets. The first sign of a prospective shift in the trend is likely to send the prices of foreign equities to much higher levels.

SUMMARY

Future investments abroad should be considered in areas which demonstrate the following characteristics: (1) progress in the expansion and improvement of the capital markets; (2) effective legislation protecting the stockholder; (3) strong and growing demand in the economy, supported by a realistic distribution of disposable income and accompanied by a firm pattern of capital formation; (4) evidence of a developed corporate structure, which is essential to a broad distribution of equities and a flexible market for them.

These conditions exist in sufficient though varying degrees in the countries of the Common Market, the United Kingdom and Japan. Thus these areas are primary future fields for investment activity. There are other countries equally interesting, although investing in them is more difficult because of their small size or the structure of their securities markets. Sweden is probably the best example in this group, followed by Australia and possibly Mexico. Once the political and economic convulsions diminish in the countries of Latin America and local attitudes become more encouraging, investments there could also be of interest to the more aggressive investor.

Part III

Analytic Approaches

11

The Valuation of Common Stocks:
The Fundamentalist's Approach

By Ralph A. Rotnem

Security analysis might be defined as an art which is trying hard to become a science, and is not likely to succeed. The reason is a simple one. As Charles Rolo observes in his introduction to this book ". . . you cannot put a stock in a test tube."

To be sure, the procedures used today by the more sophisticated security analysts are strongly oriented toward the scientific method. There are large areas of their discipline in which precise quantitative measurements can be made and

Ralph A. Rotnem, C.F.A., is senior vice president in charge of research at Harris, Upham & Co., Inc.

techniques similar to those of the scientist can be employed. But in the final count, security analysis cannot hope to be truly scientific because it is concerned with qualitative as well as quantitative judgments, and it is forced to deal with portentous imponderables.

Dan Lufkin discusses in another chapter the incalculable importance of management in the fortunes of a company, and management, clearly, cannot be put in a test tube. The yardsticks—such as return on invested capital—by which the competence of management is measured apply only to the past, and the very brilliance of a management team raises the question: How would the company fare should one or two key members of this team move to another company (a not altogether exceptional occurrence)? How, too, is the analyst to evaluate scientifically—that is to say, precisely—the effect of an actual change in top management, especially when an incoming president has built his record in a different industry? The operative point is that the security analyst is profoundly concerned with the human factor, a zone in which judgments must of necessity be highly subjective.

Among the major imponderables that affect stock prices, at least two—politics and crowd psychology—are discussed in detail in other chapters. While the serious financial analyst keeps a constant eye on these forces, the working hypotheses he arrives at certainly cannot be considered "scientific."

None of what has been said above should be construed as a reflection on the usefulness of security analysis. To recognize one's limitations and to struggle against them is surely the high road to self-improvement. The efforts of financial analysts to emulate the scientific approach, even though they cannot be totally successful, are in my opinion bound to increase enormously the seriousness and the practical value of this relatively young discipline. Indeed, it is beyond controversy that they have already done so. In the rest of this chapter I propose to describe and discuss some of the attempts that have been made—including my own—to arrive at a systematic evaluation of common stocks.

The selection of common stocks as investments has always

been determined by the relationship of current price to a seemingly intangible intrinsic value. The elusive nature of "value" has provided economists and security analysts with a quest comparable in variety and excitement to Jason's search for the Golden Fleece.

Bernard Baruch, in reply to a query whether the stock market was high in March, 1955, told the Senate Committee on Banking and Currency, "I do not think anybody is smart enough to know. Whether stocks rise or fall," he said, "is determined by innumerable forces and elements, by economic conditions, the actions of governments, the state of international affairs, the emotions of people, even the vagaries of the weather." Mr. Baruch was talking about the market price of stocks and not about their value. The role of the analyst is to determine an intrinsic value and then, it is hoped, to predict a future market price.

The proliferation of statistical studies, not only of stock prices over the years but also of the records of earnings and dividends, has provided us with more information about securities markets than we have ever had before. In addition, the analyst is becoming more and more sophisticated. The electronic computer has already caused broad changes in many areas of business and government; it is believed its use in financial analysis will further refine and qualify much quantitative material now providing the building blocks of stock valuation. If we accept Mr. Baruch's generalization that a stock's price (i.e., its anticipated future value) is determined by innumerable forces, then it is the problem of the investor to investigate as many of these forces as possible in order to discover intrinsic value.

At the present time there is no generally accepted theory for the evaluation of common stocks, yet there is a growing consensus among analysts as to which factors must be studied in any determination of value. Among these are expected growth in earning power, the stability of earnings, the degree of risk involved, the relationship of current to normal earnings, and the amount of earnings paid out as dividends. All of these are susceptible of tangible representation, and projections can be made based on a knowledge of past performance. The problems arise in relation to the question of emphasis: which factors are more significant in arriving at an estimate of value.

The analysts who will be cited in this chapter have arrived at mathematical formulae for the determination of value. In the development of these formulae, it would appear that the evaluator of common stocks is forced to assign a real value to investor sentiment. The relative effect of investor psychology can be analyzed by an examination of the actual price behavior of common stocks in relation to a normative price determined by all measurable factors contributing to their value. Thus, the serious analyst today is endeavoring to devise a numerical description of investor sentiment and to translate into technical formulae what has heretofore been a purely intuitive process.

In years past, "value" for a common stock was determined by the stability of earnings and dividends and the soundness of the financial structure of the issuing company. But the primary question asked by potential investors was, "What does it pay?" Value in this era was therefore equated with income directly received by the investor in the form of dividends. In an age of simplicity, simple responses were satisfying; in today's complex world we realize that the questions that once seemed simple are not simple, and that they demand increasingly involved and detailed answers.

As the physicist observes the behavior of molecules, which are in constant vibratory movement, so the financial analyst today is endeavoring to arrive at formulations through careful observation of stock price fluctuations and of the great variety of attendant influences. The tools of the mathematician, the sociologist, the psychologist and the economist together with the insights derived from these disciplines are all being applied to the study of the valuation of common stocks.

The authors of a leading text dealing with investment practice (Ralph E. Badger and others, *Investment Principles and Practices*) have stated that the major factors affecting the prices of common stocks are three in number: (1) earning power—amount, quality and prospects; (2) dividends—present and prospective; (3) price/earnings ratio. To what extent each of these factors goes into the valuation of common stocks has been the subject of innumerable articles and many books by highly imaginative and analytically gifted practitioners of the investment profession. As Professor Henry Sauvain stated in *Investment Management*, "When we come to the valuation of common stock, we enter a veritable 'no man's land' where battle lines are often drawn, but no one has ever achieved undisputed possession of the field."

THE "STANDARD METHOD" OF VALUATION

Benjamin Graham and David L. Dodd, in their classic textbook, *Security Analysis*, observed that the "standard method of valuation consists of capitalizing the expected future earnings and/or dividends at an appropriate rate of return. . . . The capitalization rate, a multiplier, applied to earnings and dividends, will vary with the quality of the enterprise." Several analysts have endeavored to use this rather broad general principle and amplify it with specific numerical values.

William Kurtz has elaborated on this "standard method of valuation" in a research paper, "Valuation Standards for Investments." He maintains that price/earnings ratios are a limited tool for establishing "normal values" since a stock or a stock average would still have value even if earnings fell to zero during a severe depression. Prices, therefore, must reflect *residual* values plus some multiple of earnings rather than the price/earnings ratio alone. Mr. Kurtz stated that at any given time stock market averages (e.g., Standard & Poor's, Dow-Jones, etc.) have a fixed or residual value, plus a variable which would fluctuate with earnings, and he expressed the concept of normal value as follows: Normal Value of Stock Prices = Residual Value + Multiple of Earnings × Earnings.

Working with the data for the period 1926–46, Mr. Kurtz

compared the yearly averages of the Dow-Jones Industrial Index with annual earnings. He found that the residual value of the Index, or the price at zero earnings, was 64; and that the variable portion or Multiple of Earnings was 9. Thus for the Industrial Index (in the period in question) Normal Value = 64 + 9 × Earnings.

This basic formula must be modified, Mr. Kurtz points out, since residual value would logically increase over a period of years in a growing economy and decline during a major depression. By using a previous bear market's low point Mr. Kurtz feels that one can express residual value in one figure embodying both the long-term trend and investor sentiment. In a subsequent research study, residual value was found to be closely related to the "normal" earning power of a company. Thus residual value is estimated by applying a capitalization rate to normal earnings rather than by using the price level at a previous bear market bottom.

This concept of "normal value" was then extended to include in the over-all valuation scheme the "growth factor" or lack of it, and the not so ephemeral characteristic of a stock, the "quality factor." Finding that the stocks in the Dow-Jones Industrial Index showed an approximate 5% annual growth factor, Mr. Kurtz reasoned that his original multiple of earnings, 9, would have to be reduced to a "no growth" basis. Since a dollar invested at 5% compounded annually will grow to $1.28 in five years, the earnings of the Dow-Jones Industrial Stocks will be 28% greater in five years than those of stocks with no growth rate. He therefore divided the original multiple of earnings, 9, by the 5% growth factor, or 1.28, and arrived at 7 for a "no growth multiple."

Mr. Kurtz then observed that the highest-rated stocks generally commanded a premium in price of one-third over standard equities and those of lower quality were priced at a one-third discount from standard values. For the Dow-Jones Industrial Index, the average quality factor averaged 1.10. Thus the "no growth" multiple of 7.0 was further deflated by the 10% investment quality premium for the Dow-Jones Industrial Index, resulting in a multiple of 6.4 as the standard ratio for a stock of average investment quality and non-growth characteristics. This led to his conclusive formula for arriving at normal value: Normal Value = Residual Value + Growth Factor × Quality Factor × 6.4 × Current Earnings.

Thus for arriving at normal value for a common stock one would take a past low point in the price of an issue as the residual value, or preferably apply a capitalization rate to normal earnings, and add to this the growth factor, multiplied by the quality factor, multiplied by 6.4 times current earnings. (If residual value is determined by the preferred method referred to above, the procedure is as follows: apply to "normal" earnings the same capitalization rate or multiplier (6.4 ×) as that applied in the formula to "current" earnings. Thus Residual Value = Growth Factor × Quality Factor × 6.4 × Normal Earnings.)

"PRESENT VALUE" THEORY

Over the past 35 years much work has been done by many analysts on the concept of value as equated with present worth. The pioneer studies were probably two articles by Robert G. Wiese published in *Barron's* not long after the Great Crash of 1929. More substantial contributions were made in the 1930s by Samuel Eliot Guild, who published *Stock Growth and Discount Tables* in 1931, and John Burr Williams, whose PhD. dissertation, *The Theory of Investment Value,* was brought out by Harvard University Press in 1938. Dr. Williams referred to the present value of a common stock as the sum of all its future dividends discounted to the current interest rate. Presumably, however, one does not hold a common stock in perpetuity. Therefore, present worth would be equated with future dividends to be received up to a stated point in time, as discounted, plus the capital gain realized at the time of the sale. Nicholas Molodovsky, currently editor of the *Financial Analysts Journal,* believes that the application of the present-worth theory, taken together with his monumental study, "Basic Relations in the Stock Market from 1875" (*Financial Analysts Journal,* February, 1959), will furnish greater information about the whole area of common stock valuation and better possibilities of price prediction. This study provides the investor with stock prices, earnings and dividends during periods embracing a very large variety of political and economic developments. Taken as a whole, the chart is, says Nicholas Molodovsky, "an expression of historical norms of inter-relations between prices, earnings, and dividends of common stocks."

Building on the works of Guild, Williams and Molodovsky, Dr. W. Scott Bauman has applied the present-value theory to current investment problems and has endeavored to estimate the present value of common stocks by the "variable rate method." In calculating the present worth of a given stock, it is necessary to estimate the future dividend income that a stock is most likely to produce and to select a discount rate that appears most appropriate. The fact that the earnings and dividends of many companies are growing at widely divergent rates minimizes the usefulness of current price/earnings ratios and dividend yields and forces the analyst to apply variable rates, since stock values are determined not by present earnings and dividends but by what a company will earn and pay out in the future. Dr. Bauman has presented a series of tables demonstrating variable rates which can be applied to the evaluation of common stocks of almost any category (Michigan Business Reports, No. 42, 1963, University of Michigan).

"THE VALUE LINE"

In the early 1930s, yet another analyst, Arnold Bernhard, set to work to develop an objective method of valuing common stocks. Having lived through the roaring twenties and the depressed thirties, when the market lurched from overvaluation to undervaluation with a violence sufficient to shatter the faith of millions in the rationality of the capitalistic system, Mr. Bernhard embarked on a search for a standard of value that would graphically reveal excesses in the market while they were occurring, and by so doing would, one hopes, prevent them. Professor Paul F. Wendt has observed that Bernhard might be "credited with initiating the econometric analysis of the relationship between stock prices, dividends and earnings at the practitioner level." Certainly numerous statistical formulae for evaluating stocks are now in use, whereas 25 years ago such procedures were almost unknown.

The system which Mr. Bernhard developed, "The Value Line," grows out of the assumption that individual security values are in the final analysis relative, and that the only way to determine the validity of a system of evaluation is to specify the time periods in which price forecasts are measured. The method applies certain criteria and measures their results in three different, specified time periods.*

1. Prospects for the very long pull. The 1,100 stocks in the Value Line are graded in terms of quality from A+ to C—. The quality grade is determined mainly by two factors: earnings growth over the past ten years and stability of the stock's price over the same period. The practical significance of the quality grade is to indicate the merits of a stock for the very long pull, i.e., for a period of longer than five years.

2. Prospects three to five years hence. The 1,100 stocks are divided into five categories of equal size which are ranked from I (highest) to V (lowest) for their desirability as holdings for this time period. These rankings are derived from two measurements: (*a*) a five-year moving average of cash earnings (that is to say, reported earnings plus depreciation) is fitted to the past price history of the stock; and (*b*) the multiple on the earnings curve is adjusted to take account of the change in the trend of the stock's annual price/earnings ratios divided by the price/cash earnings ratios of a broad-based market average over the past 15 years. A loose cross-sectional discipline is applied by keeping the multiples placed on the earnings curve within the limits of a band within

* Arnold Bernhard, *The Evaluation of Common Stocks* (New York: Simon and Schuster, 1959), *passim,* and p. 110.

which the price/earnings ratios of comparable companies in the same industry are found to cluster.

3. *Expected relative price performance in the next 12 months.* The 1,100 stocks are ranked in five categories for probable performance in the year ahead. The rankings are derived from three measurements. First, the nonparametric: here, the order of rank is determined by the relative position of the stock's price and earnings. Then this nonparametric rank is modified by the rate of earnings growth in the latest quarter compared to the rate of earnings growth of the market average. Finally the stock is ranked according to the percentage by which its price stands above or below its Value Line (the five-year moving average of cash earnings plotted as explained above).

Before 1965, Bernhard's method of rating stocks was based upon a correlation between average annual price, on the one hand, and earnings and book value, on the other. (For example, U.S. Steel was rated as being normally valued at 0.4 times book value plus 5 times reported earnings for the year.) Later, time series correlations included as independent variables book value, reported earnings, dividends declared, and the price one year earlier; and as the dependent variable the average annual price. The normal value thus projected was based upon earnings and dividend estimates one year in advance.

The method using projected earnings and dividends was found to be significantly successful. Yet, to his dismay, Mr. Bernhard discovered that the Value Line rating system would have worked just as well had it used the previous year's reported earnings and dividends.

This discovery led to the rating system now in use. Although the earlier methods all showed significantly successful results in practice (and fantastically successful results could they have been applied to earnings and dividends known in advance), the inability to estimate future relative earnings accurately enough forced the organization to conclude that it would be better to rely on known earnings and dividends than on estimated earnings and future dividends. In short, although the previous system was more accurate from a theoretical standpoint, the inability in practice to forecast accurately relative earnings one year ahead tipped the scales in favor of a less sophisticated method related to earnings and dividends as actually reported.

THE ROLE OF "BOOK VALUE"

An area relevant to the valuation of common stocks which, until recently, has received little attention is that of book value per share (arrived at by totaling all tangible assets, subtracting all liabilities and stock issues ahead of the common and then dividing by the number of the shares outstanding). In two articles published in the *Financial Analysts Journal* in 1964, Frank E. Block of the Citizens and Southern National Bank tried to show that book value plays both a direct and an indirect part in common stock valuation. In fact, he stated that "the ratio of price to book value is the final test of management's ability [because] effectively used assets are the basis of profitability, growth, dividends and certain other factors which establish value." On the basis of a statistical study of the 30 Dow-Jones Industrials covering the years 1949–62, Mr. Block concluded that return on equity appeared to be a direct influence on the price/earnings ratio and a major source of growth.

Price/earnings ratios have been one of the most popular tools used in shaping investment policies. Some puzzling trends are evident, however, when we examine the price/earnings ratios of the market averages. The average ratios were higher in 1930, 1931 and 1932 than in 1929, in spite of the fact that the market declined 86% from its 1929 peak to its 1932 low. Earning power also commanded a higher multiple in 1938 than it did in 1937, in spite of a decline of 53% in stock prices. Some argue that it is reasonable to capitalize earnings at a lower rate when they are unusually high and at a higher rate when they are unusually low. That tendency was evident in the bear markets that ended in 1921 and 1932, but it was certainly not apparent in the 1940s. In

1949, the average price/earnings ratio dropped to one of the lowest levels in history when the market was near its low point.

Perhaps there is some way to correct the distortions that come from a simple ratio that is affected by the two variables, earnings and prices. It is possible that we have expected too much of such a ratio, failing to realize that it does not take into consideration another important influence, namely, the fact that even if earnings dropped to zero, there would be value in the plant, equipment and net quick assets. The obvious and easiest procedure is to deduct book value from market price, since the residue gives at least a rough idea of the value of a group of stocks even if earnings were to go to zero.

There are plenty of good arguments to the effect that book-value figures are rather fictitious. But are not earnings and stock market averages themselves fictitious and, as the scientists would say, "dirty"? No one knows what *real* earnings are today. Reported earnings may be too high because depreciation rates are too low; or they may be too low because of the influence of accelerated amortization. They also can fluctuate because of changes in corporate tax rates. Nor

Chart 3. Ratio of Price (Minus Book Value) to Earnings—Quarterly

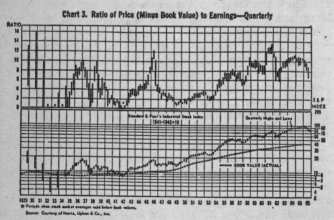

do the popular averages always indicate the real position or trend of the market, as is evident in these years when the averages rise while a majority of stocks decline. What we are trying to do in this new approach is to use the best of the "dirty" statistics that are available in the hope that the end product will be cleaner than its component parts. It is a little like the scientist who takes dirty coal and produces clean white nylon.

Chart 3 shows the result obtained when the book values of the 425 stocks comprising Standard & Poor's Industrial Index are deducted from the prices of the same index and the difference is related to earnings. The formula is *Stock Prices minus Book Values divided by Earnings*. Earnings are the last four quarterly totals; book values are the figures taken at the end of the preceding year; the prices are the highs and lows for each quarter.

The ratios that result from this method seem much easier to understand because they more closely follow market trends. This study considers the market low in price when the average sells below its book value. Instead of suggesting that the market is very high on the basis of earnings at bear-market bottoms, it shows that prices are actually low on the basis of asset values and that no premium above such values is being paid for whatever earnings are available. This chart makes it clear that good bargains were plentiful near the bottoms of the bear markets in the early 1930s, in 1942 and again in 1949. It also shows that the prices paid for earnings were high in 1929, in early 1937, in late 1938, in 1946, in 1961 and most of the time since then.

THE COST OF BUYING STOCK MARKET VALUES

Another method that should be helpful in formulating market policies shows the cost of buying values in the stock market in any given time, as compared with the average cost of buying such values during the past 25 years. By cost of values we mean the price that has to be paid for the stocks included in Standard & Poor's 425 Stocks Industrial Index in relation to: (1) average earnings of the past five years; (2) average earnings during the past ten years; (3) cash earnings; (4) current earnings; (5) book value; (6) dividends. Cost of values also includes: (7) price/earnings ratios *after* deduction of book values from market prices; (8) ratio of bond yields to stock yields.

After each of these ratios was related to its own average for the past 25 years, they were combined into a single figure, which we call "Cost of Values," reproduced in Chart 4. Clearly this yardstick, though similar in character to a price/earnings ratio, is much more scientifically constructed.

This chart shows that the best times to have bought stocks were in 1932, 1938, 1948, 1949 and 1953, when values that usually cost $1,000 were available for $750 or less. The years when such market values were selling for $1,250 or more were 1929, 1930, 1937, 1938, 1946, and 1956—all years which preceded major declines. In 1929, as the figures show, the market was priced high on values and the values themselves soon started to decline. The result was an 89% decline in the Dow-Jones Industrial Average by 1932. In 1954, the market again sold at the 1929 level of 381. But in that year it was possible to buy values *below* average 25-year costs, and the values themselves were also in an uptrend. The result was that between 1954 and February, 1966, the Dow-Jones Industrial Average rose from 381 to 995, a gain of 161%. *It is not the level of the market but the price paid for values that is significant.*

The index has been above the "High Valuation" line most of the time since 1960, indicating that the market has not been cheap for many years in terms of the historical record. On the other hand, it has not been as vulnerable as in 1929 when values cost 89% more than average. While a high cost of values in itself does not start a decline, it does mean that the market must be fed with good news and encouraged by hopes that values will increase in the future. Markets that are cheap on the basis of values can stand on their own feet; those that are overvalued are sensitive to unfavorable developments.

It is important to remember that only a tiny fraction of the nation's more than 20 million shareholders know anything about a scientific approach to security analysis, although indirectly their judgment may be influenced by the more serious analysts, investment counselors and advisory services. In the market place, however, a dollar invested by the least-well-informed person has as much influence as a dollar invested by the most brilliant financial analyst or professional portfolio manager. For this reason there will always be extremes of valuation, especially at important tops and bottoms of the market when emotional traders become more active. The behavior of the market would be quite different (and more sensible) if all the money were owned by well-informed and unemotional people.

I have not, in this chapter, tried to discuss the role of intuition, imagination, "flair"—call it what you will—in the ap-

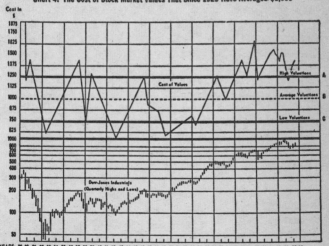

Chart 4. The Cost of Stock Market Values That Since 1929 Have Averaged $1,000

Line A – High historical valuation is represented by this line which is 25% over average.
Line B – Represents the average cost of buying values over the past 25 years.
Line C – Low historical valuation is represented by this line which is 25% under average.

Source: Courtesy of Harris, Upham & Co., Inc.

praisal of individual stocks and of the general state of the market. Let me say now, as emphatically as possible, that the importance of these qualities can hardly be exaggerated as long as they are combined with a determination and ability to seek out, assemble, and searchingly evaluate all of the available data. The "genius" who plays his hunches, whose slogan is "Don't confuse me with the facts," may well make a dazzlingly successful play which wins him a fortune. But his next play, or the one after it, is apt to end in disaster.

This leads me to conclude with a thumbnail sketch of the "ideal" security analyst, as I see him. He has an encyclopedic knowledge of business, economics and the stock market. He is dedicated to the scientific method. And he has the vision, the intuitive brilliance and the imagination of the genuine artist or the creative scientist. I have never met him, nor am I likely to, because I doubt that he exists.

12

Forecasting Stock Prices
The Technician's Approach

By Anthony W. Tabell

Technical analysis remains one of the more fascinating and controversial areas of stock market research. It has gained widespread acceptance by stock market professionals in the postwar period. At the same time, the concept has suffered at the hands of both its ardent enthusiasts, who seem to regard its goal as a magic formula for getting rich quick, and of its equally ardent detractors, who regard it as some sort of necromancy. It is, of course, neither of these things, but simply one of many important tools used in the art of investment management.

Let us begin with a definition. Technical analysis is the *analysis of past price action in order to develop meaningful projections of probable future price action.* The study of past price action is what differentiates the market technician from the security analyst or fundamentalist. The latter is engaged in the analysis of various data concerning individual companies, and most of these data relate to earnings, dividends, and finances along with products, prospects, changes in technology and so on. The technician, on the other hand, is concerned purely with the previous behavior of a given security or group of securities in the market place.

A market technician is often known, especially among

Anthony W. Tabell is senior vice president of Walston & Co., Inc.

those unfamiliar with his work, as a chartist. This definition is only partially true, and it tends to be misleading. As stated above, the technician devotes himself to the analysis of past price action. The chart—and, as we will see later in this chapter, there are many different types and varieties—is simply a useful means of setting forth price action in a conveniently analyzable form. It is the price data that are being analyzed, however, not the chart itself. This distinction becomes especially important when we consider the growing use of the electronic computer in analyzing price action.

The second part of the definition reads ". . . in order to develop meaningful projections of probably future price action." The technical analyst is not seeking a magic formula for instant profits. He is simply trying to provide an additional tool that will be useful to the investment manager in his decision-making. Like fundamental analysis, the technician's work remains as much an art as a science. Like the fundamental analyst, he will often go wrong. His contention is simply that intelligent reference to his work can improve investment results.

It may well be asked why the investment manager needs this additional tool. Will not the fundamental analysis of individual companies do the job just as well? Many, of course, believe that it will, but the technician contends that elements enter into security pricing which can be analyzed only by a study of price action. This view has been eloquently stated by Robert D. Edwards and John Magee in *Technical Analysis of Stock Trends* (Springfield, Mass.: John Magee, 1958):

It is futile to assign an intrinsic value to a stock certificate. One share of United States Steel, for example, was worth $261 in the early Fall of 1929, but you could buy it for only $22 in June of 1932! By March, 1937, it was selling for $126 and just one year later for $38. . . . This sort of thing, this wide divergence between presumed value and actual price, is not the exception; it is the rule; it is going on all the time. The fact is that the real value of a share of U.S. Steel common is deter-

mined at any given time solely, definitely and inexorably by
supply and demand, which are accurately reflected in the transactions consummated on the floor of the New York Stock Exchange.

Of course, the statistics which the fundamentalists study play
a part in the supply-demand equation—that is freely admitted.
But there are many other factors affecting it. The market price
reflects not only the differing value opinions of many orthodox
security appraisers but also all the hopes and fears and guesses
and moods, rational and irrational, of hundreds of potential
buyers and sellers, as well as their needs and their resources—
in total, factors which defy analysis and for which no statistics
are obtainable, but which are nevertheless all synthesized,
weighed and finally expressed in the one precise figure at which
a buyer and seller get together and make a deal (through their
agents, their respective brokers). This is the only figure that
counts.

No responsible technical analyst would claim that the portfolio manager should not refer to fundamentals. Technical
analysis may be compared, by analogy, to the hammer in the
carpenter's tool kit. It would certainly be impossible to build
a house using only a hammer. It would be difficult, however,
to do an efficient job of housebuilding without one.

The technician, then, analyzes the price action of individual stocks in the market place. This chapter will outline some
of the things that he looks for and considers in his analysis
and some of the techniques he uses. It is addressed to those
who seek a better understanding of technical analysis and not
to professionals, who will find it somewhat elementary.

Many of the techniques of technical analysis had their origin in the first half of this century; they were developed by a
small group of pioneers who were using them long before the
analytical profession itself grew to its present size and a large
body of analysts began to take an interest in them. Others are
the products of the computer age and mathematical theory.
All of them make certain assumptions, which we will presently examine, about the nature of stock prices.

The precursor of almost all technical work is, of course,

the ancient and venerable Dow Theory, originally conceived by Charles H. Dow, who edited *The Wall Street Journal* from 1889 to 1902. Coincident with promulgation of the theory, he created the Dow-Jones Averages. His work was later codified by his successors, W. P. Hamilton and Robert Rhea.

The theory is often explained by analogy. Let us assume that a swimmer at the beach wishes to know whether the tide is coming in or going out. It is difficult to determine this by observation, because the waves and ripples obscure tidal action. If, however, our swimmer were to place stakes in the sand at the highest point reached by the surf after a given wave and at the lowest point to which that wave receded, and then were to continue this process with each successive wave, he would soon note, if the tide were rising, a progressively higher pattern of crests and dips. He could, of course, then identify the direction of the tide with some certainty. Dow's conception of the behavior of the stock market was simply that it was similar to tides—that it was composed of major trends analogous to the tides themselves, intermediate trends analogous to waves, and minor trends analogous to ripples. He believed that it was largely impossible to predict the direction of minor or intermediate trends, but that a study of these trends could be used to determine whether the major trend was up or down. Thus, under the Dow Theory, each new high in the Averages would be noted. If, after a high, the Averages reacted, rallied to a point *below* the old high and then posted a new low *under the previous reaction low,* this would constitute evidence that an upward trend had come to an end and a downward trend had begun. Obviously, there are further complications, including the fact that both the Industrial and Rail Averages are used, and confirmation of one by the other is required. But the above is a basic summary of the theory.

Owing to differing use of this theory by various practitioners, it is difficult to compile an effective record of its performance over a period of time. Most users would agree, however, that its ability to call major turning points in the market, e.g., 1929, has been extremely good. A moment's reflection will indicate that the theory has its greatest value where long, wide upward and downward moves take place. In essentially sideways markets, it is prone to give "whipsaw" signals—buying signals near the top of a trading range and selling signals near the bottom of the range.

Regardless of its merit or lack of merit, the Dow Theory, as applied to present-day markets, is of great importance from a historical point of view. The theory was the first systematic recognition of the fact that stock prices follow trends; and that a trend, once established, tends to remain in force. It is this principle that underlies a good deal, though by no means all, of technical work. It should, of course, be made clear that when we speak of trends in the stock market we are talking of something very difficult to define. Trends in stock price action do, indeed, exist, but they vary widely in terms of both periodicity and amplitude. In other words, we have no historical guide to tell us how long a trend may continue or how far it may go. While this makes analysis difficult, it does not render it impossible.

Historically, the way of recognizing and analyzing price trends has been to set out price history on a chart. This method furnishes a handy visual record of the price fluctuations of the stock under analysis. Chart 5 presents such a record of Douglas Aircraft covering the period January, 1965, to September 1, 1966. A good deal of useful information is contained in this chart. Each of the vertical divisions represents one week. The method of charting is to draw a vertical line connecting the high and low prices at which the stock traded during the week. The price at which it closed is then indicated by making a cross-hatch on this line. Charts of this type are commonly called vertical line or bar charts, and the period represented by a single bar can be a day, a week, a month or indeed any period desired by the analyst.

The price scale on this chart is indicated on the right-hand vertical axis. It will be noted that this is a logarithmic scale as opposed to an arithmetic one. In other words, equal vertical

Chart 5. Douglas Aircraft Co. (D)

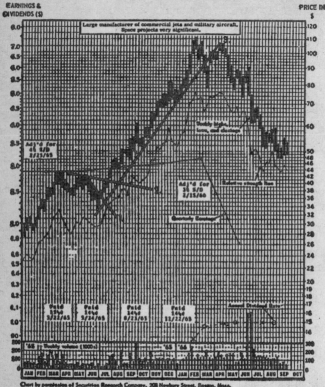

Chart by permission of Securities Research Company, 208 Newbury Street, Boston, Mass.

distances on the chart represent equal percentage changes rather than equal dollar amounts. The use of this type of scale facilitates the comparison of stocks selling at different prices.

The chart also contains a good deal of other information in easy, usable form. The heavy vertical lines, or bars, at the bottom represent the number of shares traded each week. On this particular chart, quarterly earnings are also shown by the broken horizontal line at the bottom of the chart, with the X's and O's representing the dates individual dividends were declared and payable. Also on the chart is a relative strength line, which will be discussed later.

On a chart of this type, trend analysis is a relatively simple matter; the only tools necessary are a ruler and a pencil. All we have to do is to connect successive price peaks or price bottoms with a straight line, and we have defined an uptrend or a downtrend. This has been done at various points of the Douglas chart. For example, in June, 1965, the high for each successive week touched the trend line marked 1. Finally, in early July this trend line was violated on the upside as the price of the stock rose from a low of 33 to a price above 36. The rise continued over the next few weeks, and by late July the trend line connecting the March and June highs had also been violated. Thus, an uptrend was fairly conclusively established. This uptrend remained in effect throughout the summer and fall of 1965 and early 1966, and, as time wore on, it became quite evident that it could be identified by trend line No. 3, which had been touched at no fewer than five points. Thus, the ultimate breaking of this trend line in February, after the stock had advanced to 110, had a good deal of significance. Following the breaking of the trend line, a not uncommon phenomenon occurred. The stock returned almost precisely to the trend line and moved on or just below it for a number of weeks. The downside pull-down from this line is often a confirming signal that a new trend has begun. After the trend line had been broken, Douglas in due course declined to under $50 a share. This type of elementary trend analysis is carried on regularly in the financial community. Obviously, it is fairly unsophisticated; nevertheless the penetration of a trend line in one direction or the other often proves in practice to be of considerable significance.

There is a great deal more to be derived from the charted history of a stock's price. One tremendously important concept is that of support and resistance levels. A support level is a price at which the analyst may expect a considerable increase in demand for a stock, and a resistance level is a price at which a considerable increase in the supply of stock may be expected. Support and resistance levels can normally be found in areas where a good deal of stock has previously changed hands.

The reasoning behind this is really quite simple. If many investors have bought a stock at a given price and then seen it decline below that price, the natural human tendency will be to wait to "get even" and then sell. This creates a resistance level to any subsequent upward move. Conversely, if a stock, after trading for a period of time at a given price, moves up sharply, there are likely to be many buyers who will be eager to purchase it as soon as the stock falls back to the price at which it had traded for so long. An area of support is thus formed.

Chart 6 is a price chart of General Electric, very similar to the chart of Douglas. The one difference is that the General Electric chart is a monthly chart with each vertical line showing the high, low and close for each month rather than for each week. Obviously, this permits a good deal more time to be covered and, as the lower horizontal scale will show, the chart runs from 1954 through 1966. As can be seen, the trend-line principle holds equally valid on a long-term chart such as this—note the well-defined downtrend line from 96 to 60 in 1960–61, and the equally well-defined uptrend line from 55 in 1962 to 110 in 1966. The General Electric chart, however, also illustrates the operation of the support-resistance concept.

As can be seen, in late 1954 the price of General Electric rose sharply from a low of around 42 to a high of 55, reached in February, 1955, and repeatedly touched in June, July, September and December of that year. In early 1956, the stock rose sharply above the 55 level, attaining a high of 65 in March of 1956. A broken line has been drawn on the chart across the top of the 1955 trading range. It is easy to see how many times during the next two years, in 1956 and 1957, demand or the stock materialized every time it was driven down to this level—an excellent illustration of the concept of support.

Finally, in 1958 the price of General Electric began moving sharply upward, reaching a high of 100 in January, 1960. Shortly thereafter, it began a sharp decline which extended far into 1961, and the problem again became the determination of a support level. The obvious answer was to return to the trading range of the 1956–57 period, namely the 65 to 55 area. A broken line drawn through the center of this area indicates that the stock finally did meet support at the 60 level, first in 1961 and then again in 1962. Incidentally, the sharp push through the support level in June, 1962, and the equally sharp return to above the support level in July, 1962, is a not

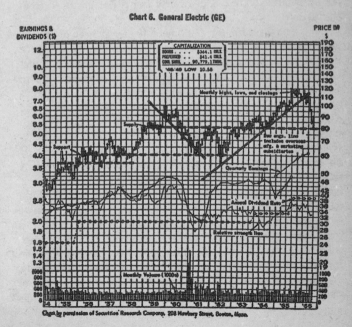

Chart 6. General Electric (GE)

uncommon phenomenon, especially at major market bottoms.

The concept of supply is illustrated by General Electric's behavior during the 1961 rally. As can be seen, the stock broke the 1960–61 downtrend line and rallied sharply during the summer and fall of that year. As indicated by the horizontal broken line at the 80 level, the rally topped out at a point where one might well have expected it to do so—underneath the overhead supply created by the 1959–60 top. It was from this level that the 1961 reaction and the test of the earlier support-level set in.

Finally, in 1963, the supply was overcome and the uptrend culminating at 120 in September, 1965, took place. This uptrend line was breached in early 1966, and a decline to 80 ensued. Here is a case where a previous level of supply becomes a support area, and a fairly sharp rise occurred from the 80 level.

Let us now return for a moment to the subject of trends. As we have seen, the Dow Theory recognized early that price action has a tendency to follow established trends and that violation of these trends often has some significance. Up to this point we have considered only actual price trends. Let us now consider a somewhat more complex concept—the trend of a stock's price *relative to the rest of the market*. The importance of relative trends—or relative strength, as the relative-trend concept is often called—can best be explained by an example. Let us consider the case of two stocks: Stock A which, over a year, declines from 100 to 90, and Stock B which declines over the same period from 50 to 40. Both, quite obviously, are in downtrends. However, on a relative basis the first stock is acting better than the second. It is down only 10%, whereas the second stock, having declined from 50 to 40, is down 20%. If the period in question were one in which the general market had been declining quite sharply, and most stocks were down at least 15%, the performance of the first stock would be truly outstanding even though it declined in price.

The important thing about relative trends is that, like actual trends, they tend to persist through time. Thus a stock which has consistently been acting better than most other stocks is, in theory, likely to continue to do so.

The problem inherent in relative strength is, of course, one of definition. It is very easy, as in the example above, to say Stock A is acting better than Stock B. When we attempt to analyze and compare the price action of more than a thousand different stocks, however, the problem becomes more difficult.

One solution is illustrated on Chart 7, which shows the weekly price history of Gulf Oil from January, 1965, through September, 1966. Below the price is another line, the ratio of Gulf Oil's price to the Dow-Jones Industrial Average. If Gulf Oil is acting better than the Dow, this line will tend to move up, regardless of whether the price itself is moving up or down. If Gulf Oil is acting worse than the Dow, the line will tend to move downward over time. As can be seen from the chart, from June, 1965, to early 1966 the relative-strength line tended to move downward *despite the fact that the price of the stock itself generally moved higher throughout most of the period.* In other words, though Gulf was rising, it was rising at a lesser rate than the Dow and was, relatively, an inferior holding. However, early in 1966, an abrupt reversal took place. The relative-strength line began to rise sharply *despite the fact that Gulf Oil's price was actually declining slightly.* This reflected the fact that, while the average stock was dropping sharply, Gulf was meeting strong demand in the 50 to 48 area and was not joining in the general market decline. This superior relative action continued with a move by Gulf Oil to a new 1966 high in October, at a time when the Dow was down as much as 22% from its high for the year.

The above example illustrates one method of deriving relative strength, i.e., by taking the ratio of a stock's price to a market average and observing the trend of this ratio. Another and somewhat more sophisticated method has been developed since the advent of the electronic computer. The computer makes it possible to observe, over a period of time, the price action of a great many stocks; to fit a trend line to each one of these stocks; and mathematically to measure the upward or downward slope of each one of these individual trend lines. It is then a relatively simple matter to assign a rank to each one of the stocks under survey, with the stock showing the sharpest upward trend being ranked No. 1, and so on down the line to the stock showing the sharpest downward trend. *What one looks for is an abrupt change in the stock's trend ranking.*

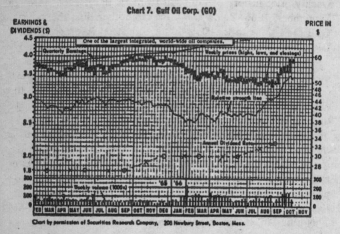

Chart 7. Gulf Oil Corp. (GO)

Chart by permission of Securities Research Company, 208 Newbury Street, Boston, Mass.

Table 10 shows how this concept worked in the case of National Airlines during the period April–August, 1966. The middle column expresses the stock's relative rank on a percentage basis; in other words, a ranking of 97 indicates that it is performing 97% better than all other stock under survey. It will be noted that by the end of June, the relative rank of National Airlines had dropped sharply from 97 to 84, despite the fact that the stock was trading fairly close to its high and at a level slightly above where it had been in April and May.

Once this drop in rank had begun, it of course continued, and by the end of August the price of the stock had declined to 56 and its relative rank to 68. Careful studies of relative rank can often anticipate such deterioration.

Table 10.
Rank of National Airlines Stock
(in 1966)

Date	Relative rank, percentage	Price
April 6	97	104
April 26	96	94
May 31	92	86
June 28	84	97
July 26	81	84
August 9	73	82
August 23	68	56

We stated at the outset that the job of the technician is to examine price data and draw conclusions therefrom. We started with some rather elementary examples of simple bar charts, illustrating trend lines and supply and support levels. We then discussed various ways in which these data are manipulated in order to determine relative strength or relative weakness. We will now examine another way in which raw price data are handled in order to make them more susceptible of analysis. This is the point-and-figure chart.

Unlike relative strength, which is a fairly new concept and one that has gained its most widespread use since the advent of the computer, the point-and-figure concept dates back more than a half century. There are records of point-and-figure charts kept as early as 1910, and such charts were in widespread use in the 1920s and 1930s. The technique involves an attempt to remove one of the basic limitations inherent in the bar charts we have been looking at in Charts 5, 6 and 7. This limitation is due to the fact that the horizontal axis on these figures is based on arbitrarily fixed time periods.

However, stock market action that is significant from a technical point of view may take place in a very short time or over a long period. The problem of the technician, ever since charts became widely used, has been to separate important action from that which is unimportant, *and to make the important fluctuations stand out prominently on the chart.* The point-and-figure method was developed to accomplish this. It is the firm belief of the writer that the point-and-figure chart constitutes the most valuable and accurate method of setting down the price history of an individual security. For this reason Walston & Co., maintains some 4,000 individual charts on this basis covering every security listed on major United States Exchanges.

The rationale behind point-and-figure charting is simple: it is that *price action is significant only when accumulation or distribution is taking place;* in other words, when stock is passing out of the hands of weak speculative holders into those of strong investment buyers, or vice versa. If a stock is being accumulated by powerful buyers, this accumulation must, of necessity, be accompanied by price fluctuation, as the buying forces the stock up, abates, and then re-enters the market as the stock recedes in price. The object of point-and-figure charting is to make periods in which many price fluctuations take place more prominent on the chart than periods in which few price fluctuations take place.

Chart 8 illustrates the construction of a point-and-figure chart. The majority of such charts are constructed on a one-point unit basis; in other words, the chartist is interested in fluctuations of one point or more. Chart 8 begins with the X in the box opposite the figure 20. After the stock has sold at 20, the chartist is interested in two things only, whether the stock sells at or above 21, or whether it sells at or above 19. This stock subsequently sold at 19, so an X was made in the 19 square just under the previous posting at 20. This X established a downtrend and, as long as this downtrend remained in effect, all subsequent postings were made in the same column. In this case, the downtrend continued until a price of 17 was reached. The stock then reversed one point by selling at 18 and the chartist moved over into the next column to post 18. Once this 18 posting had been made, a sale at 19 or 17 would establish a trend. The next recordable sale was 17 and the trend carried down to 15 in the second column. Subsequent fluctuations produced the pattern shown.

Thus, on a point-and-figure chart the width of a horizontal trading area is not an arbitrary axis based on time but is the direct result of the amount of price fluctuation which has taken place.

What are the advantages of point and figure as compared to other types of charts? The point-and-figure chart retains the features noted in Charts 6 and 7. It is possible to draw trend lines and to seek out areas of support and resistance. However, the most important feature of the point-and-figure chart is one which cannot be derived from any other method of charting—that is, the principle of "count" or congestion-area analysis.

Chart 8. A Point-and-Figure Chart

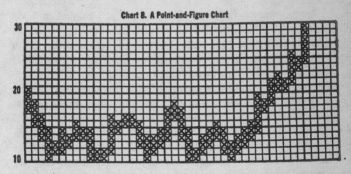

As a stock fluctuates within a narrow price range, a congestion area is formed on a point-and-figure chart. Such congestion areas are usually set off by "walls," sharp vertical moves on either side of the area. Point-and-figure analysts hold that there is a direct relationship between the horizontal width of a congestion area and the vertical extent of a subsequent upward or downward move. In other words, it is possible to count across a congestion area and arrive at an upside or downside objective or price target for the individual stock under study.

Congestion areas are commonly called either bases or tops depending on whether they precede an upward or a downward move. It is never certain whether a congested area is a base or a top until a "breakout" takes place, either upward or downward out of the congestion area. However, the analyst can often derive significant clues from the shape of the area prior to the breakout.

Let us analyze a particular chart to indicate some of the possibilities inherent in point-and-figure work. The chart we are using is shown in Chart 9 and is a chart, not of a stock, but of the Dow-Jones Industrial Average covering the period from 1958 to 1966. It is on a ten-point-unit basis, meaning that each box represents a fluctuation of ten points rather than one point as in Chart 8. Otherwise, the principle is exactly the same.

As we can see from the chart, in the bull market of 1958 the Dow climbed in an almost straight line, reaching a high of 670 in early 1959. Following this, it remained in a congestion area or sideways trading range between a low of 620 and a high of 680. Early in 1960, it broke out sharply on the downside, reaching a low of 610. In order to formulate a downside objective, it was necessary to count across the upper part of the congestion area across the 650 level. This count is illustrated between A' and A", and since we presume that a downside move will be equal to the lateral extent of the congestion area, we arrive at a downside objective of 590. The low reached on the Dow in early 1960 was 600.

However, all examples are not that simple. In late 1960, the Averages broke sharply on the downside, reaching a low of 570. At this point, it became tempting to count across the entire congestion area between 600 and 670 from C' to C". If this had been a valid count, it would have indicated a substantial further decline to the 450 level.

However, this was not the proper interpretation. The downside breakout to 570 was the beginning of what has come to be known as a "delayed ending" type of formation, leading not to a downswing but to a major upward move. Although it was difficult to ascertain this at the time through pure point-and-figure technique, other technical evidence pointed against a further extension of the decline in September, 1960.

The point-and-figure chart confirmed this when, after some hesitation in the latter part of 1960, the Dow moved sharply back into the 600 to 650 area and then penetrated this area on the upside. The base count was quite clear, running from B′ to B″ and indicating an upside objective at B of 740. This was the approximate intra-day high reached by the Dow. The next

Chart 9. Point-and-Figure Chart, Dow-Jones Industrial Average
(10-Point Unit Basis)

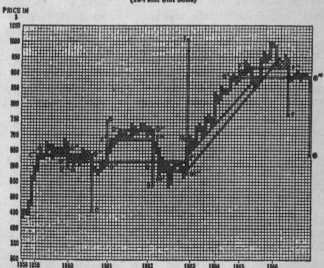

major problem arose in early 1962 when a new congestion area formed and was penetrated on the downside. For this particular area a number of counts was possible. The most conservative appeared to be across the 710 line from D′ to D″, indicating a downside objective at D of 590. A more pessimistic count ran from E′ to E″, indicating a downside objective at E of 530. This latter objective proved to be the correct one.

By the end of 1962, a small base had formed, and this was measured at M′ and M″, affording an upside objective at M of 680. This, at the time, appeared to be quite plausible for a number of reasons, among them being the fact that it coincided with the heavy overhead supply at 690 to 700. However, the Dow moved quickly through this supply and by mid-1962 it was evident that a broader count had to be taken. The only solution to the problem was to consider the entire trading range between 1960 and 1962 as a base and extend the count from B′ across the 610 line to I″; this indicated an upside objective of I of 1,000, which was just about the level ultimately reached in February, 1966. As the uptrend went on into 1964 and 1965, two trend lines appeared to define it. The first was breached in June, 1965. This breakout proved to be false, however, and a lower trend line connecting the October, 1962, and June, 1965, bottoms was not penetrated until March, 1966. By this point a definite top had formed. One plausible count at this top was from J′ to J″, giving a downside objective at J of 760, slightly above the low actually reached in October, 1966. A more pessimistic count could have been taken across G′ and G″, affording a possible downside objective of 630—an eventuality which appeared unlikely in the light of other considerations.

There are a great many other ways in which the technician can manipulate price data in order to observe, analyze and predict. For example, price trends may be smoothed through the use of moving averages and exponential smoothing techniques in order to eliminate short-term fluctuations and get a more clearly defined picture of an up or down trend. A great deal of work has been done of late on analysis of upside and downside volume in individual issues and with various methods of accumulating this volume to discover underlying buying or selling pressures. While this work is highly intriguing in theory, practical results to date have been mixed. There is no doubt, however, that as more and more data are poured into the indefatigable "brain" of the computer, a great many relationships and tendencies, which we do not now suspect, will be discovered.

All the techniques we have discussed so far have their foundation in the observed behavior of stock prices. The principle of trend was discovered as early as the 1900s by Dow and other theorists. The concept of support and resistance was also arrived at from observed phenomena as were relative-strength techniques and the point-and-figure concept. We can apply other methods of analysis to the market as a whole also based on its observed behavior in the past. For example, a major market peak is a phenomenon that is readily identifiable. There have been relatively few of them in recorded market history, and it is a fairly easy matter to go back and isolate certain phenomena that have tended to appear at most of these tops. Two of the most noticeable are breadth and volume deterioration, which have usually occurred well in advance of a peak in the popular averages.

These terms require some definition. Market breadth, first of all, refers very simply to the number of stocks advancing and declining. It is generally given concrete form through the use of a breadth index, or advance-decline line, which is derived from the raw data on the number of stocks advancing daily and weekly. The record of one such breadth index is shown in Chart 10. In this chart the vertical lines represent the weekly range of the Dow-Jones Industrial Average, and the breadth index is represented by the fluctuating solid line below it.

Computation of this breadth index is very simple. It is necessary only to take the number of advances and declines for each week, arrive at the difference, and divide this difference by the number of stocks remaining unchanged. The resulting figure is added to or subtracted from the previous reading (depending upon whether it represents advances or declines). If, for example, in a given week 800 stocks advanced, 400 declined and 200 were unchanged, the computation would be as follows: 400 is subtracted from 800, giving 400. This is divided by 200, giving 2. This is then added to the previous week's total since more stocks advanced. If more stocks had declined, the figure would have to be subtracted.

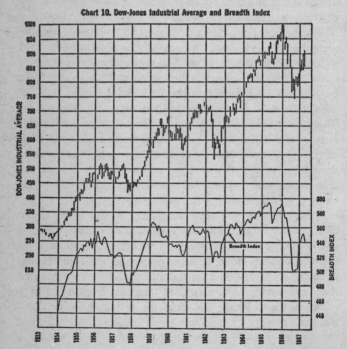

Chart 10. Dow-Jones Industrial Average and Breadth Index

It will be noted that, during the period covered by the chart, there have been four major declines in the Dow—in 1957, 1960, 1962, and 1966. In each one of these declines, as the chart clearly shows, the breadth index started to decline well before the peak in the averages. Thus a decline in this index, or a failure by the index to confirm a new high in the averages has, over the years, tended to signal a lower market. This reflects the simple fact that as a market rise reaches an advanced stage, fewer and fewer stocks continue to move ahead. That is what is meant by breadth deterioration.

As market breadth deteriorates toward the end of an advancing market, volume tends to deteriorate also. Chart 11 shows the history of the Dow-Jones Industrial Average from 1946 to 1966. The solid line represents total volume on the New York Stock Exchange on a 25-week moving total basis.

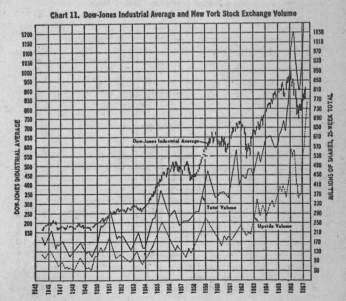

Chart 11. Dow-Jones Industrial Average and New York Stock Exchange Volume

In other words, each posting represents total trading volume for the most recent 25 weeks. The dotted line below it represents upside volume, or volume on days when the market advanced—also shown on a 25-week-total basis.

A few very interesting points can be gleaned from this series. First of all, as can be seen, the volume line has been in a secular uptrend, reflecting the large increase in the number of shares listed. Within this uptrend, however, there have been numerous peaks which stand out sharply on the chart. The peaks in *total volume* tend to coincide with the peaks in *upside volume*. In other words, there has been a marked tendency at various points in market history for total volume to decrease sharply when upside volume decreases. Now let us observe what happened after these peaks occurred. Like peaks in the breadth index, they have invariably anticipated declines or

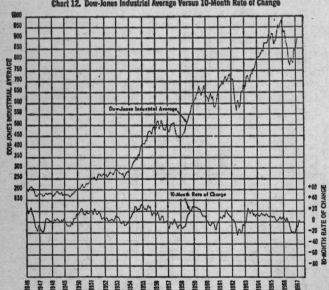

Chart 12. Dow-Jones Industrial Average Versus 10-Month Rate of Change

sideways trading ranges often by a considerable number of months. Thus, prolonged volume deterioration, especially when accompanied by declining upside volume, tends to be a danger signal.

In the foregoing description of volume and breadth we referred only to their action at market tops. Because of the nature of the stock market cycle, an entirely different set of indicators is generally used to pinpoint bottoms from that used to pinpoint tops. Market peaks, the historical record shows, reflect a process of gradual disintegration, and the deterioration generally shows up over a period of time in decaying volume and breadth. Bottom reversals, however, have a tendency to be more abrupt. For this reason, at major bottoms, analysis of rate of change often proves helpful.

The rationale behind this is rooted in the fact that selling generally tends to run its course without too much interruption. Therefore, when the market has declined to an extent consistent with past declines, and fails to follow through on the downside, a reversal is often imminent. Chart 12 shows the Dow-Jones Industrial Average since 1946, together with a simple ten-month rate of change, i.e., the percentage change in the Dow at the end of each month versus ten months ago. In a bear market, quite obviously, this line will decline to a point below the zero level and, generally, a reversal is signaled by a subsequent rise toward or through zero. As can be seen from the chart, this action has occurred close to the bottom of every major upswing during the period. It has also occurred on a number of occasions when the market did not move up immediately, but subsequently moved sideways— most notably in the 1946–49 period. And on one occasion (1957), a false signal was given which shortly afterward reversed itself.

This chapter has outlined the sort of things that the market technician is concerned with and some of the methods he uses in his analysis of stock price data. No formulae or rules have been presented; rather, an attempt has been made to show the principles which underlie technical work. Technical analysis is an exciting field and a useful one. Like all other disciplines, it requires the application of intelligence, common sense and much hard work. Properly used, it can be both fascinating and rewarding.

13

Contrary Opinion Theory: The Psychological Approach

By Bradbury K. Thurlow

Virtually every serious student of stock market phenomena has passed through that delightful sophormoric stage in his career when he discovers he is no longer a member of the investment public. He has learned that the stock of a company is not always a good buy when the dividend has just been raised and the forecasts all point to higher earnings, or a good sale when the management is gloomily predicting six more months of depressed operations. He has seen with his own eyes the follies committed by otherwise intelligent human beings when they become part of a crowd, and he can smile with inner satisfaction at Hamilton's dictum that "the public is a great stupid beast" or at Bismarck's pithy observation that "there is no such thing as public opinion; there is only public sentiment." If he is studiously inclined, he can relish the charming histories of human irrationality in Charles Mackay's 126-year-old classic: *Memoirs of Extraordinary Popular Delusions and the Madness of Crowds*, the trenchant observations on human nature in Gustave Le Bon's little masterpiece. *The Crowd,* or the modern and practical sagacity of Humphrey Neill in his *Art of Contrary Thinking* and his *Letters of Contrary Opinion*.

Once his eyes have been opened and he has seen into the

Bradbury K. Thurlow is vice president of Winslow, Cohû & Stetson, Inc.

vast gulf that separates human wisdom from mass behavior, no person is ever quite the same. Call it professional cynicism, loss of innocence, or what you will; one who has studied and understood speculative behavior must be a skeptic. It is this knowledge, this attitude of mind, that I regard as the essential prerequisite for becoming a good contrarian. It is only a prerequisite, however, as I shall endeavor to show in the rest of this chapter. Contrary opinion analysis, like its counterparts, security analysis and technical analysis, is a valid professional discipline calling for rigorous mental training and broad experience. Properly understood and applied, it is an invaluable, indeed irreplaceable, tool in forming stock market judgments and opinions on security values.

The standard oversimplification of contrary opinion as a theory is that the public (or the majority) is always wrong and therefore an opinion contrary to that being widely held is likely to be right. Such a conception is a good symptom of the sophomoric level of attainment described above. There is undoubtedly more truth than falsehood in it, but it is too crude and superficial to be used in practice. Therefore most students, after a brief flirtation, give up contrary opinion theory without ever having understood that it could be a serious and useful discipline.

As I see it, the most important general assumption of contrary opinion theory is that all information is necessarily imperfect and all human judgment is necessarily fallible. In proportion to the dissemination of information and judgments, the extent of their imperfections increases, until an idea that may have begun as the intelligent appraisal of known facts can, by being popularized, degenerate into a foolish slogan based on fantasies. Popular sentiment is far more responsive to rhetoric than to fact. An original idea, precise in character and limited in scope, gains in appeal what it loses in accuracy when the wordmen and hucksters turn it into a good sales pitch. The professional contrarian, accepting this as a normal evolutionary process, decides at what point the original idea has lost its validity, and he is not dismayed by the likelihood that few people will agree with his judgment. Contrary opinion does not assume that the majority (or the public) is always wrong. It would not, for example, take issue with the widely held belief in the right of free speech, or the popularity of the President of the United States, or the preponderant hostility toward Communism, or with the prevailing view that American Telephone is a high-quality investment issue. At the same time, contrary opinion has challenged, and eventually triumphed over, such widely held beliefs as that women should not be allowed to vote, that Huey Long was a great public benefactor, that Hitler's Germans were a superior race, and that the stock of American Telephone was a prudent investment purchase in the summer of 1929. Contrary views (as defined in this chapter) are those that take exception to arguments based on prejudice, ignorance or unwarranted assumptions—in other words, to arguments based on what one would call crowd psychology rather than individual reason.

The majority, then, is not necessarily the *crowd,* at least in the unfavorable psychological sense which that term will connote in this chapter. The majority is capable at times of acting rationally and intelligently. It is only when it succumbs to irrationalism that its behavior invites a contrary attitude. It is moreover clear that, although crowd thinking plays some part in the social behavior of most of us, it cannot damage our welfare in most of our pursuits as much as it can in the fields of investment and speculation. In these areas, crowd thinking characteristically plays a dominant and indeed respectable role. Failure to recognize it for what it is can result in financial disaster. The discipline of contrary opinion analysis is therefore peculiarly valuable for anyone who will be called on to make investment judgments.

A crowd differs from an ordinary aggregation of human beings in that it is psychologically unified and, in its unity, takes on peculiar characteristics of its own. As Le Bon wrote,

Whoever be the individuals that compose it, however like or unlike be their mode of life, their occupations, their character, or their intelligence, the fact that they have been transformed into a crowd puts them in possession of a sort of collective mind which makes them feel, think, and act in a manner quite different from that in which each individual of them would feel, think, and act, were he in a state of isolation. There are certain ideas and feelings which do not come into being, or do not transform themselves into acts, except in the case of individuals forming a crowd. The psychological crowd is a provisional being formed of heterogeneous elements, which for a moment are combined, exactly as the cells which constitute a living body form by their reunion a new being which displays characteristics very different from those possessed by each of the cells singly.

A crowd per se is neither good nor evil. It is gullible, emotional, unthinking, acutely sensitive to suggestion, unpredictable, impulsive and irresistible. A crowd can consist of two or three normally shrewd businessmen suddenly waxing enthusiastic over the luncheon table or of millions of people reacting in horror to the assassination of a President. Through the medium of the ticker tape it communicates its sentiments clearly without using words. Membership in the crowd is open to all comers. Indeed the greatest difficulty in the training of a contrarian is learning to recognize when he is already part of a crowd so that he can extricate himself from its psychological meshes and regain the use of his individual intelligence.

Once one has learned to recognize the character and influence of crowds and one's own tendency to become a part of them, the next step is to find and master a dialectic by which one can disengage oneself from crowd psychology.

Some 2,300 years ago, Aristotle attached great importance to the classification of ideas into series of extremes and means. (To take a modern example: state socialism, laissez-faire capitalism, welfare state). Fichte in the nineteenth century modernized the series into his "triad" of *thesis, antithesis,* and *synthesis,* which Hegel further developed into a system of philosophical analysis. In this were three steps: (1) establish and unify the idea; (2) challenge it and break it down; (3) form a final judgment for what survives. Mr. Humphrey Neill, in his *Art of Contrary Thinking,* applies the Hegelian system to contrary opinion analysis in the following three states: (1) general opinion (prevailing thesis); (2) the contrary, or skeptical analysis (the antithesis); (3) the conclusion you arrive at (or synthesis of the common and contrary viewpoints).

With a little practice, this process of thinking can become habit. It should lead not only to more cogent judgment on investment problems, but also to an increased perception and understanding of other events and ideas far removed from the narrow fields of finance. If one wishes to arrive at a mature, balanced judgment of one's own, it does no harm to submit any and every thesis offered to contrary interpretation. After doing so, one may well agree with the original thesis or may accept it with only slight modification. But it has then at least passed through one's own mind and is not a parrotlike repetition of something one may have imperfectly gathered from someone else whose understanding may have been faulty. "Contrary opinion" is the name given to the process by which we validate for ourselves the ideas we receive from others. Understood in this sense, it is anything but a negative exercise.

APPLICATIONS OF CONTRARY OPINION TO SPECULATIVE ABERRATIONS

Washington Irving, in his genial essay "The Great Mississippi Bubble," observed that there occurred from time to time in our society "those calm, sunny seasons in the commercial world, which are known by the name of 'times of unexampled prosperity,'" and which invariably produce excesses of optimism followed by a shattering collapse, as "the whole superstructure, built upon credit and reared by speculation, crumbles to the ground, leaving scarce a wreck behind." It would be pleasant to believe that, in this enlightened age of computerized decisions, institutional leadership, and broad dissemination of information, the old boom-and-bust cycle was a thing of the past. All the evidence, however, appears to point in the opposite direction. The human animal, as a member of a crowd, is still primarily motivated by the emotions of greed and fear, which still succeed each other in the market place with sufficient frequency to make the pattern worth studying.

In what might be called a "normal" stock market, at the midway point of its speculative cycle, stocks of good quality with average growth prospects might be selling at around 15 times current earnings to yield 5% or so. Their more dynamic and faster growing brethren might command price/earnings ratios of around 20 times, while the respectable but unpromising issues might sell for ten times earnings to yield 6% or more. The prevailing view on the long-term market trend would be mildly optimistic and that on the economic outlook might be slightly cautious. There might be occasional excitement over a few specialty issues from time to time, but by and large speculative interest would be dormant.

Then, as corporate earnings begin to improve, forecasts as to the outlook will begin to follow suit, buying comes into relatively neglected issues, whose fortunes are felt to depend on general economic progress, and into the more dynamic growth issues, whose prospects would be further enhanced by the better business conditions envisioned. Large profits are made in some of the market leaders, and public attention is directed to the attractions of other issues that could duplicate these performances. The tempo of trading rises, price/earnings ratios expand, and economists' forecasts keep improving until it appears almost self-evident that anyone can make money by being fully invested in common stocks. At this stage, numerous new issues are floated and inexperienced speculators try their hand in stocks of lower quality and higher volatility. At some point, warnings are sounded about accumulating speculative excesses, but they are disregarded, as time after time stocks show an ability to recover quickly from temporary setbacks.

At this point in the proceedings, the contrarian would be thoroughly skeptical, but in mass movements of this sort there is what Le Bon has called a "special logic," which cannot be successfully countered by rational argument. One must wait until the barrage of optimistic projections no longer produces a stock market response in the form of rising prices. Decreasing sensitivity to good news, declining volume on rallies, increasing response to bad news, and a general feeling of speculative lethargy are all signs that the period of illusion is coming to an end. The contrarian who is sensitive to these developments will undoubtedly sell too soon, and may indeed have to repurchase at higher prices if the prevailing optimism is able to reassert its market effectiveness after what proves to be only a temporary failure. He may have to repeat the selling-repurchasing process several times before he is successful, but each time he will be taking out cheap insurance against the possibility of a drastic decline in prices.

When optimistic sentiment and propaganda are no longer able to push stock prices higher, the stock market will begin to decline. In the early stages of a bear market, optimism will tend to increase during declines as technical "support points" are approached. Market letters and services will call attention to the "bargains" available at hefty discounts from recent highs, and rallies taking off from widely recognized support levels will be sharp and will generate reassuring comment. However, as the basic trend continues to carry prices downward, optimism will begin to give way to fear. Support levels will be seized upon as selling opportunities by investors who wish to get rid of large blocks of stock without destroying their market. Those who were bargain hunters in earlier declines will become sellers during rallies. The adages of Jesse Livermore will regain their currency: "Of all speculative blunders there are few greater than trying to average a losing game. Always sell what shows you a loss and keep what shows you a profit. . . . The semisucker is the type that thinks he has cut his wisdom teeth because he loves to buy in declines." *

* These remarks and many others popularly ascribed to Jesse Livermore are quoted in Edwin Lefevre's *Reminiscences of a Stock Operator*, a new edition of which was published in 1964 by the American Research Council, Larchmont, N.Y.

As these experiences accumulate and illusions are shattered, conditions become ripe for panic. Selling climaxes follow one another with ever increasing intensity and frequency. Distress selling from underprotected margin accounts takes a murderous toll of the once popular bull market leaders. Everyone is generally aware that stock prices are now cheap, but no one dares guess how much lower they may be carried by public demoralization and necessitous liquidation. It is even darkly hinted that the investment trusts, which have been the bulwark of optimistic sentiment, may have to sell heavily themselves because their shareholders are liquidating. Rumors of every description fill the air and all rational judgment seems to be suspended.

Again the contrarian is faced with a situation of "special logic." Unless he wishes to gamble or "day trade" (buy a stock and sell it on the same day), he must wait for the panic to subside, watch prices recover sharply, and wait to see how prices and psychology behave when the short-term recovery peters out and desultory selling comes in from those who were determined not to liquidate during the panic phase. The chances are good that prices will return at least to their panic lows, and they may go considerably lower if speculative optimism has not been completely destroyed. Major market bottoms occur when there is no apparent hope of recovery. To the contrarian, where there is hope there is also risk. When hope is extinguished and public pessimism reigns supreme, the contrarian is ready to enjoy his finest hour. Having endured ridicule for being "of little faith" before the collapse, he can now assume the heroic posture and assert that the speculative pendulum is ready to swing back toward normal. Of course, no one will pay any attention to him (that is, if he is right), but he will savor the rare pleasure of being able to exude courage and confidence when everyone around him is demoralized. It is at such times that those who have the daring and the funds to commit themselves to the stock market can gain the fastest and largest rewards.

APPLICATIONS OF CONTRARY OPINION TO SECURITY ANALYSIS

The foregoing paragraphs have described what might be called the popular (and for the general public the only) uses of contrary opinion analysis. In this and succeeding sections, I propose to suggest how this tool may be used by a professional or sophisticated investor in his dealings with various professional sources of investment opinion. Of these no group is more widely followed and respected than the security analysts. Indeed one might venture to say that to be a contrarian without being a security analyst as well would be a meaningless undertaking. The security analyst is rigorously trained to interpret earnings statements and balance sheets, to form opinions as to the relative investment quality and appeal of various companies within an industry, to express judgments as to the merits of one industry as opposed to another, and to have more than a smattering of knowledge on general economics. In his lower stages of development, he is a data-processing machine; in his maturity, he is an "expert" and sometimes a walking encyclopedia. He is the principal transmitter of information and investment opinion to actual or would-be stockholders.

The major flaw which the contrarian would find in the approach normally taken by the security analyst is that it tends to be exclusively fundamental and therefore tends to make absolute value judgments. To the extent that common stock prices reflect such irrational influences as "fashion" or general stock market sentiment, the security analyst's judgments, if they are based solely on fundamentals, are going to be incomplete and inaccurate. The technique of the art has been developed through the years to function in a "normal" stock market environment, which means that for about half the time during any given ten-year period it will not be fully efficient. The learned investment recommendations of bowling and electronic stocks published during the 1960–62 period are an embarrassing case in point. They reflect a basic structural weakness that security analysis by itself cannot correct: one cannot apply investment criteria to stocks that are speculative either because of their very high price/earnings ratios or because of the basically unpredictable nature of the company's business.

A second criticism of security analysts as a group—it does not apply to the better practitioners of the art—is that, being called on constantly to furnish opinions or recommendations on stocks of which they have no deep knowledge, they tend to use short cuts. Since the typical analyst now spends a good deal of time at meetings of the local Analysts' Society, special luncheons organized by corporate managements, field trips, business cocktail parties, and so on, he will normally have a fairly wide circle of acquaintances within his field. Over a period of time, he will discover within this circle a number of specialists with whom he can exchange information, thereby relieving himself, when his working schedule is overcrowded, of the burden of preparing an original opinion on some stock with which he is not particularly familiar. Such capsule opinions tend to circulate rapidly from firm to firm until they solidify into a sort of "group think."

In this same category must be placed many of the industry surveys that circulate around the financial community. As often as not these emanate from one original study that has been copied, excerpted and paraphrased by a number of imitators until it has attained general currency. At this point any cogent observations made in the original study will certainly have been reflected in the prices of the stocks discussed. The contrarian must therefore be careful to judge research material on the basis of its originality and timeliness as well as by its relevance to prevailing psychology. Much material will certainly pass these tests, but a surprising amount will not.

CONTRARY OPINION AND TECHNICAL ANALYSIS

The old-line, "pure" security analyst might well claim that by studying the balance sheet and earnings statement of a company he could give an investment opinion on its stock without knowing its name. His technical analyst counterpart would certainly be willing to give such an opinion merely by looking at a chart. The technician is not concerned with investment value but with price trend. His art (for like all other approaches in the securities field, it cannot be called a science) runs the gamut from scholarly research to outright charlatanry. In recent years, it has gained a position of respectability in investment analysis, partly because it has won a wide following which has made its theories and interpretations a major influence on short- and even intermediate-term stock market fluctuations.

There is always the question in looking at a technical analysis whether it should be followed *literally,* because it seems rationally (that is, empirically) sound, or *contrarily* because a large number of uninformed individuals are following it literally and will probably be trapped. In recent years, the proliferating popularity of chart reading has rendered almost impossible the technical interpretation of individual stocks according to classic chart patterns. "Head and shoulders tops," once the surest sign of an impending major trend reversal, are now often continuation patterns followed by powerful rises. "Breakouts" from trading ranges are often cruelly deceptive, when the newly assumed trend turns out to have been a false move and the "trading range of accumulation" is discovered (too late) to have been an area of major distribution. The number of these freak distortions of conventional patterns has in fact reached such proportions of late that one is forced to view wide areas of technical analysis with considerable skepticism. A contrary opinion against prevailing short-term technical views will often produce highly profitable trading results, but these are outside the scope of this chapter.

Point-and-figure technique falls into roughly the same category, although there are a few practitioners who have achieved consistently profitable results over a long period of time. Amateur and widely followed point-and-figure analyses are of some value to the contrarian in that well-advertised "breakouts" are often false moves, and stocks in well-recognized uptrends often make important tops just short of their point-and-figure objectives. Trend projections, as made by both point-and-figure and conventional chartists, are valuable guide points for the contrarian who sees a possible sharp trend reversal in the making and is looking for the event that might set it off. The orthodox chartist never anticipates his signals. The contrarian may often do so with great profit.

An interesting and practical application of contrary opinion techniques was shown in the mid-1965 stock market break. When the Dow-Jones Industrials made their high of 944.82 on May 14, fundamental and technical opinion was virtually unanimous in its optimism. Fundamentals, as must be expected at major tops, were exceptionally favorable. Technical conditions were similarly regarded. The Dow-Jones Industrial Average had held in a narrow rising channel for two and one-half years, during which period the upper and lower limits of the channel had been well defined. From November, 1964, through April, 1965, there had been a noticeable decrease in upward momentum, which gave a chart of the Averages the appearance of an incipient rounding top. Then, in late April, the Industrial Average suddenly came to life and spurted some 35 points in three weeks, giving the preceding three months of indecisive action the appearance of a classic consolidating trading range. The only suspicious element to be found in the advance was its lack of breadth and volume. The Averages were actually being marked up on the basis of strength in four or five high-priced blue chips, while the rest of the stock market was obviously not following along.

To the contrarian, unanimity of technical and fundamental short-term optimism is always basically suspect. If one looked at the above performance with a contrary view, it became obvious either that the rest of the stock market had to follow the blue chips to higher levels or that the blue chips had to come down again to rejoin the rest of the stock market. In the latter event, which was contrary to general expectations (and was therefore the more probable), the April–May rise in the Industrial Average could be provisionally interpreted as a false "breakout" (of the type discussed earlier). If this were so, the whole trading range subsequent to January could then be regarded as an area of distribution, an interpretation directly contrary to the prevailing technical view that the April–May rally, by carrying the market to new highs, had eliminated the possibility of distribution at lower levels. Technical orthodoxy (and opinion was virtually unanimous) held that since there had been no time for distribution in the April–May advance, therefore no serious price decline could come out of it. To spice this opinion many technicians added the observation that stock prices had only once (in 1946) recorded an important top in the month of May, and only once (in 1929) made an important top without a long prior period of lateral price movement.

Contrary opinion in this instance disclosed a technical interpretation diametrically opposed to prevailing views, but just as rational in its logic. Armed with this weapon, the contrarian was free to ignore the views of "sophisticated" technicians and proceed further to question whether their less educated counterparts might be setting a similar psychological trap for themselves. Here the prognosis was obvious and simple: if the trend line that marked the lower limit of the two-and-one-half-year channel were broken, the technically oriented but unsophisticated public would sell. The trend line could be broken merely by a return to the prices prevailing in mid-April just before the "false move" began. The technicians' bear trap was thus baited and set, and the contrarian could assume that any close approach to the Dow-Jones Industrial trendline would trip the mechanism. This is precisely what happened early in June.

By understanding the technique and rationale of the majority view and by working out an intelligent antithesis to it, the contrarian, if his reasoning is sound, has the unique advantage of being able to anticipate the sudden change in sentiment that will leave both fundamentalists and technicians confused and demoralized. As his minority view gains increasing acceptance, he is richly rewarded by the stock market, and, following his initial success, it should be easy for him to abandon his original view when it becomes the new orthodoxy and to strike out in search of a new contrary evaluation that will again anticipate an important turn in sentiment. The 1965 experience is worth bearing in mind, because, of all the various approaches to stock market analysis, contrary opinion was then the only one to achieve any measure of success.

In some of the more recently developed branches to technical analysis (interpretation of breadth figures, volume correlations, studies based on some of the less commonly used indicators, etc.), the contrarian will often find corroboration for the views he already holds. He and the technician are, after all, working toward the same goal: to measure and anticipate the force of speculative sentiment. A contrary approach in conjunction with technical analysis can be useful in reducing the necessarily high percentage of error implicit in this kind of work by casting a healthy suspicion on any technical interpretation *that appears too obvious to too many*. Moreover, by inoculating the analyst with a permanent dose of skepticism, it will protect him against the dogmatism and narrowmindedness that are the occupational diseases of the trade.

CONTRARY OPINION AND ECONOMIC FORECASTING

The pitfalls of economic forecasting are so obvious as hardly to require comment. The classic errors of optimism and pessimism at every major turning point are virtually a necessary consequence of the fact that any widely accepted forecast tends to become self-defeating. Optimism breeds overconfidence and pessimism excessive caution. The degree of the excess is unpredictable and the time lag in recording its statistical progress is often so great that the new trend is recognized only long after it has started and has been fully reflected in the stock market. Add to this the complication that the stock market itself frequently moves counter to an obvious economic trend for purely psychological reasons, and the resulting conclusion must be that as a stock market forecasting tool, the economic forecast is, to say the least, quite unreliable.

Economic indicators, in my opinion, are principally useful in serving as rationalizations for stock market opinions already formed. As such their study is a useful adjunct to technical and fundamental stock analysis and can often be used as statistical support for the contrary interpretations taken from these other approaches. The economic forecaster usually confines his projections to the immediate future, three to six months ahead, while the stock market characteristically attempts to see six months to a year ahead. There is thus only a slight correlation between the two areas of interest. The stock market analyst tends to criticize the economist for not forecasting further ahead, and the economist quite correctly accuses the stock market forecaster of making a large number of unwarranted assumptions.

The contrarian, assuming that the future is basically unknowable, will do well to avoid these interdisciplinary squabbles, and concentrate instead on those relatively rare instances when both stock market sentiment and the Standard Economic Forecast are in agreement. Here the ideal basis for a contrary view is present: a consensus of sentiment without rational foundation. If, under these conditions, the forecast turns out to be correct, in all likelihood it will already have been discounted in the level of stock prices. If the forecast proves incorrect, the stock market will be subject to significant price changes when the error of the prevailing view is recognized. In studying a situation of this kind, it is again useful to build up a rational case by scrutinizing those leading, coincident and lagging indicators that are found to support a contrary interpretation.

Parenthetically it may be observed that economic forecasts, particularly of the more popular variety emphasized in the columns of daily newspapers, have a built-in inertia. That is, they tend to justify the *status quo ante* and equate themselves with the recent or current state of the stock market. Thus, characteristically, economic forecasts tend to be most outspokenly optimistic in the late stages of a market rise and the early stages of a decline and most pessimistic a few months before and after a major low is reached. Recognized as such, they can be a valuable tool in forming a composite stock market judgment.

CONTRARY OPINION AND THE INSTITUTIONAL INVESTOR

The notion that the combined opinion of ten or twenty "experts" is likely to be better than that of a single individual is widely accepted, but it is directly contrary to the observations of Gustave Le Bon cited earlier in this chapter. The problem arises not from any lack of expertise on the part of the individual security analyst making the selection, but from the difficulty of arriving at an intelligent selection of recommendations via an investment committee. As often as not the individual members of the committee will have widely differing and irreconcilable views on investment strategy and will find that their areas of general agreement are those in which they feel least competent to express their own views. Thus the element of individual talent tends to be submerged in the homogenized mediocrity of "group think."

An additional problem peculiar to mutual funds arises from the competition with other funds and the publicity given their transactions. An "odd-ball" fund that buys an unfashionable stock and subsequently loses money will inevitably be subjected to criticism, while a dozen funds that lose just as much money in a respectable or fashionable stock will be above reproach. This situation has led to mass blunders in investment judgment that not only lost money for the mutual funds involved, but had far wider repercussions since they were piously followed by the public at large. It is seriously to be questioned whether the "growth stock" mania of 1960–61 would ever have attained the disastrous proportions it reached had it not been for the publicity given to the investment tactics of the growth funds and the enthusiastic support they received from Wall Street research departments.

The contrarian, then, must be alert to irrational excesses

emanating from institutional investors. Cults of any class of securities, be they growth stocks or blue chips, lead to excesses that will be corrected in the same way as the speculative aberrations of the small investor. The analyst must be careful not to allow the size and influence of an institution to deflect him from the exercise of his own best judgment. He may find it difficult when he confronts the barrage of statistics that are invariably marshaled in support of the current fashion, but he can be sure that any trend carried to extremes will be corrected, and his discipline as a contrarian should give him the courage to disagree when he has good reason for doing so.

CONCLUSION

In the course of his business, the professional will find many other opportunities to use a contrary opinion approach to his advantage. In studying individual companies, for example, he will often find significant remarks by top management in company reports, interviews with the press and meetings before analysts, that will give him a qualitative as well as quantitative idea of the philosophy and abilities of management. By subjecting these impressions to close scrutiny and contrary analysis he may well develop a number of original views with real relevance. He will also, in his dealings with salesmen and customers, learn to be instinctively sensitive to irrational elements in the ideas he hears and will find opportunities for testing both thesis and antithesis in his attempts to arrive at a solid judgment.

It might appear from the foregoing that contrary opinion is essentially a negative art, best suited to sour, misanthropic individuals whose main concern in life is to find fault with others. It is not in fact so, for the simple reason that in this, as in other walks of life, success ultimately depends on the ability to formulate and execute positive decisions. Contrary opinion is an intellectual discipline that makes its practitioner an adult individual who thinks for himself. In no walk of life is such independence of thought more essential to success than in the study and analysis of stock market phenomena. The habit of contrary thinking, once it is mastered, will show itself useful in thousands of applications, and where it is least expected. To reject it is to follow the crowd and to be satisfied with mediocrity.

14

Economics and Investment Management

By Edmund A. Mennis

A significant development in the postwar period has been the growing use of economic analysis and the increased employment of professional economists in government and business. This trend has been helped by the greater availability of economic data and the improved analytical tools at the economist's disposal. Moreover, the increased role of the federal government in economic policy-making as well as a better understanding by both the professional economist and the businessman of how the economy operates have focused increasing attention on economic analysis as a guide to policy formulation and decision-making

Economic analysis has been used in the investment field as well, particularly in the banking community, where interest rates and the money market require constant attention. However, more recently a marked increase has occurred in the use of economic analysis in common stock investment. A good part of this application of economics undoubtedly stems from the growth in the number and size of institutional investment portfolios and the development of institutional research staffs in the financial community to serve these important clients.

Edmund A. Mennis, C.F.A., is a senior vice president of the Republic National Bank of Dallas.

It would be an overstatement, however, to claim that economic analysis has received widespread acceptance as a tool in common stock investment. In the United States, the abundance of financial data on individual companies and the increasing willingness of corporate management to speak with financial analysts have made industry and company analysis the area of major concentration for financial analysts. A further difficulty facing the economist in the investment field is the characteristic lead of the turning points in stock prices ahead of the turning points in business. If the market leads business, what is the advantage of following business trends? Moreover, yesterday's stock market prices are known and will not change. Business data, however, are invariably reported several weeks or months after the fact, with the perennial hazard of subsequent revision and adjustment, so that it is difficult to determine where the economy has been recently, let alone where it is now and where it is going. For promptness in obtaining economic data, precision is sacrificed; for precision, revision is inevitable.

More important than all of these difficulties, in my opinion, is the problem of linking economic analysis to investment decisions. This problem might be compared to an hourglass, with a vast quantity of economic data on top and an equally vast array of corporate data on the bottom, and only a narrow channel of communication between. It is frustrating, for example, to find that the traditional classification of industries used by the government in reporting economic information does not particularly match the conventional industry classifications of stock prices. The wealth of industry information provided by various federal government agencies, not to mention the gems that occasionally come to light in Congressional hearings, are not used nearly enough by the financial analyst. The lack of familiarity with economic data and with the new methods of economic analysis, particularly among the older members of the financial analysts profession, also has prevented full utilization of the tools available. But the major obstacle lies not in the data but in the failure to find common ground where both the economist and the financial analyst can meet.

To reach this common ground, it is necessary to recognize that an investment is the purchase of future economic performance. The economist can provide information about the current or probable future economic environment, the analysis and projection of monetary and fiscal trends, international developments, and a variety of other economic information that can assist the investment manager and the financial ana-

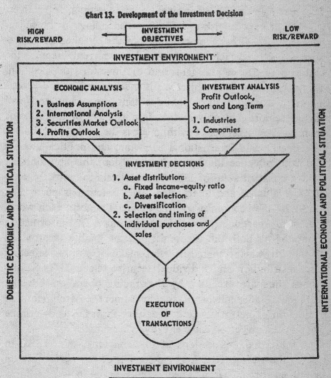

Chart 13. Development of the Investment Decision

HIGH RISK/REWARD ← INVESTMENT OBJECTIVES → LOW RISK/REWARD

INVESTMENT ENVIRONMENT

DOMESTIC ECONOMIC AND POLITICAL SITUATION

INTERNATIONAL ECONOMIC AND POLITICAL SITUATION

ECONOMIC ANALYSIS
1. Business Assumptions
2. International Analysis
3. Securities Market Outlook
4. Profits Outlook

INVESTMENT ANALYSIS
Profit Outlook, Short and Long Term
1. Industries
2. Companies

INVESTMENT DECISIONS
1. Asset distribution:
   a. Fixed income-equity ratio
   b. Asset selection
   c. Diversification
2. Selection and timing of individual purchases and sales

EXECUTION OF TRANSACTIONS

INVESTMENT ENVIRONMENT

PERFORMANCE EVALUATION

lyst. However, unless this information is directed toward the goal of determining the profitability of the economy, a particular industry, or a company, the economist will not satisfy the needs of the financial analyst.

ECONOMICS IN THE INVESTMENT PROCESS

Let me see if I can summarize briefly the position of the economist in the investment decision process, using Chart 13. The first step is the determination of investment objectives, which will vary in risk-reward ratio depending on the objectives selected. Other factors enter into the selection of investment objectives, including the need for current income, the desire to realize capital gains and the investor's tax position. This determination of objectives is independent of the investment environment in which decisions are made and will change seldom and only as the circumstances of the investor change. The investment environment is the broad background of domestic and international economic and political factors that will influence the investment decision; this environment is in a constant state of flux. The environment must be analyzed, evaluated and interpreted. This function is performed jointly by the economist and the financial analyst, each working in his particular area of competence. The information generated by both the economist and the analyst is provided to the investment manager, who makes decisions affecting asset distribution and individual security selection. These decisions then are executed by the trading operation. Finally, and again independent of the investment environment, an evaluation of performance is necessary in order to determine whether the objectives have effectively been met.

In the remaining sections of this chapter I should like to discuss the various functions the economist can perform in an investment organization. Then I will describe how this information can be combined in a logical way in order to show

how economic analysis can be integrated into investment management.

THE BUSINESS FORECAST

Analysis of current economic developments and forecasting the future usually are considered the primary contribution of the economist in the investment field; sometimes this is his only function. The stock market may lead current business developments, but if you can forecast business accurately and sufficiently far ahead, presumably you can get a lead on the stock market.

In performing his forecasting function, the economist ordinarily provides quarterly estimates, usually for the succeeding year, of economic data such as gross national product and its components, industrial production, personal income and aggregate corporate profits. These forecasts are presented in neat, tabular form, usually accompanied by a description of where the economy is, with perhaps a statement of the assumptions that underlie the projected figures. These forecasts most frequently are made toward the end of each calendar year. They may be revised at regular intervals, or they may be used until the next forecasting season rolls around, regardless of how they age in the interval. This approach assumes that the function of the economist is "to win the numbers game," that is, to provide in advance a set of numbers that will accurately project the future.

This practice does not seem to me to be the most advantageous use of the economist's talents. I consider it an unwarranted expectation that an economist or anyone else can provide even a reasonably precise numerical forecast, four quarters or more in advance, of what future business statistics will be. Periodic revisions of data, although necessary and desirable, place the economist in the difficult position of standing on a most shaky and uncertain platform as he launches into the future. Another reason for lack of enthusiasm for this approach is my belief that there is nothing magic in numbers. These neat, tabular presentations of economic data are no more than the quantifying of a large number of qualitative assumptions and evaluations that often change, sometimes quite suddenly. A perfect example of how abruptly business conditions can change materially was the sharp drop in automobile sales in the spring of 1966, when sales fell from a seasonally adjusted annual rate of 9.3 million domestically produced cars in the first quarter to an 8.0 million rate in April and a 7.5 million rate in May. Such an unexpected decline clearly calls for a reassessment not only of automobile demand but also of consumer buying attitudes generally. A forecast, therefore, is not something done by the calendar; rather, it should be a daily reappraisal of the future as new information becomes available. In addition, many factors besides economic developments affect stock prices, so that even the best economic forecast may not provide the clue to stock price performance. The unusually sharp drop in stock prices in 1962, unaccompanied by a business contraction, is a good illustration.

How, then, do I believe economic forecasts should be used in the investment field? One suggestion, and not an insignificant one, would be to stop labeling such exercises "forecasts." The word "forecast" implies a prediction of what the future will be. Personally, I much prefer the word "assumption," which clearly announces that the economic information provided is not a prediction but rather an assessment of the most probable outcome based on what we know now and where we are today. Assumptions can be changed, but forecasts are expected to come true.

But if assumptions are not useful to predict stock prices, for they can at best be only part of the factors influencing stock prices, what purpose can they serve? In the first place, they describe the probable business environment in which investments will be made. Aided by this information, the investment manager is better able to appraise the investment climate; that is, in what kinds of investments is he most likely to make money? Should he be moving from bonds to stocks? Should he be more or less conservative in his equity selections? What industries should he favor? How should he balance his portfolio to take advantage of the most probable developments and also retain some hedges in case the assumptions have to be changed? In addition, the financial analyst is given guidelines to assess the profitability of the industries and companies he follows.

The nature of the assumptions is important also. The economist can provide a perspective far broader and for a longer time period than either the investment manager or the analyst is likely to have in his preoccupation with daily events. The economist's assumptions not only provide an overview but can also extend horizons out three to five years, indicating the trends as well as the dimensions of possible downturns during that period. With this background, the investment manager is better equipped to meet the challenge of sudden market movements or the distortions caused by overemphasis on near-term developments. For the large institutional investor, where the accumulation or sale of large positions takes time, the longer-term view obviously is most important.

Flexibility and willingness to change are vital if the economist is to perform his function effectively. His usefulness is enhanced if he avoids the temptation to substitute his ideas of what should be for his best appraisal of what probably will be. The latter obviously is of greater importance. Moreover, a purely economic analysis is not nearly so effective as one which includes the political climate as well. Political decisions are often not economically based, but they can have an important influence on economic activity. Consumer attitudes also may not be economically rational, but they have an important impact on spending and investment. A properly trained and experienced economist will be aware of these requirements, all of which are necessary to make him a useful member of the investment team.

How should business assumptions be prepared? My own experience suggests that business assumptions should be prepared initially in the late summer to cover the remaining quarters of the current year and the four quarters of the succeeding year. In addition, it is extremely useful to have an estimate of the economy for a good business year about five years away as well as an estimate of the probable dimensions of any downturn in that period. This procedure provides not only a fairly detailed analysis of the year ahead but also the trend for the next several years and some measure of the possible pitfalls in between. The starting point for this work is a review of where the economy is believed to be and a qualitative evaluation of such critical areas as expected consumer durable demand, plant and equipment spending trends, the residential construction outlook, probable inventory developments, and federal government monetary and fiscal actions. With these essentials determined, a numerical forecast then can be prepared.

The data contained in these assumptions should include the details of gross national product and its components; the Federal Reserve Index of Industrial Production; plant and equipment spending; automobile sales, production and inventories; housing starts; personal income and personal disposable income; and aggregate profits. The economic assumptions, together with assumptions about the money market and the stock market, summarize the most probable future investment environment and form the basis for investment policy. In addition, the results should be used uniformly by all of the industry analysts in preparing their company earnings estimates. This approach provides a consistent framework for investment decisions and avoids the internal conflict and confusion that might result if, for example, the steel analyst anticipated production of 130 million tons of steel, and the automobile analyst expected production of only seven million cars.

Having prepared the detailed business assumptions, the monitoring process begins. Current economic information, both published and unpublished, should be gathered daily and analyzed in order to determine if the assumptions still are valid. When necessary, rather than at stated intervals, a new set of numbers should be prepared. While assumptions should not be changed unnecessarily, whenever substantial economic shifts occur the assumptions should be adjusted rapidly.

To summarize, then, economic assumptions may not be the best guide to future stock price movements. However, they should provide the broad perspective of the environment in which investments will be made and the fundamental ingredients to determine the relative profitability of particular industries and companies. Effective use of these services of the economist can, I believe, make a vital contribution to successful investment performance.

MONEY MARKET TRENDS

In addition to providing business analyses and assumptions about the future, there are other areas in which the economist can be effective. Although frequently considered a part of general economic analysis, the financial sector really deserves separate treatment, particularly where investment in fixed-income obligations is important. Money market trends must be followed because of their impact on the business picture, because of their impact on the timing and selection of bond purchases and sales, because of their influence on shifts in the equity ratio of a balanced investment portfolio and, finally, because of their influence on investment in financial institutions, the earnings of which depend fundamentally on the difference between the interest rates they must pay and the rates that they can earn.

In addition, money market analysis provides an important feedback to business analysis. The effect of high interest rates and tight money in the economy in 1966 is a fairly recent reminder that fiscal policy has not completely displaced monetary policy as an economic regulator. Tight money may cause a slowing of economic expansion and raise questions about future profit stability and growth. Tight money has an influence on investment attitudes and alters the yield relationships and relative attractiveness of bonds and stocks. The trend of commercial loans gives an indication of business demand. The pattern of institutional investors' forward investment commitments provides a clue to the willingness of businessmen to make future investments and to the strength of the housing market. Thus you can see that the contribution of monetary analysis to business analysis is significant.

The specialized nature of the research in the money market area can be touched on only briefly. Fundamentally, this work requires an analysis of the supply and demand for funds. It includes a detailed evaluation of savings flows and the demand for funds by the business sector, the mortgage market, and the government sector—federal and state and local. An essential part of this research is an analysis of the attitudes, objectives, and actions of the Federal Reserve System and the U.S. Treasury, both of which are critical forces in the money market. Federal, state and local budgets and projected financing plans are other essential ingredients in effective money market analysis. Not to be overlooked is the balance of payments, which in recent years has acted as an important inhibiting factor on the money managers, curtailing action that might otherwise have been indicated were only domestic considerations important. The result is not only an evaluation of the future course of interest rates, both long- and short-term, but also additional evidence from the financial side of current and prospective business activity and the investment climate.

INTERNATIONAL DEVELOPMENTS

A good economics staff in the investment field also must be aware of what is happening in the world outside of a country.

Analysis of foreign developments is essential for a variety of reasons. Money rates are affected by changes in the balance of payments and competitive interest rates abroad. Developments in the balance of payments can lead to restrictions on direct investment, such as the voluntary restraints on corporate investing abroad or indirect restrictions such as the interest equalization tax. Devaluation losses in foreign currencies can have a significant impact on the earnings of American corporations, sometimes eliminating one or two years' growth in earnings. Devaluation of the dollar or the pound, whether actual or feared, will have important repercussions on domestic companies as well as an impact on security values, both short and long term. Foreign companies provide competition for American companies, which must be assessed. Wage and price developments abroad influence both the effectiveness of this competition and the operation of foreign subsidiaries of American companies. Finally, in spite of temporary inhibitions such as the interest equalization tax, investment is becoming more international, and securities of foreign companies will continue to find a place in the portfolios of American investors.

Obviously, the kind of research done in the international field is different and may not be as thorough as that done on the U.S. economy. Distance and the lack of available data make this type of analysis less comprehensive. Nevertheless, at a minimum, economic and political developments abroad, the balance of payments for the United States and foreign countries, trends in prices and wages, and major industry and company developments should be followed. Foreign periodicals and statistical reports can be helpful, but much useful information also can be provided by reports from, and personal contacts with, research organizations and banks, both in the United States and abroad. This information should be integrated into the preparation of the economic assumptions and also be reported to the research staff to assist it in the evaluation of its industries and companies.

CORPORATE PROFITS RESEARCH

Although all the information the economist can provide may be helpful, the most valuable contribution he can make is to focus and interpret this information as it bears on the outlook for corporate profits. The remaining section of this chapter will indicate an approach for accomplishing this task of fully integrating economic analysis and investment management.

The detailed set of business assumptions described earlier can be used to outline for the analyst the probable business environment in which particular companies and industries will operate. These business assumptions are therefore a very helpful guide in making estimates of sales volume for the period ahead. Some industry sales are closely related to cyclical factors, others to aggregate activity, others are influenced by population and income trends, still others by financial forces. A skilled analyst will know which inputs are most useful.

In addition to help in estimating sales trends, the economist can also assist in estimating changes in factors affecting costs and prices and therefore profit margins. Aggregate data are available on trends in labor costs and productivity not only in broad areas of the economy but also in many specific industries. In addition, the economist has available a wide variety of data on price trends that cover the economy generally as well as many particular areas and products. More importantly, with his broader perspective he can evaluate the economic and political forces affecting prices and give valuable clues to future price trends. His perspective may help the analyst to determine whether a price change is in the offing or whether a given price change will stick.

An economist who is aware of the changing trends in the business scene and the political forces at work also can advise whether changes in the tax structure should be considered in making estimates. Economic assumptions have definite implications for the federal budget and the flow of funds into and out of the Treasury. This information, combined with knowledge of the political attitude of the Administration and of Congress, can be important determinants of fiscal policy, an area most financial analysts usually are willing to leave to someone well acquainted with this field.

With this information to guide him, coupled with his knowledge and experience and the additional benefit of contacts with companies, the analyst can now prepare earnings estimates for individual companies. However, this ordinarily is not the ultimate object of an investment organization; from these individual earnings estimates an investment policy and program must emerge. Most institutional investment is done with some concept of relative investment values in mind rather than by concentrating on the earnings and market value of individual securities taken in isolation. Consequently, some procedure must be used to obtain benchmarks against which any particular company can be compared.

Many analysts use the Dow-Jones Industrial Average as a yardstick, although its composition does not make it particularly suitable for this purpose, in my opinion. The Standard and Poor's Average would seem more useful, particularly since historical data are available covering a large number of industries. However, using the Standard and Poor's Average requires making a great many individual company earnings estimates. My own experience suggests that earnings of the Standard and Poor's Average can be approximated by a smaller sample of 125 to 150 companies. Individual earnings estimates can be aggregated by industry, by economic groupings and in total, in order to determine general earnings trends as well as trends in specific investment areas.

Here is another place where the economist can be helpful. These earnings estimates can be compared with the economic assumptions in order to see if the estimates seem reasonable. They can also be compared with estimates of other broad aggregates of corporate profits that the economist can prepare, such as the Department of Commerce profits figures or those of the Federal Trade Commission-Securities and Exchange Commission in the manufacturing area. Differences in the expectations for some of these broad profit aggregates and any sample of large, successful companies should not be surprising, because the profits performance of companies that are of primary investment interest usually is better than that of companies generally. However, comparison of trends and turning points is useful.

Two further steps can be taken. The first would be to aggregate data for particular industries into groups, the earnings of which are affected differently by changing economic conditions. A possible division might be cyclical, cyclical growth, growth, and defensive (relatively non-cyclical) industries. Others will occur to the sophisticated analyst. In this way, broad divergence in earnings trends can be ascertained that may indicate shifts in investment emphasis.

A second step would be to add data on prices in order to compute price/earnings ratios and yields. This step provides a basis for relative value comparisons, because a stock can be compared with its industry, with the group of which it is a part and also with a broad measure of the market in terms of the two fundamentals of security analysis, earnings and their valuation. This comparison can be made at a point in time and, if the historical data are available, a comparison may also be made with past relationships over time. This perspective provides invaluable insight for investment selection. Admittedly, the historical data are not easily prepared, although the computer has simplified the task materially.

These last two steps are not necessarily the function of the economist. They have been described, however, in order to indicate the logical steps in investment decision-making and to show the flow from the broad economic assumptions to earnings to their valuation. Such a logical, step-by-step approach will give the framework in which investment policy is set. It also will assist in the investment program—that is, the selection and timing of individual security purchases and sales. At each point, critical judgments must be made, and a constant review is necessary in the light of the flow of new information. The economist, with his background and perspective, can play a key role in interpreting the information and assisting in making better investment decisions. I am convinced that more rather than less use of this kind of analysis will occur in the years ahead.

15

Politics and the Stock Market

By Eliot Janeway

Gresham's Law, which teaches us that cheap money drives out good, applies as well to the value of the various techniques for quantitative analysis of the stock market: the inflation in the supply of competing techniques erodes the value of all of them. In fact, the multiplicity of competing methods for doping and predicting the stock market, by definition, makes each of them suspect—recalling the theological controversies of the Middle Ages. The medieval fashion of advancing a half dozen to a dozen simultaneous and different arguments for the existence of God proved less persuasive than reliance upon just a single approach deemed to command confidence would have been.

A retreat to the less recondite approach of qualitative analysis may very well prove more analytically satisfactory and more pragmatically useful than the intricacies of contemporary charting and technical quantification; and I think it does. Certainly, once political factors are recognized—and today they universally are—as formative and, above all, continuous influences on the pattern of stock market performance, reliance upon qualitative analysis becomes indispensable. By the same token, preoccupation with quantitative analysis can be-

Eliot Janeway is syndicated financial writer and publisher of the Janeway Service.

come distractive; for, notwithstanding the numbers games played by pollsters and with political polls, and notwithstanding the election-day arithmetic to which the political competition is subject biennially and quadrennially, the fact remains that the impact of political factors upon market performance is essentially qualitative. It calls for analysis in the intellectual sense, and for diagnosis in the clinical sense, as contrasted with mere measurement.

To pursue the contrast between quantitative and qualitative analysis a step further, the reliance of conventional stock market analysis upon the quantitative approach invariably gets bogged down in the historical approach. Charts and tables, by definition, measure past performance. But the questions posed for decision-making in the present and in the unfolding future involve a constant judgment as to what is best called "the fractional relevance of historical phenomena." Thus, again and again, the masters of quantitative market analysis miss trend-making turns because their studies lead them to expect predictable effects to follow from familiar causes—and in a familiar historical pattern. The classic criticism of generals—that they are forever preparing to win the last war—can be turned as fairly against stock market quantifiers. They are caught in a fundamental dilemma: either to base forecasts on the future reliability of past performance (and to take their charts at face value); or, alternatively, to make allowance for a fundamental historical rule that history never repeats itself in the same way (and to play guessing games with their charts).

Qualitative analysis, by contrast, offers a double advantage. Politically, it is tailored to fit the times because it comes to grips with the influence of the political factor upon the stock market. But it is useful intellectually as well as pragmatically because the second advantage it offers is that of being historically trustworthy. In qualitative analysis of the political pressures responsible for making and changing stock market trends, the historical factor can be trusted to serve as a reliable and continuous guide to future performance.

There is one rule and one rule only to heed in anticipating a market rise after a political change for the better, and vice versa; and it is a rule which, once formulated, can readily be seen to have applied with equal force today. Indeed, it is a rule which, once fathomed and followed, supersedes all the more fashionable rules of conventional market analysis and frees the political analyst of stock market behavior to relegate them to marginal roles.

The rule, simply stated, holds that when the President and the Congress work in harmony together, and when the President proposes and the Congress disposes, no negative pressures to which the stock market is subjected can keep it down; and that, contrariwise, when a breach develops between the President and the Congress, when the President moves but doesn't lead, and when the Congress advises but doesn't consent, no expansive pressures which conventional analysis identifies as constructive can hold the stock market up.

To state the rule is to put the premium for market judgment where, indeed, the premium has always been: on information. Every schoolboy and every schoolteacher knows the story of how the founding Rothschild father struck it rich. He wasn't distracted from the premium on information by a cumbersome clutter of charts measuring buying vs. selling pressures up to the moment of decision-making in the present. Instead he counted on his own political orientation and savvy—specifically, in his case, on an accurate report of whether Napoleon was up or down. He placed his reliance on political information and on a reading of it that was realistic at the time.

The premium on political information in the contemporary American market—and the contemporary market is preeminently the American market—is, by definition, elusive and requires continuous professional reading of the rhythm of change, of alternate improvement and deterioration, in the Presidential relationship with Congress. Progress toward teamwork has never failed to assert itself as the decisive bullish force upon the stock market. Contrariwise, neither has the lack of this teamwork failed to assert itself with equal force as the decisive bearish offset to an otherwise plausible array of bullish economic factors whose reach is primarily limited to the market place but falls short of the trend-making areas in our political economy; and, in fact, the deterioration in President Lyndon B. Johnson's relations with Congress late in 1965 and all through 1966 first caused and then accentuated the corresponding deterioration from bull-market climax into bear-market breakout.

The apparent conflict dramatized by the interplay of money conditions and stock market conditions is really seen, on analytical scrutiny, to work out as only a variant of the eternal triangular interplay among the stock market, the President and the Congress, with the trend and tone of the stock market following the trend and tone of the Presidential relationship with Congress. Taking at face value the financial axiom—and axiom it is—that stock market conditions follow where money conditions lead, the analytical problem reduces itself to an essay in reconciliation between the financial and political elements of the market equation.

On the political side, like Keynes or not, the fact is that certain of his cardinal working premises have long since become institutionalized in the contemporary structure of things. Significantly enough, it was that most talented conservative contemporary economist, Professor Milton Friedman of the University of Chicago, who summed up the institutionalization of Keynesian premises with his well-known comment, "We are all Keynesians now." The central premise of Keynesianism proceeds from his classic work, *A Treatise on Money*, which lays it down that the price of money is what government says it is. Keynes's formulation of his premise referred to government in Hobbes's sense of the sovereign; and, indeed, in the European scheme of things the structure of sovereignty is unitary. Even in England, the executive arm of government and the legislative arm are one and the same.

In America, however, money happens to be more than just what government in the abstract or in any unitary sense says it is. It happens to be, over any given period of time, what Congress decides to make it. The political realities reinforce the Constitutional fundamentals: in whatever other areas of governmental decision-making the President remains supreme (such as in his role of Commander in Chief), the Congress is supreme and unchallengeable in its control of the money value-setting process. While, for example, most writers on the subject popularize the running relationship between the Federal Reserve Board and the President, or the Treasury, the fact is that the Federal Reserve Board is an agency of the Congress. And while the President exerts obvious influence over the Board and its policies through his right of appointment, it is a large question whether the Executive Branch or the Congress is the primary source of influence over the Board's operational management of the banking system and the money supply.

Though all parties to all controversies insist they want the Board to be independent, the practical operating question for the Board at any given turning point in financial and market history is not a question about the independent operations of the Board itself but, rather, about the relations between the President and the Congress. When the President and the Congress are working in harmony, and when the Secretary of the Treasury enjoys acceptability and ascendancy on Capitol Hill, the Board is not likely for very long to assert its independence of the Congress which created it.

During the Eisenhower years, a short-lived exception developed to this rule which, however, was quickly followed by a decisive reaffirmation of it. Secretary of the Treasury George Humphrey was the strong man of the first Eisenhower administration on the home front, and his intellectual and emotional sympathies expressed and activated sympathies which inspired Federal Reserve Board Chairman William McChesney Martin but which he had not managed to assert on his own. But, unlike Chairman Martin, Secretary Humphrey enjoyed an unusual degree of personal acceptability (as distinct from political plausibility) with the Democratic leaders of Congress, who controlled its machinery. The jumble which ensued found the Congress highly critical of the Federal Reserve Board. It also found the Federal Reserve Board in the intellectual ascendant with a Republican President; but, at the same time, it saw the nonpolitical Republican President and, more particularly, his conservative Secretary of the Treasury, enjoy personal interchanges across party lines of unusual warmth and camaraderie with the Democratic leaders of Congress, notwithstanding their suspicions and notwithstanding their critical and cool attitude toward the Federal Reserve Board.

The result of this confusion between cordiality on the part of personalities and conflict on the part of policies was not long in exploding into the debacle of 1957. With Secretary Humphrey's departure, the Johnson-Rayburn Congress limited its cooperation with the Eisenhower administration to the area of foreign relations and went to work on the Federal Reserve Board with a vengeance, and with dramatically bullish results: witness the 1958 stock market recovery. In sum, when the Federal Reserve Board managed to assert a temporary ascendance over the Executive Branch, during a period of Congressional passivity, the outcome was dramatically bearish. But once the Congress reasserted its primacy in the financial area, and made its own monetary preferences the condition of its continuing accord with an alarmed and acquiescent Executive, the Board itself became acquiescent; and the stock market became strong again.

Thus the stock market trend at any given time is invariably a resultant of the Board's ability to fit itself into the Presidential relationship with Congress. In phases when the Board is asserting its ascendance over the market and is out of step with Congress, and when Congress is out of step with the President, the prognosis for stock prices is invariably bearish, as in 1966. When, however, the Board is moving with the Congress, and the President and the Congress are moving forward in step with one another, the direct impact of the

Board upon the stock market trend is invariably and trustworthily beneficial—as was the case, for example, in 1964.

This proposition is admittedly general in its reach, but it suggests a corollary which is more specific: that when the President and the Congress are moving forward in step with one another, money is never too tight for comfort in the economy—nor, consequently, too tight for stability in a bull market.

Taking Congress, then, as the money-controlling participant in the partnership in which sovereignty centers under our system, it is apparent that when breaches occur between the Congress and the President, they inevitably concern money matters. This is more than a matter of theory: again and again the central theme of our political and financial history illustrates and reinforces the point. The Congress by itself cannot govern—no center of money power can. Whenever Congressional revolts against the Executive have exceeded the limits of dissent, when they have tried to usurp the responsibilities of the Executive Branch to govern, they have not only failed: they have positively boomeranged.

But just as the Congress cannot govern, neither can any President govern without the active, willing and, indeed, participating concurrence and cooperation of Congress. These axioms stated, there emerges this operating reality for political analysis and for stock market analysis alike: when the President and the Congress have a falling out, whatever the origin of the quarrel, its climax and its point of conflict inevitably center on money matters. And when the President and the Congress disagree about money matters, it is the beginning of a bad day—more than that, of a bad chapter—for the stock market.

However suspect the invocation of the historical pattern may have become in the area of financial and economic analysis, the influence of the Presidential-Congressional relationship has not outgrown the reach of history. Nor is it likely to. Thus, no looking back to the long drawn-out crisis that struck our emergent stock market structure during the middle of the last century can bring the problem into full focus without reference to the breach between the Presidency, bastion of the gold dollar that it was, and the Congress, happy hunting ground of "the sons of the wild jackass" that the rise of populism made it: lest we forget, the Lower House, prime mover that it is in the spending and rationing of money, served William Jennings Bryan as his springboard into national prominence. The Presidents, Democratic as well as Republican, were for gold; the Congress was for paper for the people; and the market, caught in the middle of this crossfire, got hurt.

While comparisons between contemporary experiences and those which punctuated our history during the last century are by definition suspect as irrelevant, the modern era begins with the crusades which made the administration of Theodore Roosevelt so characteristically colorful, and their impact upon the Presidential relationship with Congress and, through the Presidential relationship with Congress, upon the modern history of the Executive-Congressional-market triangle is highly relevant.

At the time of the panic which marred our progress in the first decade of this century, the national scene was dominated by the first Roosevelt to serve in the Presidency. He was a Republican rebel, on the other side of orthodoxy from the financial establishment. A power struggle which coincided with the panic of 1907 found him aligned foursquare against the pillar of Republican orthodoxy, Senator Nelson Aldrich, who enjoyed a degree of domination over the Senate not duplicated until the heyday of Lyndon Johnson's leadership in the mid-1950s. TR's clash with Senator Aldrich not only prejudiced his reputation for soundness, but cost him control over the machinery of power. When he retaliated by splitting away from his own party, his revolt cost the Republicans control over the machinery of power centered in the White House—but not over the parallel power center in the Senate. On the contrary, the Republican hierarchs in the Senate dug into their entrenched bastions and laid siege to Woodrow Wilson until, finally, they beat him politically and broke him physically and emotionally.

In Lyndon Johnson's era of Senatorial domination, which coincided with the period of George Humphrey's ascendancy in the Executive Branch and with the prelude to the 1957 bust, just about all the dictatorial powers attributed to LBJ by his Senatorial critics were required to muffle Congressional criticism of the Federal Reserve Board in the interest of bi-partisan harmony. It is no exaggeration to say that the grievances left over from Johnson's fights with Senatorial liberals in the interest of going along with Eisenhower and Humphrey on a personal basis contributed to the difficult position which he created for himself in 1959 and 1960 (thanks to which he compromised and defaulted on the initiatives that would have been required to bring him within reach of the 1960 Presidential nomination in his fight with Kennedy).

Going back to the chapter that followed in the historic pattern, the modern American conscience has been so entirely dominated by the traumatic shock of America's retreat into isolationism during the 1920s that attention has necessarily been diverted from the financial to the political consequences of the historic breach between Henry Cabot Lodge and President Wilson. Wilson's defeat by this first Lodge to sit in the Senate precipitated the cataclysmic postwar bust that followed the Armistice and, more than incidentally, it broke the stock market. The crash of 1929 has obscured memories of the pattern-making crash of 1920. As we look back on this, the chapter is more political than financial. The financial consequences were incidental.

But to the extent that America's retreat into isolationism followed directly from the Wilson-Lodge feud, so did the postwar bust and the chain reaction of financial dislocation that were set in motion during the early 1920s. Lest the contemporary thrust of this breach be doubted, it is inarguable that America's post-World War I bust led directly to the collapse of the German currency during the early 1920s; and, because what at the time was accepted as the boom of the 1920s was in fact an imperfect and overspeculative recovery from America's postwar bust, the postwar collapse of the 1920s opened the door for the rise of Hitler and the unleashing of World War II. In the sense that we have not yet finished solving the problems posed for us by World War II, and that we have not yet resolved the peace its end ushered in, it is the better part of historical responsibility to admit freely that we have not yet finished paying for the cost of the bust which followed the boom of World War I—which is to say that we have not yet finished absorbing the cost of the breach between President Wilson and Senator Lodge. Forerunner that it was of the later, less costly confrontation between Senator Robert A. Taft and President Harry S. Truman, it nevertheless demonstrated that a Presidential failure to lead Congress cannot be compensated for by Congressional usurpation of the right to govern when Presidential powers have broken down. The fact that any such Congressional assertion is foredoomed to disaster merely accentuates the bearish stock market consequences of a breach between the Congress and the President.

During the next formative chapter of political and parallel market history, a chapter within the memory of the senior generation holding the decision-making power today, it was President Herbert Hoover's breach with Congress that made the bear market of the 1930s inevitable. Nineteen-thirty, it is well to remember, was a year of business performance plausible by every standard of conventional economic bullishness; and the bear market rally, as it proved to be, of 1930 was plausible too (which explains why it was such a big rally, and proved so costly to those who took it at face value). What broke the back of the resistance to the bearish pressures making for disintegration and collapse was the political verdict rendered in the elections of 1930 on President Hoover's inability to deal with the Congress of his own party.

When the Democratic opposition took control of the

Lower House, custodian of the money power that it is, the trend of the market did not turn toward recovery even though Democrats had taken over from Republicans. On the contrary, it broke in recognition of the irreparable breach between the President and the Congress. Subsequent history was not long in confirming the wisdom of the market; for the duel in our Constitutionally balanced government between the Presidential policy-proposing center and the Congressional money-disposing center came to a head on the financial front. The President was for using the money power of the federal government to reactivate business investment. But he was against using federal funds for purposes of humanitarian relief. Unfamiliar though this historic confrontation may seem to contemporary readers, the Democratic opposition in Congress was against federal spending for purposes of economic pump-priming, although it was for directing federal funds to the relief of depression victims. From this confrontation evolved the winning Democratic issue embodied in the rhetoric directed against the "trickle-down" theory. Never mind that many of the agencies subsequently institutionalized into the New Deal were in fact started by Hoover. Never mind, either, that Franklin D. Roosevelt based his winning campaign on his absurd charge—which, however, "took"— that the depression was directly attributable to Hoover's profligate spending. The fact, which is decisive for purposes of historical analysis as well as for contemporary analysis, is that the President and the Congress were in a fight and that the stock market was caught in the middle and was broken.

The controversy between President Truman and Senator Taft, which dominated the 80th Congress, precipitated the stock market debacle of 1946: it stands as a monument to the historical analysis of the impact of Presidential-Congressional relationships upon the stock market. Still more recently in this sequence, as per the foregoing, the sharp market break of 1957 reflected the end of President Eisenhower's ability to deal with, and to accommodate himself to, the dual power center on Capitol Hill. The definitive work of Washington correspondents Rowland Evans and Robert Novak, *Lyndon B. Johnson: The Exercise of Power*, documents the political origins of this far-reaching stock market break all the more authoritatively because the book's emphasis is entirely political, centering as it does upon the Presidential-Congressional relationship, and not at all financial.

The latest chapter in the recurrent drama was written by the bear market of 1966. Just as the stock market in December, 1963, was quick to sense, and to strengthen in response to its intuition, that President Johnson would get the country moving again because, as I put it at the time, he would get the Congress moving again (in the wake of Kennedy's failure to do exactly this), so it was uncanny in its genius for ferreting out the roots of the unpublicized row between Johnson and Congress late in 1965, to which the market reacted with its sophisticated and decisive break early in 1966.

Any comprehensive castback across the broad range of the Presidential-Congressional relationship, and its parallel impact upon stock market history, should take notice of the 1962 market break, which signaled the end of John Kennedy's honeymoon with Congress. The imperfect and suspect recovery from the 1962 break was overshadowed by the emergence in still preliminary form of the United States balance-of-payments problem, which tended toward a confrontation between Presidential political policy-making and Congressional monetary policy-making, if only because of its direct impact on monetary and fiscal policies expressed in the implied pressure to raise domestic interest rates. The Congressional apparatus is rank-conscious; and the balance-of-payments problem ranks lower in the Congressional scheme of things than the structure of domestic interest rates.

Politics under the contemporary American system has evolved into two separate and distinct forms of the art. The first, and most familiar, is the politics of normalcy practiced in peacetime. The other is the politics of emergency invoked in time of war. Any view of politics and the stock market comprehensive enough to be realistic must necessarily take account of this fundamental distinction between these two forms of politics. For not only do the broad historic trends of the stock market parallel the cycle of Presidential-Congressional relationships in the political arena; they also parallel the activation and deactivation of the war-emergency cycle.

To state this phase of the problem, to add the dimension of emergency to the problems of normalcy is to invoke memories of the era of Franklin D. Roosevelt. As a young man, he had made his debut on the national scene in Woodrow Wilson's "little war" cabinet as Assistant Secretary of the Navy during World War I. Contrary to legend and popular impression, FDR was not economically or financially oriented (on the contrary, his judgments and analytical arsenal in this area were decidedly amateurish). Nevertheless, the Wilson Administration's mismanagement of the problems of war finance left an indelible impression on him. Toward the climax of his own career in the Presidency, as the dangers of World War II drew close, memories of the fiscal and monetary mismanagement of World War I and its costly and tragic aftermath were agitated; and FDR asserted, again and again, his determination not to permit any war Presidency of his to precipitate another postwar bust. Whatever other criticisms may be leveled against Roosevelt's leadership during World War II, and on whatever other fronts, although his strategy may have failed to win the war in a lasting or political sense, no one can question the decisive success with which he carried out his determination to win it on the economic and financial front. It is indeed ironic that, political animal that he pre-eminently was, Roosevelt should have been fated to lose World War II on the political front while, amateur at economics that he remained to the end, he should nevertheless have contrived to win it on the money front. In fact, the monument to Roosevelt's historic achievement in avoiding any repetition of Wilson's failure on the money front is the term "postwar boom." An entire generation has come to use the phrase casually and uncritically. In fact, it marked a revolution in the fiscal, monetary and economic direction of home-front resources in time of war; and it certainly marked the advent of a new era in the influence of the cycle of emergency politics upon the stock market.

But not necessarily a bullish new era: rather a new era of cyclical fluctuation in response to new stimuli. War, by definition, unleashes inflation—that is, inflation of costs. Looseness of language, unfortunately, has invited a corresponding looseness of assumption. Because the impact of war upon costs is inflationary, the deflationary influence of cost inflation upon values has been obscured. As a matter of fact, it is not merely in time of war that the pernicious deflationary erosion of values set in motion by the inflation of costs takes its toll. This cross-current between the inflation of costs and the deflation of values has been most clearly and painfully apparent in postwar Europe, where the spiral of cost inflation has outrun even the inflationary pressures within the United States; and, predictably and inescapably, the consequent deflation of values there has broken the European stock market (leaving property as the only inflation-proof haven for cash). In Europe, the appreciation of property values—and this appreciation alone—has significantly and, moreover, safely outrun the inflation of costs.

The world-wide cost inflation set in motion by World War II is merely a special, because a quantitatively accentuated, case of cost inflation of any kind on any scale. During wartime, while the impact of emergency inflation is maximal, and while the obvious qualitative risks to values are too, the stock market is necessarily quiescent. The historical pattern, before Roosevelt found the way to win the peace of 1945 on the money front, called for peace to compound the damage inflicted upon the stock market by war; for it assumed a postwar bust in the economy. But the end of World War II signaled an unprecedented postwar boom—which, as cannot be repeated too often or with too great emphasis, reverses the familiar historical pattern. Thanks to the wartime measures which built up the reservoir of liquid savings, the post-World War II boom was liquified by rich accruals of savings which made money easy enough to satisfy a prime requirement for a bull market in an expansive economic situation.

This same pattern occurred during the Korean War emergency. The war itself put the quietus on stock market expansion, but it created a prodigious potential of effective, because liquid, demand. True to the market maxim that the major moves take shape as big surprises, the Korean armistice of 1953 found the prevailing psychology of the period resigned to slump in the economy and contraction in the stock market. Instead, the new cycle of emergency politics triggered another postwar boom and sent the stock market surging into orbit. The market boom of 1953 coincided with the liquidation of Truman's troubles with Congress over whether to win the war or to call it off, and with the onset of the new Eisenhower era of good will. While a number of economic and financial obstacles stood in the way of a strong market revival in 1953, nevertheless the auspicious atmosphere of Congressional relations which marked the advent of the Eisenhower era set the tone and determined the trend of the post-Korean bull market.

Seen against this background, the great market break of 1966 confirms the new political pattern of stock market susceptibility to emergency pressure. The "McNamara escalation" of the war in Vietnam was ordered in June, 1965. Its first repercussions hit the money stream toward the end of 1965, by which time the President's failure to follow through on his new war plans by formulating a corresponding new plan of war finance had involved him in his historic breach with Congress. The escalation of the war itself would have been enough to break the bull market. So would the President's breach with Congress, which resulted from his failure to recognize its rights as the coordinate arm of government responsible for sharing with him the management of a plan for financing the war. This failure to formulate a plan of war finance left the Johnson Administration with no alternative but to rely on the free workings of the money market for the financing of its escalated war. And this, climaxing and confirming as it did the Presidential breach with Congress, delivered the *coup de grâce* to the bull market and explains the underlying force of the bear market which threatened to follow. If it threatened to develop into a big bear market, the reason was that the war which made it a bear market had become a big war. Once a wartime bear market developed, it was fated to remain a bear market so long as we were fated to remain at war.

Not that the rise or fall of the stock market is itself a governing or even a relevant reason for a national decision to start or to stop a war: it is simply that the cycle of emergency politics has become the prime pattern-making influence upon the stock market, working in exact reverse to the popular notion that inflation is a benign influence upon stock market values. For the biggest inflation of all, that resulting from war, has proved to be the biggest deflator of values, while relief from war equates with relief from market slump and with expectations for market recovery.

If any special case of the bearish impact of war inflation upon stock market values could be derived from an academic casebook, it would be the one which confronted America in 1966. The bearish impact of war inflation was compounded by reversion to World War I's ill-fated reliance upon free market finance in time of war, which in turn compounded the bearish impact of a Presidential breach with Congress over the absence of both a popularly intelligible war plan and a plan of war finance. The prognosis was for all of the special circumstances responsible for 1966's "Vietnam" bear market to remain operative until the fundamental requirement for a bear market bottom and a bull market start—a harmonious team relationship between the President and Congress—was again in force.

In time of war, or in time of peace, whether prevailing political pressures are those of war emergency or of peacetime normalcy, the overriding fundamental political influence on stock market stability and buoyancy is the presence or absence of harmony in the Presidential relationship with Congress.

16

Price/Earnings Ratios: A Critical Reappraisal

By Nicholas Molodovsky

In the July-August, 1960, issue of the *Financial Analysts Journal*, S. Francis Nicholson, then vice president of the Provident National Bank in Philadelphia, published a study which made a deep impression on financial analysts. It opens with the following three paragraphs:

> Within three to ten years, will the better price performance be in common stocks, with the current price/earnings multiples of over 25 times, or in those under 12 times?
>
> Answers to this question as posed to sophisticated Financial Analysts and businessmen, in the past year, have been nearly ten-to-one in favor of the high multiples. It is assumed they are bought for growth, and the low multiples only for income.
>
> The results of certain studies, covering data for past years, would indicate a contrary conclusion; i.e., that on the average the purchase of stocks with low price/earnings multiples will result in greater appreciation in addition to the higher income provided.

We propose, in this chapter, to present in some detail Mr. Nicholson's provocative study, and several others which document a similar thesis—a thesis to which we do not subscribe

Nicholas Molodovsky, C.F.A., is a vice president of White, Weld, Inc., and editor of the *Financial Analysts Journal*.

—and later to examine critically the subject of price/earnings ratios and their use in the formulation of investment policy.

Mr. Nicholson's article contains two statistical explorations, which reach identical conclusions. Nicholson's Study No. 2 is limited to a sample consisting of only 29 stocks, all belonging to the chemical industry. Moreover, out of these 29 stocks, 7 were not available for all of the 18 years of the period used. In their own right, industry studies are of great interest. However, Nicholson attempts to prove an investment principle of over-all significance. For this purpose, the sample is too small. A mitigating circumstance may be mentioned. In Mr. Nicholson's demonstration, Study No. 2 plays only a supporting role. The cast of leading statistical characters appears in Study No. 1. We shall accordingly concentrate our critical attention on that study.

Study No. 1 is based on a sample of 100 predominantly industrial issues of trust investment quality. It covers the time span 1939–59, divided into 11 subperiods. The 100 stocks are arranged into five groups in the ascending order of their respective price/earnings ratios at the beginning of each subperiod and show the price appreciation in each subperiod according to price/earnings ratio groups. The results are not ambiguous. The 20 lowest multiples show more appreciation in all 11 subperiods than the 20 highest multiples. Accordingly, Mr. Nicholson concludes that investors should do substantially better by buying low price/earnings ratio stocks.

In an article, published in *The Commercial & Financial Chronicle* of September 16, 1965, in which he reviewed a number of statistical experiments aimed at the selection of undervalued stocks, Professor Paul H. Cootner of Massachusetts Institute of Technology referred to the Nicholson study. He pointed out that the 100 stocks—all of them high grade —had been selected from the vantage point of 1960, the year in which Mr. Nicholson made his study. His selections might have been quite different if they had been made at the beginning of the entire period, i.e., in 1939. Many of the stocks would possibly not have been included in Nicholson's sample because in 1939 they lacked a high investment rating. Dr. Cootner thought that if there is a fallacy in Mr. Nicholson's results, it is likely to arise from the use of hindsight in determining what is a high-grade stock.

Professor Cootner's concern does not imply that the validity of the experiment is dependent on a high investment rating of a sample's component stocks. His fear that the results might be biased—and even biased quite substantially—is undoubtedly aroused by the possibility that good profits could have been derived from the stocks which stayed high grade; and that large losses could conceivably have been suffered by stocks which might have descended to a low-grade status. Many of such possible losses could have occurred in the highest price/earnings group, which, by its very nature, is the most vulnerable.

One of the observations made by Nicholson in connection with his Study No. 1 reads as follows: "If an investor bought the 20 lowest multiples in 1939, changed in 1944 to the 20 lowest in that year, and again in 1949, and 1954, his investment would have appreciated in 1959 to 14.7 times his original investment. Similar procedure with the 20 highest multiples in these years would have brought the value to 45 times the original investment. (These figures are, of course, not adjusted for broker commissions and taxes.)"

Even allowing for brokerage commissions and taxes, we are impressed by the magnificent cumulative profits achieved by purchasing the lowest multiple stocks and consistently reinvesting, at stipulated intervals, the actually (or hypothetically) realized proceeds of a terminal year into stocks whose multiples had at that time become the lowest. The results exceeded by better than 3:1 those of an analogous procedure applied to stocks with the highest multiples. (This implies, of course, that in the same terminal year the proceeds realized from the previous purchase of the same number of stocks with the highest multiples were reinvested in an equal number of stocks whose price/earnings ratios still were, or had become, the highest at that time.)

OTHER TESTS OF PRICE/EARNINGS
    RATIOS AS INVESTMENT GUIDES

The distinguished investment banking firm, Drexel & Co.,
of Philadelphia, which recently became, through merger,
Drexel Harriman Ripley Incorporated, applied the
price/earnings ratio criterion to the ten highest and ten lowest multiple stocks within the 30-stock sample of the Dow-
Jones Industrial Average. The stocks were held for one year,
the starting and the target date being June 30. To make the
experiments more conclusive, two sets of computations were
made, based respectively on actual reported earnings of the
preceding year and estimated earnings of the year still in
progress. These studies convinced the authors that the
price/earnings criterion for the selection of stocks gives excellent results and that the lower multiple stocks consistently
outperform the higher multiple groups—especially the highest
—by a wide margin.

Drexel Harriman Ripley investigations of the respective investment merits of stocks with the lowest and highest
price/earnings ratios have continued, from time to time, over
the last several years. The recent studies are more sophisticated than the earlier. All calculations are made by an electronic computer. The findings are unchanged: the lowest
multiple stocks outperform the highest.

The September 20, 1966, issue of *The Commercial & Financial Chronicle* contained an article entitled "Price Performance Outlook for High and Low P/E Stocks" by Paul F.
Miller, Jr., C.F.A., and Ernest R. Widman, respectively senior vice president (now president), and economist of Drexel
Harriman Ripley Incorporated. The co-authors describe a
study in which they took data from 1948 through 1964 for
industrial companies included in the Compustat tapes with
annual sales exceeding $150 million, grouping the stocks into
five different price/earnings ratio classes. The selection was
confined to companies with fiscal years ending between September 30 and January 31. Their number increased from 110

in 1948 to 334 in 1964. (Companies showing no earnings or registering deficits were excluded.)

Price/earnings ratios were computed, using year-end prices and fiscal-year earnings. The price performances of the qualifying companies were calculated for all one-year periods following the year-end price/earnings ratio calculations. Then an average price performance was derived from each price/earnings quintile. Price performances were similarly compared for all three-year and five-year segments within the 1948–64 period. To quote the authors, "The low price/earnings group has consistently outperformed the high price/earnings group. In fact, there is a distinct tendency for the groups to fall in a pattern of inverse rank correlation with the height of the P/E ratio."

To make sure that the better performance of the low price/earnings group was not caused by a few stocks with wide gains, which offset a possibly poor performance by the rest of the group, the authors examined the statistical distribution of the stock price performance within the lowest and highest price/earnings quintiles. They found that the distributions of both quintiles were almost identical.

There is a significant difference between the early and the latest Drexel studies. The investigations of the investment results of the 30 stocks in the Dow-Jones Industrial Average were conducted on a cumulative periodic basis determined by the differential price/earnings approach. The recent studies did not use the cumulative reinvestment process.

None of these studies were open to the question of a possible hindsight bias, which Dr. Cootner raised in commenting on Mr. Nicholson's paper. The 30 Dow-Jones Industrial Average stocks are blue chips with an established history. The 334 stocks used by Drexel Harriman Ripley in their study's terminal year of 1964 probably did not all deserve the highest investment rating. All were, nevertheless, undoubtedly quality stocks. For only stocks of companies with a large dollar volume of sales were admitted into the sample, while all companies showing deficits, or even a lack of earnings, were denied representation.

SUPPORTING EVIDENCE

Additional evidence supporting the Nicholson-Drexel conclusions is to be found in the work done by James D. Mc-
Williams, investment officer in charge of computer approaches to common stock analysis and portfolio selections in
the Trust Department of the Continental Illinois National
Bank and Trust Company of Chicago. In an article which appeared in the May-June, 1966, issue of the *Financial Analysts
Journal,* Mr. McWilliams evaluates the usefulness of the
price/earnings ratio as an analytical tool. He uses Compustat
tapes from which he extracts a sample of 390 industrial
stocks. The study, which covers the period from 1953
through 1964, reveals that a portfolio composed of low
price/earnings ratio stocks registered a better performance
than a portfolio made up of high price/earnings ratio stocks.

The McWilliams investigation is broad and deep. It employs many statistical techniques and constraints. In con-
structing his sample, McWilliams admitted only those listed
industrial stocks which had a complete 12-year history of
April 30 prices and had calendar fiscal years. Unlisted stocks
were not admitted. The price/earnings ratios were calculated
by dividing April 30 prices by per-share earnings for the
fiscal year ending the preceding December 31. The data were
classified into price/earnings deciles; and mean returns, as
well as standard deviations about the means, were computed.
Numerous exhibits were embodied in the presentation. The
study was done on an IBM 7010 machine using the Fortran
language.

A sum of $10,000 was hypothetically invested, as of April
30, 1952, in each price/earnings decile and continually reinvested on an annual basis. In this respect, Mr. McWilliams
followed Mr. Nicholson's method of periodic cumulative
reinvestment.

It was found that the $10,000 originally invested in the
highest price/earnings ratio decile stocks would have grown
to $45,329 by April 30, 1964. The same amount of $10,000
originally invested in the lowest price/earnings ratio decile

stocks, and continually reinvested on an annual basis, would have grown to $103,960 during the same period.

In no case was any adjustment made for commissions that would have been incurred in actually implementing these original investment and annual reinvestment techniques. Had commissions been allowed for, adds McWilliams, the results would have been substantially poorer in all of the price/earnings deciles.

GROWTH EXPECTATIONS

It is of course clear that when investors are willing to pay more for $1 of current earnings of some stocks, as contrasted with other stocks, they expect to derive investment benefits from this premium. The most common expectation is faster relative growth of future earnings. This expectation may be reinforced by another: the assumption that the more rapid earnings growth could also prove to be more stable in relation to the basic trend.

John E. Hammel and Daniel A. Hodes submitted this double expectation to empirical verification in their article, "Factors Influencing P/E Multiples," published in the January–February, 1967, issue of the *Financial Analysts Journal*. Their findings were based on a comprehensive statistical study which used correlation-regression techniques and computer processing to analyze the financial data of over 400 major companies. The analysis related *selected measures of growth* and *variability in earnings* per share to the price/earnings multiples of the companies studied. This double analysis shows that variability in past earnings is a fairly important influence on the price/earnings multiple and that expected growth in earnings is a strong influence on the multiple.

It stands to reason that the prices of stocks with characteristically high earnings multipliers are more fragile. Only confidence that earnings growth will be sustained at high compounding rates for an extended period can keep them aloft. When investors lose faith that a high-flying stock will continue to make money at a rapidly growing rate, the same thing happens as when an aircraft loses speed: it starts falling.

The stock of a company enjoying greater than average earnings growth is bound to suffer more from unrealized growth expectations. As long as the expectation is fulfilled, it strengthens the anticipation of a continued favorable trend and this widens the differential spread between the earnings multiple of this stock and those of stocks whose profits are growing at slower rates. But when confidence begins to wane, the decline of a growth stock's price will be related to its anticipated rate of earnings growth.

Since, by definition, the gap between current price and current earnings widens when the price/earnings ratio rises, a group consisting of the highest price/earnings ratio stocks will obviously contain a larger proportion of stocks destined to disappoint investment hopes than the groups with lower price/earnings ratios. This should be particularly the case when stocks included in all the groups are endowed with sound earnings, and when equities showing even temporary deficits are either completely or largely excluded. This tends to strengthen the performance of the lowest price/earnings group by eliminating from it stocks with flat or negative earnings trends which may often account for the very existence of a low multiple.

Needless to say, not all stocks will perform alike. In the high price/earnings group, the hope of rapid future earnings growth may be vindicated or even exceeded. By the same token, the more modest expectations of rising earnings, which are characteristic of the low multiple samples, may reveal some pleasant surprises. The reverse may also occur in either group. It seems unlikely that, in either case, the average group performance will be greatly affected. Under the conditions of stock selection stipulated by the studies described above, there is good reason to expect that the group comprised of the highest price/earnings ratio stocks will register the greatest proportion of price casualties. And the probabilities will have more time to work themselves out as the period of the experiment is extended. Empirical verification is welcome, but simple reasoning points toward the likely outcome. The reasoning is strengthened further when it is applied to the cumulative periodic reinvestment process.

STRUCTURE OF PRICE/EARNINGS RATIOS

There are ten possible combinations in the respective changes of prices and earnings that can bring about a rise or a decline of a price/earnings ratio. Three combinations can cause it to remain unchanged.

A price/earnings ratio will rise under five sets of conditions: (1) When both prices and earnings are rising, but prices are rising relatively more than earnings. (2) When prices are rising, but earnings remain stationary. (3) When prices are rising, but earnings are declining. (4) When prices remain stationary, but earnings are declining. (5) When both prices and earnings are declining, but prices are declining relatively less than earnings.

A price/earnings ratio will decline under five sets of conditions also; they will be symmetrically inverse to the foregoing. There will be no change in the price/earnings ratio when prices and earnings are rising at the same rate, or both declining at the same rate, or when both remain unchanged.

When an original amount is invested in a group of stocks characterized by the highest price/earnings ratios and periodically *cumulatively* reinvested—be it at annual, three-year, or five-year intervals—in those stocks whose price/earnings ratios have, in the meantime, become the highest, what result will be achieved? Such a high price/earnings ratio sample is becoming increasingly vulnerable to a price setback after each successive reinvestment. On each such occasion, stocks eliminated from the sample are replaced by others whose prices have outdistanced earnings even more than in the case of all or some of the stocks contained in the original sample (which was, from the outset, selected because its price/earnings ratios were the highest). Cumulatively, earnings fall further and further behind prices, thereby com-

pounding the exposure to any loss of confidence in the
mounting demands which are made by this procedure on
earnings growth rates. The sample is also rendered systematically weaker in terms of the defense it could put up against
any random market shock, because its earnings base is chron-
ically shrinking in relation to price.

The contrary of the above applies to the sample with the
lowest price/earnings ratios. It is growing in strength all the
time, since its earnings base is enlarged at the time of each
successive reinvestment. Those equities which fall by the
wayside, at each periodic revision of the composition of the
lowest price/earnings group, are replaced by others whose
earnings have demonstrated stronger action than their respective prices. In this group, relative weakness is consistently
eliminated in favor of strength, whereas in the highest
price/earnings group, strength invariably yields to weakness.
Once again, individual exceptions will occur in all the groups
classified by their respective price/earnings ratios, but they
are unlikely to alter the average group effect.

Nobody can deny that the most profitable investment results will be secured by paying the lowest possible multiple
for earnings which will grow in the future at an increasingly
rapid rate. A successful investment strategy can be developed
by purchasing low multiple stocks—which means paying less
for each $1 of their respective per-share earnings—and sell-
ing them when their multiples reach heights which, in the
judgment of the investor, exceed acceptable risks of further
holding. Such a policy, however, must be quite flexible at
both ends of its operation.

When the original investment is made, it may be desirable
to set some limit on the price/earnings ratio at the time of
the acquisition. It should not be applied, however, in an iron-
clad manner but should be extended to a higher multiple if
the earnings trend of a particular stock warrants such a decision. Investment criterion constraints should be provided with
respect to earnings. Only those stocks should be included
among the candidates for purchase which have demonstrated
a consistently high earnings growth rate for several years and

which offer, in addition, persuasive evidence that growth is unlikely to fall off in the reasonably foreseeable future.

In such a strategy, there should be no time limitations for the period of holding. If an upper price/earnings limit is set as a selling signal, it must remain flexible. It can only serve as a target for re-examination. No fixed rule can supersede constant surveillance and analysis. If the rule is applied mechanically, the portfolio will never contain any holdings of Avon Products, Corning Glass Works, Litton, International Business Machines, Polaroid or Xerox.

We find no kind words to say about the application of an investment policy based on price/earnings ratios for periods shorter than one year. A tabulation in the November, 1966, issue of the Cleveland Trust Company *Business Bulletin* has shown that low price/earnings multiples were no protection during the decline of stock prices in 1966. Since the turn in the stock market came early in October, the November issue of the *Bulletin* encompasses the entire bear market. The *Bulletin*'s tabulation is limited to the 30 Dow-Jones Industrial Average stocks. But as they represent the market's core, they offer an important illustration. The Cleveland study shows that from their 1965 highs to their 1966 lows, the tendency has been for stocks with low price/earnings ratios to fall the furthest—further than the stocks with higher price/earnings ratios.

To be fair, we should recognize that many stocks in the Dow-Jones Industrial Average are sensitive to cyclical influences. Still, in dealing with ratios of current prices to current earnings, we must remember that we are in the presence of a complex measurement. Any analyst who uses current price/earnings ratios must have a clear insight into their structure and meaning.

THE PRICE/EARNINGS RATIO AS AN INVESTMENT CRITERION

It is completely futile, and even misleading, to conduct elaborate studies of the action of price/earnings ratios, as is sometimes done, without relating them to an exhaustive analysis of the movements of stock prices and earnings. The latter are independent economic variables. Price/earnings ratios have no existence of their own. As their name implies, they are nothing but quotients reflecting any of the 13 possible different combinations of the numerator and the denominator.

Attempts are made to construct average price/earnings ratios; or to show intriguing but irrelevant patterns of bull and bear swings in price/earnings ratios. None of these things can be done without making sure that prices and earnings are in significantly related phases. Otherwise, we are playing meaningless arithmetical games instead of engaging in effective financial research. Investment analysis is difficult enough without confusing it by the injection of ghosts.

To illustrate, we will take the 1957 bear market in stock prices and the bull market of 1958. From its July high to its October low in 1957, the Dow-Jones Industrial Average lost 100 points. Soon thereafter it not only retraced the entire decline, but established, by an impressive margin, new and then unprecedented highs. The progress of this new bull market was looked upon with much distrust. Fear gripped many investors' minds. Stock prices seemed to have lost all contact with any reasonable measure of value. The price/earnings ratios were high and kept rising, while earnings went from bad to worse.

Not only individual investors but professional commentators and investment advisory organizations reacted in much the same way to the rising stock prices. To place them within a framework of reference, let us remind ourselves that, in terms of the Dow-Jones Industrial Average, the bull market took off from a low of 416.15 in October, 1957, and advanced to a high of 688.21, which it reached in January, 1960. Throughout the winter of 1957–58, and the spring and summer of the latter year, bearish opinions reigned. As late as July 31, 1958, when the Dow-Jones Industrial Average had advanced some 90 points from the 1957 low to the level of about 505, a famous service wrote: "Some of the old line fundamentals about price/earnings ratios and other traditional measures of proper prices for the time being, at least, do not seem to be doing people much good."

In August, 1958, as the Dow-Jones Industrial Average was again approaching its 1957 high, a financial writer of *The New York Times,* surveying the collapsing earnings reported for the first two quarters, commented that the securities markets were caught in one of the most confusing economic experiences of recent history. He even found it apropos to quote from *Macbeth,* "For the moment," he said, "the ticker tape is spinning out what seems to be best describable as 'a tale told by an idiot, full of sound and fury, signifying nothing.' . . . The babel of prices coming from the securities ticker is so incongruous that there is little of extravagance in the statement that today in Wall Street nobody seems to have any definite idea of what an investment grade common stock is really worth."

"Many Are Mystified by Continued Rise of Stock Prices" asserted a headline in the financial pages of the *New York Herald-Tribune* in mid-September, 1958. The article was accompanied by photographs of customers in a brokerage office. The mood predominant among them was described by the caption, "Market Baffles Tape Watchers."

Two days prior to this report, an editorial in *The Wall Street Journal* entitled "Puzzle at Broad and Wall" stated, "If you look at the usual statistics—the relationship of earnings to stock prices, for example—the booming market makes little sense."

This statement notwithstanding, there was really no mystery about the "strange" action of price/earnings ratios. Changes in price/earnings ratios are sometimes the result of a time lag in the respective movements of stock prices and earnings. In 1958, prices were already rising while earnings were still declining. This confused many people who were anxiously watching the action of price/earnings ratios. Unhappily for the observers, price/earnings ratios were then only in part capitalization factors. They carried a substantial superstructure, which was the arithmetical reflection of the numerator and denominator moving in opposite directions.

The price of a stock would be no more than a meaningless number if it did not represent an attempt to express the stock's value, i.e., its capital worth. Capital is a store of wealth. Current earnings do not offer a basis broad enough for erecting on it a capital structure. Capital is substantial. Its income-producing mass cannot be appraised or estimated from so slim an indication as the earnings of a single year. Nevertheless, despite the fact that the ratios of stock prices to current earnings are, by their nature, quite unsuitable for such a role, in practice they are often treated as capitalizers. This attitude toward them has developed out of their handiness as financial yardsticks, even though these yardsticks are mercurial and uncertain in the extreme.

Much of the analytic work being done in Wall Street measures up to high standards and is constantly improving. Some of the reports prepared by competent financial analysts, especially when they have a training in science and engineering, make impressive reading. Indeed some firms have built their business and their reputation on exhaustive studies which may take many months of research. Yet business life moves fast, and, to keep up with it, Wall Street often resorts to short cuts. This applies particularly to hurried daily financial "intercom." Just as telegraphic language has to be brief, rapid-fire financial communication uses abbreviated concepts.

When individual ratios of prices to current earnings are computed for quick ready reference, they carry a limited meaning with respect to the outlook for future earnings. To acquire greater significance, they must be dissected with a surgeon's skill. The first problem which the analyst faces in dealing with current earnings is to determine their relation to *basic earning power*. When a company's current earnings stand below its estimated normal earning power, the price-to-current-earnings ratio will rise to compensate for the deviation from the norm. When current earnings rise above the basic earning power, the ratio will fall.

This compensating mechanism produces another phenomenon: the countermovements of current earnings and price/earnings ratios. Their existence confirms the presence of a valuation process in the stock market. The principle of compensation and the rule of countermovements were studied by the author of this chapter in great detail in *The Analysts Journal* of November, 1953, in an article entitled "A Theory of Price/Earnings Rations."

From time to time, financial writers rediscover this phenomenon and marvel at it. On January 16, 1967, a well-known weekly publication carried in its Business and Finance section a piece headed "Wall Street: Up On the Down Staircase." The article contained a table showing that the price/earnings ratio on Dow stocks has invariably climbed in years when earnings were actually declining. The author was wondering hopefully whether the stock market might not continue rising in 1967 even if corporate profits should fall.

Increasingly, analysts avoid using price-to-current-earnings ratios. Whatever label they may apply to it, they reason in terms of basic earning power. As an example, we may quote a passage from an article, "The Stock Market—From One Viewpoint" (*Investment Dealer's Digest*, May 30, 1966) by Waid R. Vanderpoel, vice president of the First National Bank of Chicago:

> Does it follow that many groups are now attractive due to the combination of price decline and earnings rise? Before we meet this question head on, let us look at the price/earnings ratio relationship from another viewpoint. If we include 1966, earnings will have risen for five consecutive years. Yet a study of past results would indicate rather frequent variance. It is our contention that investors must take average earnings, or what we call "trend line" earnings, into consideration. Dow Jones Industrial Average earnings have advanced about 60% from the 1955–62 plateau. What is the relationship between current market levels and five-year average earnings? On this basis, stocks are still high—higher than in late 1961 from which level the Dow Jones Average plunged more than 25%. Since late 1964, stocks have commanded a higher multiple of five-year average earnings than at any even reasonably prosperous time since 1929.

A more advanced concept of the price/earnings ratio was introduced into the financial literature by W. Edward Bell, past president of the Security Analysts of San Francisco. In "The Price-Future Earnings Ratio," a paper published in *The Analysts Journal* of August, 1958, Mr. Bell made a significant contribution by bringing in the dimension of time, an essential element of all investments, into the conventional price/earnings ratio. He looks at the ratio as a figure showing the number of years of prospective earnings contained in the current price. Bell's article presents a table, reproduced as Table 5 of this volume, showing the corresponding price/earnings and price-future earnings ratios for various assumed constant annual rates of growth.

By suggesting that we view the price/earnings ratio as a payout and that we add a quantifiable element of time, Bell rendered a great service to investment thinking. Except for the absence of the rate of discount applied to future earnings, Bell's concept comes close to that of "present worth."

The current price/earnings ratio is too deeply imbedded in financial practice to allow the hope that its use will soon disappear. We should learn at least to understand more clearly its theoretical nature and its practical limitations. It would be still better if we could train ourselves to use capitalization *rates* instead of capitalization multipliers. They would tie in with rates of discount and rates of return on common stocks, which are the pillars of valuation and sound investment thinking. It is a remarkable fact that such famous treatises as *The Valuation of Property* by James C. Bonbright, who was professor of finance at Columbia University, and *Financial Policy of Corporations* by Arthur Stone Dewing, who was professor of finance at Harvard University, do not even mention the term "price/earnings ratio." Nor can the term be found in the respective indexes of their two-volume works. Yet both these scholars devote considerable space in their books to discussions of the appraisal of common stocks.

In our opinion, the best solution to the problem of the valuation of common stocks lies in methods which completely sidestep the use of price/earnings or earnings/price ratios. We must reaffirm our faith in a doctrine that is not of our own creation, but which we have many times defended: *it is* *the thesis which holds that the value of a common stock is the present worth of its future stream of dividends.* This method is completely free from any injection of price, the variable which investors seek to measure in their search for underpriced stocks.*

CONCLUSION

We do not wish to leave readers under the impression that the eminent professionals who engaged in recent studies of low and high price/earnings ratios relied blindly on the conclusions to which these studies led. In their investment practice, these analysts also use many other tools that are not open to criticism.

An unpublished study of price/earnings ratios dated March 26, 1963, which S. F. Nicholson distributed to his bank's clients and correspondents, ends with a caveat. *"Caution!* In observing the significance of data in this report as in previous price/earnings studies, attention is called to the need for analytical judgments on factors other than earnings ratios; and the preference for good earnings in relation to prices should not lead to using price/earnings ratios as an all-conclusive formula for sound investment."

In the course of a brief correspondence between Paul F. Miller, Jr., and the writer last August, Mr. Miller wrote:

> Please don't misunderstand our emphasis on these studies. We have never claimed that selection by P/E ratios is a substitute for earnings growth in determining investment success. In fact, several studies which we have conducted prove conclusively that there is no substitute for earnings growth in successful investment selection. However, I am somewhat wary of

* See, in particular, Nicholas Molodovsky, "Valuation of Common Stocks," *The Analysts Journal,* February, 1959. This article was reprinted in Eugene M. Lerner's "Readings in Financial Analysis and Investment Management," Richard D. Irwin, Inc., 1963. Also, Nicholas Molodovsky, Catherine May and Sherman Chottiner, "Common Stock Valuation: Principles, Tables and Application," *Financial Analysts Journal,* March–April, 1965.

earnings projections and even short-term earnings estimates. I think you will agree that even one-year estimates of earnings can be woefully inadequate and inaccurate.

You will notice in our more recent studies that we have shown that the market tends to be correct in appraising high price/earnings ratio and low price/earnings ratio stocks as groups, that is, the high P/E stocks do indeed tend to have better earnings growth over a period of time than do the low P/E stocks. Quantifying this very roughly, it appears that approximately 65% of the issues in the high P/E categories do turn out to have superior trends; likewise, 65% of the stocks in the low P/E categories tend to have drab or declining earnings trends. It is the balance of the 35% that makes the difference in the average price performances of the two groups. In the high P/E ratio group, 35% of the issues proved to be disappointments, and evidently record substantial losses. In the low P/E ratio group, 35% of the issues turned out to have very good earnings trends, and, of course, record substantial investment profits. Of the 65% of the issues in the high P/E group that turn out well from an earnings standpoint, profits are normally realized at an above-average rate; and in the 65% of the low P/E stocks that experienced drab or declining earnings, the market results are below average although not, as a rule, very heavily in the negative column.

It is evidently the penalty concept as it applies to the high P/E stocks, and the reward concept applied to the low P/E stocks, both in those cases where surprises occur, that causes the advantage on average to be in favor of the low P/E ratio issues.

We have never said that the odds favor investment in any one low P/E stock versus any one high P/E stock or even a select group of low P/E stocks versus high P/E stocks. All we have commented on is the action of relatively large groups of stocks in these P/E ratio categories.

At the end of his article, which we have discussed earlier in this chapter, Mr. James D. McWilliams also limits the significance of his conclusions. Rearranging his samples into the best-performing stocks, he finds that the very best performing common stocks can be found in any price/earnings ratio decile. He does not, however, obtain the same result by rearranging the stocks by the poorest performers. The latter predominate in the highest price/earnings decile. McWilliams remarks in this connection: "Weaving the results of the extremely good and the extremely poor performers together in the analytical decision-making process, it appears that we can find good performers anywhere, but if you are looking at high P/E stocks, great care must be exercised to determine that the company is going to keep on growing. This is the area where it appears that the investor frequently bids multiples and prices up too sharply in relation to actual growth and the investor is subsequently disappointed." We couldn't agree more.

In sum, S. Francis Nicholson, who pioneered the confrontations of the high and low price/earnings ratios, rendered a service to investors at a time when the "growth stock" cult was transgressing the bounds of financial analysis. Yet his method contained a statistical flaw. A periodic cumulative reinvestment into the highest and lowest price/earnings ratios, when it is effected on a group basis, reinforces the overpricing and underpricing of the respective groups. His research influenced in this respect some of his followers.

Even in those studies which had no recourse to the cumulative reinvestment method, the results would have been more convincing if no constraints had been used for the selection of stocks. All listed stocks should have been included, as was done for a different purpose by James H. Lorie and Lawrence Fisher. However, despite these shortcomings, recent studies of price/earnings ratios have at least confirmed statistically the rather obvious fact that, on the average, investors profit more by paying less for one dollar of earnings of sound stock.

This does not alter the fact that excellent values may be found among the highest price/earnings ratio stocks as well. The fiftieth issue of *Vickers Favorite 50* presents data, as of December 31, 1966, garnered from the common-stock holdings of about 500 investment companies with combined assets of close to $50 billion. Ranked by dollar value, the two largest holdings of these funds were International Business Machines and Polaroid. Among the 15 largest holdings, we also find Eastman Kodak, Xerox, Minnesota Mining & Manufacturing, International Telephone & Telegraph, General Telephone & Electronics, and Avon Products. We leave it to our readers to figure the price/earnings ratios of these stocks—they certainly qualify as high!

Part IV

An Over-all View

17

The New American Capitalism

By Armand G. Erpf

It is only in the United States, the United Kingdom, and Japan that there exists a broad, highly developed, capital investment market which has the structure to elicit widespread public investment in corporate enterprises. This new concept has given rise to a democratic capitalism, or a people's capitalism, where purely private ownership and dictation have yielded to a mixture of family and public ownership. This trend has been, and is, modifying the nature of traditional capitalism, transcending the doctrinaire ideologies enunciated so eloquently and emphatically in Europe in the nineteenth century by both the Right and the Left. It bids fair, when

Armand G. Erpf is a partner of Carl M. Loeb, Rhoades & Co.

more fully grown, to be importantly different from the theories of Socialist dogma or the views of the laissez-faire school.

In 1966, there were approximately 3¾ million farms in the United States and over one million incorporated companies. There were some 26,000 companies whose securities were quoted and had some degree of trading. Approximately 6,000 had 300 shareholders or more and accounted for the bulk of the trading in the over-the-counter markets and on the Stock Exchanges. Of these about 3,000 were listed on recognized Exchanges, nearly half being on the New York Stock Exchange—the Big Board—which handles over 90% of the listed transactions in this country.

THE U.S. INVESTMENT STRUCTURE

The 1962 Census of Shareowners made by the New York Stock Exchange showed that share ownership in the United States had dramatically increased since the first census of 1952. Then an estimated 6.5 million Americans owned shares in the nation's publicly held companies. By early 1962, that figure had grown to 17 million, and by 1967 it was believed to be in excess of 21 million. Common stocks are now universally favored. They are included in the endowment funds of universities, charitable institutions, and pension funds, and in the portfolios managed by the trust departments of the banks. Normally, a portion of the savings of the people and of institutions steadily find their way into common stock investment. The investment trusts (mutual funds), developed over recent decades, had $35 billion worth of securities at the end of 1966. These are owned largely by small shareholders the length and breadth of the land, many of whom utilize an automatic procedure for increasing their holdings. Thus, savings not only go into insurance, savings banks, and bond purchases—which along with mortgages were the principal vehicles of the past—but also into equities; and, if anything, the propensity for equities is rising.

On the New York Stock Exchange, at the end of 1966,

there were nearly 11 billion shares listed and they had a value of nearly $500 billion. As an example, the American Telephone Company, with 538 million shares outstanding, had about three million stockholders and 834,000 employees. General Motors, with 285 million shares outstanding, had 1.3 million shareholders and about 700,000 workers. It is normal for the major corporations each to have hundreds of thousands of shareholders, to whom information, dividend checks, and annual reports are distributed through massive, mechanized operations. Stockholder relations are taken seriously by management and directors; and corporate officers and departments are directly assigned to the task of responding to the inquiries of stockholders and of the financial community. Stockholder meetings may be heavily attended and, in the case of the large national corporations, there is a trend towards holding the meetings in different regions of the country to permit accessibility.

The members of the New York Stock Exchange and their branches, and the underwriting houses and over-the-counter houses who may not be members of the New York Stock Exchange but are members of the National Association of Securities Dealers, together have a network of several thousand offices serving all the cities of the country. These offices are linked to a communications network which permits transactions and information to move with electrical speed. An order to purchase or sell securities, transmitted from any part of the country to the floor of the Stock Exchange, can be consummated in a matter of minutes. Through a system of correspondent relationships, even the smallest securities concern has on tap research information from major brokerage houses.

The professional investment community, whether dealers in securities or managers of funds, employs more than 14,000 security analysts. This discipline, which began early in the century in the important insurance companies and the trust departments of banks, has over the last 30 years attained professional status. The important institutions of higher learning of the United States have established graduate schools in business, which give masters' and doctoral degrees in the several aspects of business administration and analysis. This corps of university-trained personnel regularly interviews the managements of the U.S. corporate enterprises in which there is any sizable degree of public interest. There ensues widespread dissemination of descriptive material, commentary, analysis, comparison, and even criticism for the enlightenment of existing or prospective investors.

The Securities and Exchange Commission, an organ of the federal government of the United States, maintains a nationwide surveillance of all the Exchanges and all transactions. Security issues must be registered and, in general, no public offering can be made without full disclosure of pertinent information concerning the nature of the company, its financial position, and the financial relationship of interested principals. The over-all purpose is to maintain honest dealings, free of manipulation, to prevent fraud, and to authenticate the truthfulness of the information presented by the company to the public. Speculative risk and judgment as to the success of the company remain with the individual. The uniformity of reports, the quarterly submission of financial data and the disclosure of corporate developments all purport to assure the public of the seriousness, integrity and validity of the corporate process. In effect, with due regard for company secrecy and confidential matters, the idea is that corporate activity should take place in a goldfish bowl. As a consequence, there is confidence in the corporate capitalistic process, and the corporations therefore have ready access to the savings of the public for financing. Hence, by and large, they have acquired an autonomous existence in a plural society and are free—to a major degree—from financial liens or pressures.

The existence of a large and relatively liquid market strengthens the proclivity to invest, makes the common stock a store of value relied upon by the public at large, and puts in the hands of the managers and owners the resources with which to acquire new assets or productive activities. This capitalistic innovation is an important ingredient in the creation of a dynamic economy.

THE U.S. CORPORATE STRUCTURE

Having broadly surveyed the U.S. investment structure and the implications of the changing ownership pattern of private property through the massive diffusion of wealth, I will now examine the corporate structure. Corporate enterprises in the United States can be divided into two broad categories: (1) the large-scale institutional type of corporation, organizational in character and having management in depth; (2) the private, entrepreneurial type of corporate enterprise, clustering around the personalities of owner-managers.

In the first category, the corporate operation is carried on by trained professional management. The organizational setup has some resemblance to a military establishment, with a line-and-staff concept of operational and functional responsibilities. The cadre is underpinned with echelons chosen on the basis of training and experience to assure continuity of the institution. In a way, this type of organization constitutes a private bureaucracy motivated by profit, and accountable to the shareholders and to the public for the performance of its duties and for the profitability and growth of the business. As a bureaucracy, the operation is rational, and each step must be clearly understood before it is acted upon.

In the second category—which in a way constitutes the purely private capitalism operating underneath the institutional organizational capitalism—the management, while professional to a degree, is less bureaucratically organized. It moves on a quickened decision basis, dominated by talents which can act upon phenomena intuitively, and before the operation and sequence can be fully outlined and scientifically justified.

The interplay of these two broad categories of corporate activity in the United States makes for stability and strength, on the one hand; and for innovation, trial and error, and brilliance, on the other. Obviously, these characteristics are not mutually exclusive but they touch upon some of the main-springs of action of each group.

For my own purpose, I tend to subdivide these two broad categories further, each into three groups which again are not mutually exclusive but tend to blur one into the others.

In the first category, the *first group* is comprised of the great institutions—multi-billion dollar in scope and equity valuation—which may dominate some of the basic industries, and whose fortunes are tied into the welfare and fabric of the whole nation, and in some cases of the world. These are gigantic. For example, in 1966, the American Telephone & Telegraph Company was valued at $35 billion; Standard Oil of New Jersey at $17 billion. General Motors, with a turn-over at $20 billion, was roughly the size of the entire Dutch economy. U.S. Steel, valued at nearly $3 billion in the market, had a capacity as large as the whole steel industry of West Germany. Indeed many of our multi-billion-dollar corporations have become multi-national in scope, and their policies and plans are influential factors in world trade.

A second characteristic of these institutionlike corporations is that they maintain large staffs and highly equipped laboratories for basic, applied, development and process research. Of the $23 billion spent on research and development in the United States in 1966, of which perhaps two-thirds was financed by the U.S. government, the large corporations accounted for a substantial percentage; and they account for the preponderant percentage of research paid for by corporations out of their own funds.

A third characteristic is that the cash flow of this type of corporation—that is, depreciation and retained earnings—is huge and furnishes the basis for annual stabilized long-term capital expenditures and for acquisitions and investments overseas.

A fourth characteristic is that, in general, because of the provisions and interpretations of the antitrust laws, our institutional corporations are estopped from easy acquisition of domestic companies or assets. In effect, the tenor of our law and the climate of our governmental opinion is that these corporations—being huge, powerful, financially self-sustaining and maintaining large staffs of scientists—should grow from within by the application of their resources to those fields in which they wish to expand their endeavors.

In the *second group* of my first category would come the large corporations—let us say those which are valued in the market somewhat below or above $1 billion. Their attributes are similar in nature to those of the first group, but not quite so extensive, and many of them may represent industries which were organized more recently than oil, utilities, steel, automobiles and so on. Some of the companies within this second group have only come on the market as publicly held institutions with masses of stockholders in recent decades.

The *third group* in the first category constitutes in large measure service companies, which had had long historic association in the public-service area. Many of them have come on the market as publicly owned companies since the war. By and large, they are professionally managed and their organizational setup is on a perpetuating basis. In some cases, capital requirements are negligible since the assets and good will revolve around their performance and their franchises. In the case of banks, finance companies and insurance companies, capital requirements range from moderate to several hundred million dollars.

Turning, now, to my second broad category, I would describe the *first group* in it as "enterprises." Here the management and ownership may coincide to a significant degree and the public shareholders are carried along on the shoulders of the central body of management ownership. They may have organizations and research in some depth but the topmost echelon of the company will be thinner; and the company's fortunes revolve to a greater degree around the talent and drive of individual personalities. Judgment is to a greater extent intuitive and may reflect the artistic as opposed to the scientific approach. These enterprises are aggressive and represent private capitalism before it becomes institutionalized. Their long-term objectives often are to grow into an institutional type of business corporation; or to combine with other enterprises to create an impregnable structure; or to diversify to the degree necessary either to neutralize or to diminish economic vulnerability.

The *second group* of my second broad category consists of "venture" corporations which, if they succeed, may become enterprises. If they do not, they are liquidated at a profit or a loss and disappear.

The *third and final group* are "wildcatters," the term applied to proprietors, or an association of proprietors, who drill in unproven territory—and I am not just referring to oil and mining but to industry in general. In this group the mortality is great, but occasionally fortunes are made through a stroke of genius or a play of luck.

Let me now cite a few numbers that indicate the proportions of the economic canvas I have been discussing. The 30 companies constituting the Dow-Jones Industrial Average had a stock market valuation at the end of 1966 of roughly $137 billion, more than one-third of the total valuation then of all stocks on the Big Board. Similarly, the 500 companies comprising Standard & Poor's Composite Index, which includes 75 utilities and covers many industries, had an aggregate valuation of $374 billion, or 78% of the New York Stock Exchange total. Thus, the organizational institutional corporate category dominates the corporate scene. However, the virility, versatility and variety of the lesser groups is astounding in the sum total of their decision-making in the course of a year, and it is here one finds the incubation of many new projects, products, and processes. The trial and error accompanying these tens of thousands of decisions is an enormous stimulus and creative irritant to the whole body of capitalistic activity. The probing and prodding of the entrepreneurial, truly private capitalistic group has a profound impact on the more stolid and more stable larger organizations which, of necessity, must proceed with greater caution, with more fully proven ideas, and more thoroughly developed and tested plans. Obviously the research laboratories of the major corporations account for a great innovative outpouring. Nevertheless, the inventiveness and creativeness of the entrepreneurial category are the source of a host of new industries which have appeared on the scene relatively recently, and have already, in a number of instances, achieved substantial stature. We need only point to drugs, broadcasting and air transport; to a Polaroid, a Xerox, a Texas Instruments, to say nothing of the defense-inspired electronics series of industries, and the awe-inspiring computer.

All of these groups constitute the two major categories broadly defined above. They have a public following in the form of investors and financial houses sponsoring and counseling them. They have a market for their securities. And they distribute relatively accurate information about their activities.

GOVERNMENTAL STRUCTURE

I now turn to our governmental structure in terms of its economic and financial influence and supervisory powers.

Our capitalistic structure operates in a society in which the government is the largest single economic force and segment. In 1966, the federal government of the United States collected and disbursed about $140 billion of taxes, of which nearly half went for defense, atomic energy and the space program. The fifty states and the thousands of counties receive or raise and also spend about $76 billion. Thus the three echelons of government, allowing for overlapping, account for nearly $200 billion, or about 27% of the gross national product, which amounted to an estimated $740 billion in 1966. However, the actual purchase of goods and services *directly by government* was equivalent to only 20% of the gross national product. In this sense, our economy can be considered 20% socialistic and 80% private.

Beyond this, the regulatory laws affecting wages, hours, pensions, unemployment insurance, transfer payments, steeply progressive income taxes; the swings of fiscal policy determined by whether the budget is in deficit or in surplus; the management of the federal debt of over $300 billion; and the overseeing of credit by the Federal Reserve System affecting in one way or another the 13,000 commercial banks—all these factors have their impact on the economy, and depending upon how they are operated, the cycle of business is either smooth, ameliorated or aggravated. In this framework of democratic capitalism there is the convergence of expanding public and private capitalism, along with extensive social welfare programs and selective government intervention. In a real sense this is a synthesis of nineteenth-century capitalism and socialism—two systems considered mutually antagonistic which nonetheless, in the afternoon of the twentieth century, are being pragmatically applied in a plural society in such a way as to overcome their contradictions and nourish an affluent and democratic culture.

The American society—despite the huge tax load it is carrying—was recently putting aside in the form of savings or the equivalent some $100 billion per annum. This $100 billion can be broken down as follows: roughly $27 billion was saved by individuals; $66 billion was cash plowback by the corporations; and the remainder represented contributions to pension funds and other elements. This capital formation in one way or another finances business expenditures for plant, machinery and equipment of $61 billion (1966) and private individual capital expenditures for homes and consumer durables.

INVESTMENT OUTLOOK

With this background, we are in a position to take a brief look at the long-term investment outlook. As my late friend, Imre De Vegh, used to remark, "We can take a look at the stock market exogenously and endogenously."

Among the external influences are the economic analyses and projections which we receive from the professional economists and which we review and relate to our particular frame of reference. For the rest of the decade the projections are constructive, taking into consideration the increasing labor force, government policies and the social conscience.

These projections, by and large, envisage a growth rate for gross national product of around 4% per annum in real terms (i.e., excluding the effect of price increases). Whatever the flurries, obstacles or delays, this appears to represent a valid expectation; and if this premise is accepted, it constitutes a good base for a secular trend in the dance of values reflected in the stock market mirror.

Naturally the economic factors are enmeshed in the political scene. It was under Wilson that the great conceptual debate in our country began when the Federal Reserve System was laid down, marking the beginning of a long and painful transition from an agricultural, rurally dominated political economy to an urban and industrialized society. While there was little change under the three subsequent Presidents, the great transition was finally effected under Franklin D. Roosevelt in a mixed program of reform and revenge. The debate nonetheless continued, as subsequent Administrations were surrounded by honorific figures still imbued by *laissez-faire* philosophy and ignorant of and horrified by modern fiscal flexibility and monetary management. Finally, the country was ready for the deliberately planned tax cut of 1964 and the investment-inducing modifications of depreciation allowance. This meant the acceptance of revolutionary fiscal and monetary measures as a guide to political supervision of a capitalist economy. Presumably this orientation makes for growth rather than inertia. That a majority of the people so believe was suggested by the defeat of Barry Goldwater, which also removed elements in the House and the Senate that since 1937 had—for good reason or bad—been frustrating the efforts of the Chief Executive to carry domestic legislation through Congress. This points toward a concert of power between the Executive and the Legislature, making for a managerial type of government which can apply itself wholeheartedly to putting into practice the philosophy which we have been debating for a half century, placing the emphasis on management rather than on the endless debate of principles. As long as much of this philosophy remains to be fulfilled, there should be an ample reservoir of governmental stimulation—both to encourage growth of the economy and to counteract possible pauses or setbacks. This should create a politico-socio-economic climate which could endure until the potential is fulfilled or exhausted. By that time, a new philosophy, a new frame of reference, a new order of projections may be called for.

However, our domestic developments are not immune to the play of international forces. Without going into a long rigmarole about the international outlook and our relationship thereto, a few brief observations will be proffered.

As to Russia, the October, 1962, nuclear confrontation resulted, I believe, in a financial stabilization of the Cold War vis-à-vis that challenger, and furthered somewhat the probability of coexistence and lessened tensions within the Atlantic area.

The Chinese threat, while important, is of a different magnitude—at least for the foreseeable future. It may involve us in war of a kind for a long time to come, but war of a relatively low intensity—a struggle different from being on the brink of a general holocaust. While the Chinese threat may delay the stabilization of defense expenditures which was taking place in 1963 and 1964, it should not strain our capabilities sufficiently to detract from the growth of the economy. Nor should it interfere too seriously with the application of the $50 billion of additional revenues projected for the rest of the decade to lower taxes, raise social expenditures, and finance experimentation by our three echelons of government on a relatively vast scale.

A third external consideration revolves around the international monetary problem which, after a half dozen years of simmering, has come to a boil and is receiving a great deal of attention on the part of the Free World sovereignties. One can be optimistic or pessimistic as to the rapidity with which a so-called monetary solution is reached, and one can be hopeful that decision-making will take place along the lines of the various eminent plans proposed. Presumably, *gouver-*

ner c'est prévoir. Even granting that international monetary accommodations of a progressive nature come into being, there are several structural strains which must be sweated out. The presence of 700,000 American soldiers and dependents in Europe, despite lowering tensions, still constitutes a severe payments drain. Moreover, Europe and other portions of the globe entice direct investment on the part of American capitalistic enterprises seeking to benefit from unsaturated markets, weaker competition, organizations not comparable in scale to ours. One must also take cognizance of the influence of our antitrust laws which tend to encourage, one might almost say incite, expansion abroad. These monetary uncertainties and global structural strains represent important imponderables before us. They constitute hazards which might very well bring about a severe buffeting of the stock market.

Still, on the whole, the exogenous influences on balance appear favorable. Let us now turn to the endogenous, or largely internal, factors influencing the stock market.

An important ingredient in stock market psychology and in the propensity to invest savings in stocks rather than to place them in savings banks and fixed-income instruments is the fear of inflation. This has been present for the past two decades throughout the world, in Communist as well as capitalist economies. Despite the fact that, unlike the other major industrial nations of the Free World, and perhaps even Russia, we have been able in recent years (at least until 1966) to contain unit costs and to keep the advance in consumer prices to not more than 1½% per annum (I refer to retail prices, of course, since only in New York does everybody buy wholesale), the apprehension that inflationary pressures might increase persists in investment psychology and undoubtedly adds a multiple or two to the evaluation of common stock earnings. To an extent this argument in favor of common stocks is justified, even by the modest erosion of purchasing power witnessed in recent years. After all, a 5%

yield in a bond amounts to only 2½% after income taxes in the 50% bracket (which is reached all too soon); if you deduct the erosion in purchasing power (which amounts to at least 1½% annually) compounded over the years, the ultimate return is certainly quite unsatisfactory.

All this leads to a fair amount of confusion in the public mind as to what is prosperity and what is inflation. The confusion is compounded by stock pushers who try to recommend their wares, not on the basis of prosperity values but of presumably accelerating inflation.

The switch from bonds to equities, particularly on the part of individuals, has increased the demand for common stocks and has forced upward their evaluation—that is, the willingness to discount future earnings more generously than might otherwise be the case. All the qualifying factors entering into the appraisal of common stocks—the whole gamut of security analysis, industry analysis, and evaluation—are popularly subsumed in the price/earnings multiple. This is an attempt to relate a rate of growth more or less intellectually determinable as reasonably valid to an equity situation which has found structure and place in its industry and in the economy. The emphasis on the growth factor by security analysts in our country has, to a degree, superseded the traditional criteria of balance-sheet position, fundamental tangible assets, book value, and dividend yield. These have given way to the entrepreneurial characteristics of the company—to its creativity or innovative talent in product and process, and to new combinations of factors, notably the cash flow to finance capital expenditures, the nature of franchises (whether by virtue of brand, market acceptance, captive or entrenched outlets), and the quality of its relations with its distributive intermediaries or channels.

The high-water mark of multiple-itis was reached in the winter of 1961, and it was followed by the May–June crash of 1962. The Dow-Jones Industrial Average late in 1961 was selling at about 24 times current earnings. After the stock market recovery toward the end of 1962, the earnings multiple fluctuated around the 18–19 level; and after the February–October decline in 1966, the multiple receded still further to less than 13 times estimated 1966 earnings. Since earnings and earnings estimates were rising, stock prices advanced between the end of 1961 and the end of 1966 even in the face of the sharp contraction of price/earnings ratios.

The price/earnings multiple purports to evaluate the growth trend of the economy and the growth trend of stocks. In 1963, 1964 and 1965, growth was at a good rate and profits were rising. Cash flow, capital expenditures and expansion were in balance, and the supply of stocks was not being increased, since virtually no new equity financing was needed. Indeed the supply contracted somewhat because of company purchases of their own shares. This led to a recovery of the prevailing multiple, although it remained substantially below the levels of 1961 and early 1962 when euphoria was rampant and expectations were wild.

At the end of 1966, when the preponderant belief was that the rate of growth might slacken, the multiple for the Dow-Jones Industrial Average was down to about 14 times current earnings. If, however, the rate of growth should actually rise, it may well be that current cash flow of over $60 billion or thereabouts after dividends may not be sufficient to sustain plant expenditures and working capital needs; and in that case a supply of equities, or the equivalents, would come on the market. Thus we arrive at a conclusion that, if in the period ahead of us the rate of growth of the economy should be less than expected, the multiple should be sober or might even decline. On the other hand, if the rate of growth is on the optimistic side, the multiple might very well be restrained by additional supply. Only in those rare intervals when these forces are in balance—when demand persists with no supply of new stocks—should the multiple be firming. In brief, one must look to earnings growth for improvement in share prices in the face of a possibly stable or declining price/earnings multiple. If the bull market in multiples were over, which in my opinion it is, this would be a salutary development in modern capitalism.

We have been talking about Averages, which include somewhat static or unprogressive kinds of companies as well as dynamic enterprises. Over the past two decades, the whole sweep of revaluation has beneficially affected the stock market as a whole and, by and large, earnings and multiples have both risen. While one can make a case for continuous progress in earnings, whatever the interruptions may be, it is difficult to envisage a further over-all rise in the multiple. This should not, however, apply to industries or individual companies where the entrepreneurial ingredient is strong and the growth rate superior—in some cases vastly superior to the hoped-for real growth of 4% per annum for the economy as a whole. To the extent that the long-term view of such companies is validly based on solid entrepreneurial characteristics exhibited in that portion of the economy, substantial appreciation potential may be hoped for, provided the relationship of earnings growth to the current multiple is attractive. Thus a distinction must be made between the entrepreneurial equities and the run-of-the-mill capitalistic equities, where one should not expect more than a wage for the resources used, including ordinary management, labor, capital and technology.

Pedestrian companies in an expanding economy need not be static but they may not be particularly alluring. Such stocks, in effect, may simply be somewhat better than fixed-income instruments in view of the virtually regressive return on fixed-income investment. But to the investor who will employ his savings resources in an entrepreneurial way—that is, in astute speculation in the best sense of the word—the opportunities for an exceptional return over the years still exist.

In the present phase of modern U.S. capitalism, there are about $700 billion of equities extant, of which some $500 billion are listed on the New York Stock Exchange and the rest on other exchanges and over-the-counter. This is a huge storehouse of values, more than twice as large as demand and time deposits put together; and in the minds of most people, whether they be right or wrong, these values constitute money or quasi-money. Because of the high rates of income taxes, this storehouse is dipped into by the American people to purchase all sorts of things—a house, a work of art, a trip around the world; and it is used by corporations as a better medium than money with which to buy other corporations, since the seller can make the sale on a tax-free basis. Thus it is important that this stock of national wealth be authentic, meticulously audited, free of manipulative practices (whether inside or outside the corporation), properly under public supervision (though some of the supervision may be unnecessarily sadistic) and soberly appraised. In another highly developed capitalist economy, Japan, the equity market got out of hand, and the intervention of the Bank of Japan itself was required to support security prices and the solvency of the economy. This is the complete circle. In Japan, the difficulties were touched off by the payments restrictions imposed by the U.S. government to redress the structural strain in our relations with the rest of the world, an indication of the sensitivity of stock markets to the international payments problem.

In the United States, two great developments affecting the equity market have taken place in the postwar period. In the first place, the pension funds have emerged and have grown to a tremendous size. These institutions warehouse equities, presumably for decades, on behalf of a mass of contributors and for the benefit of an anonymous group in the future. This kind of "abstract" ownership of common stocks accounts for a substantial and growing percentage of the total. Second, there are the mutual funds, with assets of $35 billion at the end of 1966, which are growing at the rate of about $2½ billion per annum in new investments and are owned by millions of small shareholders who can turn in their shares on demand.

While millions of investors and beneficiaries are involved in mutual funds and pension funds, the decision-making in both these areas is concentrated in the hands of a relatively small number of managers. This new concentration in the financing of the modern, democratic, welfare, capitalistic society cannot fail to be a significant influence on stock price movements.

There are always imponderables but, when all is said and done, for over 30 years—through all the vicissitudes of wars, depressions, inflation (real and imagined), revolution and clashes of social doctrine—the trend of common stock prices has been upward. There have been severe and trying shake-outs: 1937; 1946; then a series of minor ones until 1962, which was severe; another minor one in 1965; and another quite severe one in 1966. There is no assurance that such setbacks will not recur; indeed whenever confidence becomes too assured, the very framework for a setback in stock prices is established. The belief in boom-bust as affecting the economy as a whole, the nervous chartists and the casino players —all contribute to instability. For funds or individuals the search for values and opportunities in individual stocks, selected industries, or broader segments of the economy should prove rewarding; and I believe that less attention should be paid to "the state of the market" in the shorter swings.

In the American investment market, there are at least 100 industries, all with varying trends. It is fatuous to try to sum up the investment potential by taking any one yardstick and attempting to apply it universally to this brilliant galaxy of investment opportunities. This is what makes for a rich harvest in speculation and investment in the American market. This market is broad, liquid, better documented than any other in the world (both in regard to industry characteristics and factual information about companies); and the economic data and statistics for the country as a whole are more precise and more up to date than those for any other economy.

In time, all this information will be computerized—full statistics on the country, complete data on the industry and accurate company figures. The retrieval of this information will be possible with little or no time lag, permitting the vast horizons of the future to emerge before the vision of the imaginative and perceptive risk-taker, who will be in a superb position to arbitrage the present with the future. This is the true function of leadership in every field—to deploy the artistic intuitions of the mind and the knowledge gained from experience within a framework of hard, scientific fact.

Appendixes

Who's Who
among the Contributors

CHARLES J. ROLO is a senior security analyst and account executive at H. Hentz & Co., members of the New York Stock Exchange, a leading Wall Street brokerage house founded in 1856. When he entered the brokerage business in 1960, he had behind him a successful career as a writer and editor. After graduating from Oxford with an honors degree in politics, philosophy, and economics, he received a master's degree from the Columbia School of Journalism. In World War II he worked for the British government and also served as a war correspondent. Out of this experience came two books: *Radio Goes to War* and *Wingate's Raiders*. Subsequently he was for 12 years the literary critic of *The Atlantic Monthly*. He has edited several anthologies (among them, *Psychiatry in American Life*) and has contributed more than 100 articles to leading magazines in this country. A member of the New York Society of Security Analysts, he writes frequently about the stock market and has done a weekly market commentary on the radio.

GEORGE J. NELSON was born in Russia and after attending schools in Copenhagen and Berlin, he entered the London School of Economics and later went to Cambridge University. He served his apprenticeship on Wall Street in two leading brokerage houses, graduated to the role of economist, and in 1955 formed his own mutual fund, the Nelson Fund, Inc. It has been nicknamed "The Millionaires' Fund" because of its high net asset value, and its shares are to a large degree held by institutions and professionals in the United States and abroad. In 1963, Mr. Nelson formed the Tokyo Fund, of which he is president. He is a member of the New York Chamber of Commerce, the American Economic Association, and the new York Society of Security Analysts.

RICHARD E. BLODGETT was for several years a reporter on *The Wall Street Journal*, specializing in coverage of mutual funds and brokerage houses. More recently he has been an assistant finance editor of *Business Week*.

ARMAND G. ERPF, a general partner of Carl M. Loeb, Rhoades & Co., members of the New York Stock Exchange, is also chairman of the executive committee and a director of Crowell-Collier and Macmillan, Inc., a member of the executive committee and director of Seaboard Air Line Railroad Company; a director of the General Instrument Corporation, the Jefferson Insurance Company of New York, the Jersey External Trust, Rayonier Incorporated, and Stein Roe & Farnham International Fund.

After graduating from Columbia University in 1917, he gained experience in a variety of areas, being associated in turn with a mining and importing company, a firm of crude-rubber brokers, and a firm of management engineers. In 1933, he became director of the statistical and research departments of Carl M. Loeb, Rhoades & Co.

During the second World War, Mr. Erpf served in the office of the Commanding General, Headquarters Army Service Forces, Washington, D.C., and for periods of duty in the western Pacific and the China theater. He was appointed to the General Staff Corps in 1944, and was awarded the Legion of Merit in 1946.

Mr. Erpf is a member of the Council on Foreign Relations, the New York Chamber of Commerce, and the Economic Club of New York, and is a trustee of the Whitney Museum. Recently, a chair named in Mr. Erpf's honor was established at the Columbia Graduate School of Business.

ELIZABETH M. FOWLER has been a financial writer on *The New York Times* for the past 12 years. After graduating from Smith College, she received her master's degree in business administration at New York University. Her subsequent experience includes a stint as financial writer for a brokerage house and copy editing on *The Wall Street Journal*. She is the author of *90 Days to Fortune*, published in 1965, an account of how an amateur investor made a fortune in the bear market of 1962.

RICHARD L. GEIGER, a licensed professional engineer, started his career in industry, and since 1956 he has devoted himself to security analysis and investment counseling. He was for several years associated with DeVegh & Co., and is now an independent financial consultant, specializing in investment planning and the study of ventures. A diector of several corporations, he is a member of the American Physical Society, the Institute for Management Science, and the New York Society of Security Analysts.

GEORGE J. W. GOODMAN is the editor of *The Institutional Investor*, a journal for professional investment managers. A former editor of *Time* and *Fortune*, he has also written several novels, including *The Wheeler Dealers*, of which he also wrote the movie script. At one time, before the word "performance" had even been coined, he was co-manager of a small "performance" fund.

PHILIP GREER, currently the New York financial correspondent of the *Washington Post*, formerly covered Wall Street for the *New York Herald-Tribune*. He came by his knowledge of stock market operations on the firing line, having been for more than six years a Registered Representative with various member firms of the New York Stock Exchange.

ELIOT JANEWAY is well known in financial circles as the publisher of the Janeway Service. He also writes a syndicated column for the *Chicago Tribune-New York News Syndicate*. The distinctive characteristic of his approach to the forecasting of trends in the economy and the stock market is its emphasis on the economic and financial impact of governmental decisions and of the political pressures responsible for them. Mr. Janeway is the author of *Struggle for Survival*, a definitive study of economic mobilization during World War II, and of *The Economics of Crisis*, published early in 1968.

MYRON KANDEL, formerly financial editor of the *New York Herald-Tribune*, is the editor of the *New York Law Journal*. He previously served as the *Herald-Tribune's* correspondent for Germany and the European Common Market, as business editor of the *Washington Star,* and as a business-financial news reporter for *The New York Times.*

JAMES KARANFILIAN is vice president of Bernstein-Macaulay, Inc., the investment management subsidiary of Carter, Berlind & Weill, members of the New York Stock Exchange. Mr. Karanfilian supervises the bond investment program for individual and institutional clients. He joined Bernstein-Macaulay in 1957 after receiving a master's degree in banking from Columbia University. He has lectured on bond investments in the New School for Social Research.

KURT I. LEWIN is vice president and manager of the Foreign Institutional Department at Bache & Co., Inc. Mr. Lewin received his master's degree in economics from Columbia University in 1956 and subsequently pursued studies there in the field of industrial engineering. Since 1962, he has been a lecturer in economics at Columbia.

Prior to joining Bache & Co., Mr. Lewin was manager of the foreign department of a leading New York brokerage house, where his activities involved him in the Common Market countries, Great Britain, Canada, Australia and Mexico. Previously he worked as a security analyst specializing in economic surveys, railroads and oil.

DAN W. LUFKIN, chairman of the board of directors of Donaldson, Lufkin & Jenrette, Inc., and a director of several companies, was born in 1931 and is one of the youngest men in the top echelons of Wall Street. He graduated from Yale University in 1953, served two years in the U.S. Marine Corps, and then took his master's degree in business administration at the Harvard Graduate School of Business. After a brief apprenticeship in the brokerage business, he became one of the founders of Donaldson, Lufkin & Jenrette in 1959, a firm which has won a reputation for the quality of its institutional research.

WALTER MAYNARD is vice chairman of Shearson, Hammill & Co., Inc. After graduating from Harvard, he studied economics and history at Trinity College, Cambridge. He joined Shearson, Hammill as a partner in 1940—just 11 years after starting his career in Wall Street "at the bottom of the ladder"—and he later was placed in charge of the Research Department. During World War II, he served on General Eisenhower's staff as a lieutenant colonel, and was awarded the O.B.E. from the British government and this country's Legion of Merit for his work on the plans for the Normandy invasion. He is a former governor of the Investment Bankers Association, a former governor of the New York Stock Exchange (1956–62), and a member of the New York Society of Security Analysts.

EDMUND A. MENNIS, C.F.A., is a senior vice president and chairman of the Trust Investment Committee of the Republic National Bank of Dallas. A graduate of the College of the City of New York, he received his M.A. degree from Columbia University and his Ph.D. from New York University. He was awarded the designation of Chartered Financial Analysts and is chairman of the Institute's Research and Publications Committee. He is also an associate editor of the *Financial Analysts Journal,* a member of the Economic Advisory Board of the Secretary of Commerce, and a Fellow as well as a member of the Council of the National Association of Business Economists.

NICHOLAS MOLODOVSKY, C.F.A., a vice president of White, Weld, Inc., and publisher and editor of the *Financial Analysts Journal,* is one of the leading scholars of Wall Street. In the course of a long and distinguished career, he has published numerous learned papers on various aspects of security analysis. He is a member of the Educational and Publications Committe of the Institute of Chartered Financial Analysts and a member of the New York Society of Security Analysts. The chapter he contributed to this symposium will be included in a book, *Common Stocks: Reality and Illusion,* published in 1968.

RALPH A. ROTNEM, C.F.A., a member of the Institute of Chartered Financial Analysts, has had a long and distinguished career on Wall Street. After taking his master's degree in business administration at the Harvard Business School in 1929, he joined Harris, Upham & Co., Inc., members of the New York Stock Exchange, and is now the firm's senior vice president in charge of the Research Department. He has been a president of the New York Society of Security Analysts, a vice president of the National Federation of Financial Analysts Societies, and an associate editor of *The Analysts Journal.* Mr. Rotnem is a director of the Nelson Fund, Inc., and a member of the Advisory Committee of the Bankers Trust Co. He has lectured and written widely on the stock market and the valuation of common stocks.

LOUIS STONE graduated from Yale University in 1931 and went to work in Wall Street as a security analyst. During World War II he served on General Eisenhower's staff and was discharged with the rank of lieutenant colonel. A stockholder in Hayden, Stone, Inc., which he joined in 1956, he is the firm's economist and author of its widely distributed *Monthly Letter*.

ANTHONY W. TABELL is senior vice president and director of technical research for Walston & Co., Inc., members of the New York Stock Exchange, and is the author of the widely circulated *Tabell Market Letter*. Throughout his career he has specialized in the technical approach to stock market analysis. Like his father—the late Edmund W. Tabell, who pioneered in this field and with whom he was teamed for many years—Anthony Tabell has pioneered in the use of electronic computers for the technical analysis of stock prices. He has addressed statistical, business and professional groups throughout the country and has written widely for newspapers and magazines. He is a member of the New York Society of Security Analysts and the Investment Association of New York.

BRADBURY K. THURLOW graduated magna cum laude in 1946 from Harvard University, where he was president of the *Harvard Lampoon* and a member of Phi Beta Kappa. After leaving Harvard, he entered the brokerage business and later formed his own firm in the mid-1950s. He is now vice president and treasurer of Winslow, Cohû & Stetson, Inc. He writes the firm's *Weekly Market Letter* and its monthly *Commentary*, and for several years he contributed a regular column to *Forbes* magazine.

The Language of Investing:
A Glossary

INTRODUCTION

The language spoken in America's investment world may sound like a strange tongue to the newcomer. It is often vivid, colorful, flavored with the idioms of many eras. Some expressions have filtered down from the day when brokers traded securities under a buttonwood tree in the open air. Others are so new that they have seldom been indexed before.

Any glossary of this special language involves certain problems. Some words and phrases cannot be defined completely without going into related background material; others have nuances of meaning which even the experts may dispute.

We have tried to define terms simply and easily, trimming subtle shades of meaning in the interest of brevity and readability.

ACCRUED INTEREST: Interest accrued on a bond since the last interest payment was made. The buyer of the bond pays the market price plus accrued interest. Exceptions include bonds which are in default and income bonds. (See: *Flat; Income Bond*)

ALL-OR-NONE ORDER: A market or limited-price order which is to be executed in its entirety or not at all, but, unlike a fill-or-kill order, is not to be treated as canceled if not executed as soon as it is represented in the Trading Crowd. Bids or offers on behalf of all-or-none orders may not be made in stocks, but may be made in bonds when the number of bonds is 50 or more.

ALTERNATIVE ORDER—EITHER/OR ORDER: An order to do either of two alternatives—such as, either sell (buy) a particular stock at a limit price or sell (buy) on stop. If the order is for one unit of trading when one part of the order is executed on the happening of one alternative, the order on the other alternative is treated as canceled. If the order is for an amount larger than one unit of trading, the number of units executed determines the amount of the alternative order to be treated as canceled.

AMORTIZATION: A generic term. Includes various specific practices such as depreciation, depletion, write-off of intangibles, prepaid expenses and deferred charges.

ANNUAL REPORT: The formal financial statement issued yearly by a corporation to its shareowners. The annual report shows assets, liabilities, earnings—how the company stood at the close of the business year and how it fared profit-wise during the year.

ARBITRAGE: A technique employed to take advantage of differences in price. If, for example, XYZ stock can be bought in New York for $10 a share and sold in London at $10.50, an arbitrageur may simultaneously purchase XYZ stock here and sell the same amount in London, making a profit of 50 cents a share, less expenses. Arbitrage may also involve the purchase of rights to subscribe to a security, or the purchase of a convertible security—and the sale at or about the same time of the security obtainable through exercise of the rights or of the security obtainable through conversion. (See: *Convertible, Rights*)

ASSETS: Everything a corporation owns or due to it: Cash, investments, money due it, materials and inventories, which are called current assets; buildings and machinery, which are known as fixed assets; and patents and good will, called intangible assets. (See: *Liabilities*)

AT-THE-CLOSE ORDER: A market order which is to be executed at or as near to the close as practicable.

AT-THE-OPENING OR AT-THE-OPENING-ONLY ORDER: A market or limited-price order which is to be executed at the opening of the stock or not at all, and any such order or portion thereof not so executed is treated as canceled.

AVERAGES: Various ways of measuring the trend of securities prices, the most popular of which is the Dow-Jones Average of 30 industrial stocks listed on the New York Stock Exchange. The term "average" has led to considerable confusion. A simple average for, say 50 leading stocks would be obtained by totaling the prices of all and dividing by 50. But suppose one of the stocks in the average is split. The price of each share of that stock is then automatically reduced because more shares are outstanding. Thus the average would decline even if all other issues in the average were unchanged. That average thus becomes inaccurate as an indicator of the market's trend.

Various formulae—some very elaborate—have been devised to compensate for stock splits and stock dividends and thus give continuity to the average. Averages and individual stock prices belong in separate compartments.

In the case of the Dow-Jones Industrial Average, the prices of the 30 stocks are totaled and then divided by a divisor which is intended to compensate for past stock splits and dividends and which is changed from time to time. As a result, point changes in the average have only the vaguest relationship to dollar price changes in stocks included in the average. In August, 1966, the divisor was 2.245, so that a one-point change in the industrial average at that time was actually the equivalent of 7 cents. (See: *Point; Split; NYSE Common Stock Index*)

AVERAGING: (See: *Dollar Cost Averaging*)

BALANCE SHEET: A condensed statement showing the nature and amount of a company's assets, liabilities and capital on a given date. In dollar amounts the balance sheet shows what the company owned, what it owed, and the ownership interest in the company of its stockholders. (See: *Assets; Earnings Report*)

BEAR: Someone who believes the market will decline. (See: *Bull*)

BEAR MARKET: A declining market. (See: *Bull Market*)

BEARER BOND: A bond which does not have the owner's name registered on the books of the issuing company and which is payable to the holder. (See: *Coupon Bond; Registered Bond*)

BID AND ASKED: Often referred to as a quotation or quote. The bid is the highest price anyone has declared that he wants to pay for a security at a given time, the asked is the lowest price anyone will take at the same time. (See: *Quotation*)

BIG BOARD: A popular term for the New York Stock Exchange.

BLUE CHIP: Common stock in a company known nationally for the quality and wide acceptance of its products or services, and for its ability to make money and pay dividends. Usually such stocks are relatively high priced and offer relatively low yields.

BLUE SKY LAWS: A popular name for laws various states have enacted to protect the public against securities frauds. The term is believed to have originated when a judge ruled that a particular stock had about the same value as a patch of blue sky.

BOARD ROOM: A room for customers in a broker's office where opening, high, low and last prices of leading stocks are posted on a board throughout the market day.

BOILER ROOM: High-pressure peddling over the telephone of stocks of dubious value. A typical boiler room is simply a room lined with desks or cubicles, each with a salesman and telephone. The salesmen call what is known in the trade as sucker lists.

BOND: Basically an IOU or promissory note of a corporation, usually issued in multiples of $1,000, although $100 and $50 denominations are not uncommon. A bond is evidence of a debt on which the issuing company usually promises to pay the bondholders a specified amount of interest for a specified length of time, and to repay the loan on the expiration date. In every case a bond represents debt—its holder is a creditor of the corporation and not a part owner as is the shareholder. (See: *Collateral Trust Bond; Convertible; General Mortgage Bond; Income Bond*)

BOOK: A notebook the specialist in a stock uses to keep a record of the buy and sell orders at specified prices, in strict sequence of receipt, which are left with him by other brokers. (See: *Specialist*)

BOOK VALUE: An accounting term. Book value of a stock is determined from a company's records, by adding all assets (generally excluding such intangibles as good will), then deducting all debts and other liabilities, plus the liquidation price of any preferred issues. The sum arrived at is divided by the number of common shares outstanding and the result is book value per common share. Book value of the assets of a company or a security may have little or no significant relationship to market value.

BREADTH MARKET: Breadth is an area of market technical study which involves the total number of stocks dealt in in the New York Stock Exchange. Most technicians use four principal Breadth Indexes, all derived and computed from the same basic data carried in *The Wall Street Journal*. The basic index is a straight advance-decline line. Two indexes are concerned with increasing and decreasing volume. And the fourth is a composite Breadth Index.

BREAKOUT: A term used in technical analyses to signify a decisive move upward or downward on substantial volume out of a consolidation area. For example, if a stock has been trading for a period of time in the 32–36 area, a move on volume to 37 or 31 would be termed a breakout.

BROKER: An agent, often a member of a Stock Exchange firm or an Exchange member himself, who handles the public's orders to buy and sell securities or commodities. For this service a commission is charged. (See: *Commission Broker; Dealer*)

BROKER'S LOAN: Money borrowed by brokers from banks for a variety of uses. It may be used by specialists and odd-lot dealers to help finance inventories of stocks they deal in; by brokerage firms to finance the underwriting of new issues of corporate and municipal securities; to help finance a firm's own investments; and to help finance the purchase of securities for customers who prefer to use the broker's credit when they buy securities. (See: *Call Loan; Customers' Net Debit Balances; Margin*)

BUCKET SHOP: An illegal operation now almost extinct. The bucket-shop operator accepted a client's money without ever actually buying or selling securities as the client ordered. Instead he held the money and gambled that the customer was wrong. When too many customers were right, the bucket shop closed its doors and opened a new office.

BULL: One who believes the market will rise. (See: *Bear*)

BULL MARKET: An advancing market. (See: *Bear Market*)

CALL (See: *Puts and Calls*)

CALL LOAN: A loan which may be terminated or "called" at any time by the lender or borrower. Used to finance purchases of securities. (See: *Broker's Loan*)

CALLABLE: A bond issue, all or part of which may be redeemed by the issuing corporation under definite conditions before maturity. The term also applies to preferred shares which may be redeemed by the issuing corporation.

CAPITAL GAIN OR CAPITAL LOSS: Profit or loss from the sale of a capital asset. A capital gain, under current federal income tax laws, may be either short-term (six months or less) or long-term (more than six months). A short-term capital gain is taxed at the reporting individual's full income tax rate. A long-term gain is taxed at a maximum of 25%, depending on the reporting individual's tax bracket. Up to $1,000 of net capital loss—that is, when you sell securities at a lower price than you paid for them—is deductible from the individual's taxable income during the year reported. If the capital loss is more than $1,000, as much as $1,000 annually is deductible annually thereafter until all of the loss has been deducted. The amount of capital loss which may be deducted is reduced by the amount of any capital gain.

CAPITAL STOCK: All shares representing ownership of a business, including preferred and common. (See: *Common Stock; Preferred Stock*)

CAPITALIZATION: Total amount of the various securities issued by a corporation. Capitalization may include bonds, debentures, preferred and common stock. Bonds and debentures are usually carried on the books of the issuing company in terms of their par or face value. Preferred and common shares may be carried in terms of par or stated value. Stated value may be an arbitrary figure decided upon by the directors or may represent the amount received by the company from the sale of the securities at the time of issuance. (See: *Par*)

CASH FLOW: Reported net income of a corporation *plus* amounts charged off for depreciation, depletion, amortization, extraordinary charges to reserves, which are bookkeeping deductions and not paid out in actual dollars and cents. A yardstick used in recent years because of the larger noncash deductions appearing to offer a better indication of the ability of a company to pay dividends and finance expansion from self-generated cash than the conventional reported net income figure. (See: *Amortization; Depletion; Depreciation*)

CASH SALE: A transaction on the floor of the Stock Exchange which calls for delivery of the securities the same day. In "regular way" trades, the seller is allowed four business days for delivery. (See: *Regular Way Delivery*)

CERTIFICATE: The actual piece of paper which is evidence of ownership of stock in a corporation. Watermarked paper is finely engraved with delicate etchings to discourage forgery. Loss of a certificate may at the least cause a great deal of inconvenience —at the worst, financial loss.

CLOSED-END INVESTMENT TRUST: (See: *Investment Trust*)

COLLATERAL: Securities or other property pledged by a borrower to secure repayment of a loan.

COLLATERAL TRUST BOND: A bond secured by collateral deposited with a trustee. The collateral is often the stocks or bonds of companies controlled by the issuing company but may be other securities.

COMMISSION: The broker's fee for purchasing or selling securities or property for a client. On the New York Stock Exchange the average commission is about 1% of the market value of the stocks involved in the transaction and approximately one-quarter of 1% on bonds.

COMMISSION BROKER: An agent who executes the public's orders for the purchase or sale of securities or commodities. (See: *Broker; Dealer*)

COMMON STOCK: Securities which represent an ownership interest in a corporation. If the company has also issued preferred stock, both common and preferred have ownership rights, but the preferred normally has prior claim on dividends and, in the event of liquidation, assets. Claims of both common and preferred stockholders are junior to claims of bondholders or other creditors of the company. Common stockholders assume the greater risk, but generally exercise the greater control and may gain the greater reward in the form of dividends and capital appreciation. The terms "common stock" and "capital stock" are often used interchangeably when the company has no preferred stock (See: *Capital Stock; Preferred Stock*)

CONSOLIDATED BALANCE SHEET: A balance sheet showing the financial condition of a corporation and its subsidiaries. (See: *Balance Sheet*)

CONVERTIBLE: A bond, debenture or preferred share which may be exchanged by the owner for common stock or another security, usually of the same company, in accordance with the terms of the issue.

CORNER: Buying of a stock or commodity on a scale large enough to give the buyer, or buying group, control over the price. A person who must buy that stock or commodity, for example one who is short, is forced to do business at an arbitrarily high price with those who engineered the corner. (See: *Short Position; Short Sale*)

CORRESPONDENT: A securities firm, bank or other financial organization which regularly performs services for another in a place or market to which the other does not have direct access. Securities firms may have correspondents in foreign countries or on exchanges of which they are not members. Correspondents are frequently linked by private wires. Member organizations with offices in New York City also act as correspondents for out-of-town member organizations which do not maintain New York City offices.

COUPON BOND: Bond with interest coupons attached. The coupons are clipped as they come due and are presented by the holder for payment of interest. (See: *Bearer Bond; Registered Bond*)

COVERING: Buying a security previously sold short. (See: *Short Sale; Short Covering*)

CUMULATIVE PREFERRED: A stock having a provision that if one or more dividends are omitted, the omitted dividends must be paid before dividends may be paid on the company's common stock.

CUMULATIVE VOTING: A method of voting for corporate directors which enables the shareholder to multiply the number of his shares by the number of directorships being voted on and cast the total for one director or a selected group of directors. A 10-share holder normally casts 10 votes for each of, say, 12 nominees to the board of directors. He thus has 120 votes. Under the cumulative voting principle he may do that or he may cast 120 (10 × 12) votes for only one nominee, 60 for two, 40 for three, or any other distribution he chooses. Cumulative voting is required under the corporate laws of some states, is permissive in most others.

CURB EXCHANGE: Former name of the American Stock Exchange, second largest Exchange in the country. The term comes from the market's origin on the streets of downtown New York.

CURRENT ASSETS: Those assets of a company which are reasonably expected to be realized in cash, or sold, or consumed during the normal operating cycle of the business. These include cash, U.S. government bonds, receivables and money due usually within one year, and inventories.

CURRENT LIABILITIES: Money owed and payable by a company, usually within one year.

CURRENT RETURN: (See: *Yield*)

CUSTOMERS' MAN: (See: *Registered Representative*)

CUSTOMERS' NET DEBIT BALANCES: Credit of New York Stock Exchange member firms made available to help finance customers' purchases of stocks, bonds and commodities.

DAY ORDER: An order to buy or sell which, if not executed, expires at the end of the trading day on which it was entered.

DEALER: An individual or firm in the securities business acting as a principal rather than as an agent. Typically, a dealer buys for his own account and sells to a customer from his own inventory. The dealer's profit or loss is the difference between the price he pays and the price he receives for the same security. The dealer's confirmation must disclose to his customer that he has acted as principal. The same individual or firm may function, at different times, either as broker or dealer. (See: *NASD; Specialist*)

DEBENTURE: A promissory note backed by the general credit of a company and usually not secured by a mortgage or lien on any specific property. (See: *Bond*)

DELIVERY: The certificate representing shares bought "regular way" on the New York Stock Exchange normally is delivered to the purchaser's broker on the fourth business day after the transaction. If a seller wants to delay delivery of the certificates, he may have his broker offer the stock "seller's option," instead of "regular way," and he may specify the number of days, from 5 up to 60, for delivery. A stock offered "seller's option" may command a lesser price than if offered "regular way." (See: *Bid and Asked; Cash Sale; Offer; Transfer*)

DEPLETION: Natural resources, such as metals, oils and gas, timber, which conceivably can be reduced to zero over the years, present a special problem in capital management. Depletion is an accounting practice consisting of charges against earnings based upon the amount of the asset taken out of the total reserves in the period for which accounting is made. A bookkeeping entry, it does not represent any cash outlay nor are any funds earmarked for the purpose.

DEPRECIATION: Normally, charges against earnings to write off the cost, less salvage value, of an asset over its estimated useful life. It is a bookkeeping entry and does not represent any cash outlay, nor are any funds earmarked for the purpose.

DIRECTOR: Person elected by shareholders at the annual meeting to establish company policies. The directors appoint the president, vice presidents, and all other operating officers. Directors decide, among other matters, if and when dividends shall be paid. (See: *Management; Proxy*)

DISCRETIONARY ACCOUNT: An account in which the customer gives the broker or someone else discretion, which may be complete or within specific limits, as to the purchase and sales of securities or commodities including selection, timing and price to be paid or received.

DISCRETIONARY ORDER: The customer empowers the broker to act on his behalf with respect to the choice of security to be bought or sold, a total amount of any securities to be bought or sold, and/or whether any such transaction shall be one of purchase or sale.

DISTRIBUTION: Selling of a large block of stock to a large group of investors. (See: *Exchange Distribution; Liquidation; Primary Distribution; Secondary Distribution; Special Offering*)

DIVERSIFICATION: Spreading investments among different companies in different fields. Another type of diversification is also offered by the securities of many individual companies because of the wide range of their activities. (See: *Investment Trust*)

DIVIDEND: The payment designated by the Board of Directors to be distributed pro rata among the shares outstanding. On preferred shares, it is generally a fixed amount. On common shares, the dividend varies with the fortunes of the company and the amount of cash on hand, and may be omitted if business is poor or the directors determine to withhold earnings to invest in plant and equipment. Sometimes a company will pay a dividend out of past earnings even if it is not currently operating at a profit.

DOLLAR COST AVERAGING: A system of buying securities at regular intervals with a fixed dollar amount. Under this system the investor buys by the dollars' worth rather than by the number of shares. If each investment is of the same number of dollars, payments buy more when the price is low and fewer when it rises. Thus temporary downswings in price benefit the investor if he continues periodic purchases in both good times and bad and the price at which the shares are sold is more than their average cost. (See: *Formula Investing*)

DO NOT REDUCE "DNR" ORDER: A limited order to buy, a stop order to sell or a stop limit order to sell which is not to be reduced by the amount of an ordinary cash dividend on the ex-dividend date. A do not reduce order applies only to ordinary cash dividends; it is reduced for other distributions such as a stock dividend or rights.

DOUBLE TAXATION: Short for "double taxation of dividends." The federal government taxes corporate profits once as corporate income; any part of the remaining profits distributed as dividends to stockholders is taxed again as income to the recipient stockholder.

DOW THEORY: A theory of market analysis based upon the performance of the Dow-Jones industrial and rail stock price averages. The theory says that the market is in a basic upward trend if one of these averages advances above a previous important high, accompanied or followed by a similar advance in the other. When the averages both dip below previous important lows, this is regarded as confirmation of a basic downward trend. The theory does not attempt to predict how long either trend will continue, although it is widely misinterpreted as a method of forecasting future action. Whatever the merits of the theory, it is sometimes a strong factor in the market because many people believe in the theory—or believe that a great many others do. (See: *Technical Position*)

DOWN TICK: (See: *Up Tick*)

EARNINGS REPORT: A statement—also called an income statement—issued by a company showing its earnings or losses over a given period. The earnings report lists the income earned, expenses and the net result. (See: *Balance Sheet*)

ECONOMETRICS: The branch of economics which expresses economic theory in mathematical terms and seeks to verify it by statistical methods. This discipline makes economic forecasts and suggests choices for economic policy by measuring the impact of one economic variable on another.

EQUIPMENT TRUST CERTIFICATE: A type of security, generally issued by a railroad, to pay for new equipment. Title to the equipment, such as a locomotive, is held by a trustee until the notes are paid off. An equipment trust certificate is usually secured by a first claim on the equipment.

EQUITY: The ownership interest of common and preferred stockholders in a company. Also refers to excess of value of securities over the debit balance in a margin account.

EXCHANGE ACQUISITION: A method of filling an order to buy a large block of stock on the floor of the Exchange. Under certain circumstances, a member-broker can facilitate the purchase of a block by soliciting orders to sell. All orders to sell the security are lumped together and crossed with the buy order in the regular auction market. The price to the buyer may be on a net basis or on a commission basis.

EXCHANGE DISTRIBUTION: A method of disposing of large blocks of stock on the floor of the Exchange. Under certain circumstances, a member-broker can facilitate the sale of a block of stock by soliciting and getting other member-brokers to solicit orders to buy. Individual buy orders are lumped together and crossed with the sell order in the regular auction market. A special commission is usually paid by the seller; ordinarily the buyer pays no commission.

EX-DIVIDEND: A synonym for "without dividend." The buyer of a stock selling ex-dividend does not receive the recently declared dividend. Open buy and sell stop orders, and sell stop limit orders in a stock on the ex-dividend date are ordinarily reduced by the value of that dividend. In the case of open stop limit orders to sell, both the stop price and the limit price are reduced. Every dividend is payable on a fixed date to all shareholders recorded on the books of the company as of a previous date of record. For example, a dividend may be declared as payable to holders of record on the books of the company on a given Friday. Since four business days are allowed for delivery of stock in a "regular way" transaction on the New York Stock Exchange, the Exchange would declare the stock "ex-dividend" as of the opening of the market on the preceding Tuesday. That means anyone who bought it on and after Tuesday would not be entitled to that dividend. (See: *Cash Sale; Delivery; Net Change; Transfer*)

EX-RIGHTS: Without the rights. Corporations raising additional money may do so by offering their stockholders the right to subscribe to new or additional stock, usually at a discount from the prevailing market price. The buyer of a stock selling ex-rights is not entitled to the rights. (See: *Ex-Dividend; Rights*)

EXTRA: The short form of "extra dividend." A dividend in the form of stock or cash in addition to the regular or usual dividend the company has been paying.

FACE VALUE: The value of a bond that appears on the face of the bond, unless the value is otherwise specified by the issuing company. Face value is ordinarily the amount the issuing company promises to pay at maturity. Face value is not an indication of market value. Sometimes referred to as par value.

FILL OR KILL: A market or limited-price order is to be executed in its entirety as soon as it is represented in the Trading Crowd. If not so executed, the order is treated as canceled. For purposes of this definition, a "stop" (See: *Stopped Stock*) is considered an execution.

FISCAL YEAR: A corporation's accounting year. Due to the nature of their particular business, some companies do not use the calendar year for their bookkeeping. A typical example is the department store which finds December 31 too early a date to close its books after the Christmas rush. For that reason many stores wind up their accounting year January 31. Their fiscal year, therefore, runs from February 1 of one year through January 31 of the next. The fiscal year of other companies may run from July 1 through the following June 30. Most companies, though, operate on a calendar-year basis.

FIXED CHARGES: A company's fixed expenses, such as bond interest, which it has agreed to pay whether or not earned, and which are deducted from income before earnings on equity capital are computed.

FLAT: This term means that the price at which a bond is traded includes consideration for all unpaid accruals of interest. Bonds which are in default of interest or principal are traded flat. Income bonds, which pay interest only to the extent earned, are usually traded flat. All other bonds are usually dealt in "and interest," which means that the buyer pays to the seller the market price plus interest accrued since the last payment date. When applied to a stock loan, flat means without premium or interest. (See: *Short Sale*)

FLOOR: The huge trading area—about two-thirds the size of a football field—where stocks and bonds are bought and sold on the New York Stock Exchange.

FLOOR BROKER: A member of the Stock Exchange who executes orders on the floor of the Exchange to buy or sell any listed securities. (See: *Commission Broker; Two-Dollar Broker*)

FLOOR TRADER: (See: *Registered Trader*)

FLUCTUATION: (See: *Point*)

FORMULA INVESTING: An investing technique. One formula calls for the shifting of funds from common shares to preferred shares or bonds as the market, on average, rises above a certain predetermined point—and the return of funds to common share investments as the market average declines. (See: *Dollar Cost Averaging*)

FREE AND OPEN MARKET: A market in which supply and demand are expressed in terms of price. Contrasts with a controlled market in which supply, demand and price may be regulated.

FUNDED DEBT: Usually interest-bearing bonds or debentures of a company. Could include long-term bank loans. Does *not* include short-term loans, preferred or common stock.

GENERAL MORTGAGE BOND: A bond which is secured by a blanket mortgage on the company's property, but which is often outranked by one or more other mortgages.

GILT-EDGED: High-grade bond issued by a company which has demonstrated its ability to earn a comfortable profit over a period of years and pay its bondholders their interest without interruption.

GIVE UP: A term with two different meanings. For one, a member of the Exchange on the floor may act for a second member by executing an order for him with a third member. The first member tells the third member that he is acting on behalf of the second member and gives the second member's name rather than his own. For another, if you have an account with Doe & Company but you're in a town where Doe has no office, you go to another member firm, tell them you have an account with Doe & Company and would like to buy some stock. After verifying your account with Doe & Company, the firm may execute your order and tell the broker who sells the stock that the firm is acting on behalf of Doe & Company.

They give up the name of Doe & Company to the selling broker. Or the firm may simply wire your order to Doe & Company who will execute it for you. In either case you pay only the regular commission.

GOOD DELIVERY: Certain basic qualifications must be met before a security sold on the Exchange may be delivered. The security must be in proper form to comply with the contract of sale and to transfer title by delivery to the purchaser.

GOOD TILL CANCELED ORDER (GTC) OR OPEN ORDER: An order to buy or sell which remans in effect until it is either executed or canceled.

GOVERNMENT BONDS: Obligations of the U.S. government, regarded as the highest-grade issues in existence.

GROWTH STOCK: Stock of a company with prospects for future growth—a company whose earnings are expected to increase at a relatively rapid rate.

GUARANTEED BOND: A bond which has interest or principal, or both, guaranteed by a company other than the issuer. Usually found in the railroad industry when large roads, leasing sections of trackage owned by small railroads, may guarantee the bonds of the smaller road.

GUARANTEED STOCK: Usually preferred stock on which dividends are guaranteed by another company, under much the same circumstances as a bond is guaranteed.

HEAD-AND-SHOULDERS: A term used in technical analysis to describe a chart pattern that signals a reverse of a trend. A head-and-shoulders top (so-called because of some resemblance to a human head and shoulders) portrays three successive rallies and reactions, with the second rally reaching a higher point than either of the others. Failure of the third rally to reach the peak of the second is interpreted as a signal that a major uptrend may have come to an end. In a head-and-shoulders *bottom,* the pattern is the exact reverse of that just described, and it suggests that a reversal of an existing downtrend is about to take place.

HEDGE: (See: *Arbitrage; Puts and Calls; Selling Against the Box; Short Sale*)

HEDGE FUND: A mutual fund or private partnership which has the contractual right to sell short as well as buy long—i.e., to hedge its market position. Most hedge funds employ a variety of speculative techniques designed to maximize possible capital gains. Among these are the use of borrowed funds to provide leverage and the use of Put and Call options.

HOLDING COMPANY: A corporation which owns the securities of another, in most cases with voting control.

HYPOTHECATION: The pledging of securities as collateral for a loan.

IMMEDIATE OR CANCEL ORDER: A market or limited-price order which is to be executed in whole or in part as soon as it is represented in the Trading Crowd, and the portion not so executed is to be treated as canceled. For the purpose of this definition, a "stop" is considered an execution. (See: *Stopped Stock*)

INACTIVE POST: A trading post on the floor of the New York Stock Exchange where inactive securities are traded in units of 10 shares instead of the usual 100-share lots. Better known in the business as Post 30. (See: *Round Lot*)

INACTIVE STOCK: An issue traded on an exchange or in the over-the-counter market in which there is a relatively low volume of transactions. Volume may be no more than few hundred shares a week or even less. On the New York Stock Exchange many inactive stocks are traded in 10-share units rather than the customary 100. (See: *Round Lot*)

IN-AND-OUT: Purchase and sale of the same security within a short period—a day, week, even a month. An in-and-out trader is generally more interested in day-to-day price fluctuations than dividends or long-term growth.

INCOME BOND: Generally income bonds promise to repay principal but to pay interest only when earned. In some cases unpaid interest on an income bond may accumulate as a claim against the corporation when the bond becomes due. An income bond may also be issued in lieu of preferred stock.

INDENTURE: A written agreement under which debentures are issued, setting forth maturity date, interest rate, security and other terms.

INDEX: A statistical yardstick expressed in terms of percentages of a base year or years. For instance, the Federal Reserve Board's index of industrial production is based on 1957–59 as 100. In September, 1965, the index stood at 142.8, which meant that industrial production that month was 42.8 per cent higher than in the base period. An index is not an average. (See: *Averages; NYSE Common Stock Index*)

INTEREST: Payments a borrower pays a lender for the use of his money. A corporation pays interest on its bonds to its bondholders. (See: *Bond; Dividend*)

INVESTMENT: The use of money for the purpose of making more money, to gain income or increase capital, or both. Safety of principal is an important consideration. (See: *Speculation*)

INVESTMENT BANKER: Also known as an underwriter. He is the middleman between the corporation issuing new securities and the public. The usual practice is for one or more investment bankers to buy outright from a corporation a new issue of stocks or bonds. The group forms a syndicate to sell the securities to individuals and institutions. Investment bankers also distribute very large blocks of stocks or bonds—perhaps held by an estate. Thereafter the market in the security may be over-the-counter, on a regional stock exchange, the American Exchange or the New York Stock Exchange. (See: *Over-the-Counter; Primary Distribution; Syndicate*)

INVESTMENT COUNSEL: One whose principal business consists of acting as investment adviser and a substantial part of his business consists of rendering investment supervisory services.

INVESTMENT TRUST: A company which uses its capital to invest in other companies. There are two principal types: the closed-end and the open-end, or mutual fund. Shares in closed-end investment trusts, some of which are listed on the New York Stock Exchange, are readily transferable in the open market and are bought and sold like other shares. Capitalization of these companies remains the same unless action is taken to change, which is seldom. Open-end funds sell their own new shares to investors, stand ready to buy back their old shares and are not listed. Open-end funds are so-called because their capitalization is not fixed; they issue more shares as people want them.

INVESTOR: An individual whose principal concerns in the purchase of a security are regular dividend income, safety of the original investment, and, if possible, capital appreciation. (See: *Speculator*)

ISSUE: Any of a company's securities, or the act of distributing such securities.

LEGAL-LIST: A list of investments selected by various states in which certain institutions and fiduciaries, such as insurance companies and banks, may invest. Legal lists are restricted to high quality securities meeting certain specifications. (See: *Prudent-Man Rule*)

LEVERAGE: The effect on the per-share earnings of the common stock of a company when large sums must be paid for bond interest or preferred stock dividends, or both, before the common stock is entitled to share in earnings. Leverage may be advantageous for the common when earnings are good but may work against the common stock when earnings decline. Example: Company A has one million shares of common stock outstanding, no other securities. Earnings drop from $1 million to $800,000 or from $1 to 80 cents a share, a decline of 20 per cent. Company B also has one million shares of common but must pay $500,000 annually in bond interest. If earnings amount to $1 million, there is $500,000 available for the common or 50 cents a share. But earnings drop to $800,000 so there is only $300,000 available for the common, or 30 cents a share—a drop of 40%. Or suppose earnings of the company with only common stock increased from $1 million to $1.5 million—earnings per share would go from $1 to $1.50, or an increase of 50%. But if earnings of the company which had to pay $500,000 in bond interest increased that much—earnings per common share would jump from 50 cents to $1 a share, or 100%. When a company has common stock only, no leverage exists because all earnings are available for the common, although relatively large fixed charges payable for lease of substantial plant assets may have an effect similar to that of a bond issue.

LIABILITIES: All the claims against a corporation. Liabilities include accounts and wages and salaries payable, dividends declared payable, accrued taxes payable, fixed or long-term liabilities such as mortgage bonds, debentures and bank loans. (See: *Assets; Balance Sheet*)

LIEN: A claim against property which has been pledged or mortgaged to secure the performance of an obligation. A bond is usually secured by a lien against specified property of a company. (See: *Bond*)

LIMIT, LIMITED ORDER OR LIMITED-PRICED ORDER: An order to buy or sell a stated amount of a security at a specified price, or at a better price, if obtainable after the order is represented in the Trading Crowd.

LIQUIDATION: The process of converting securities or other property into cash. The dissolution of a company, with cash remaining after sale of its assets and payment of all indebtedness being distributed to the shareholders.

LIQUIDITY: The ability of the market in a particular security to absorb a reasonable amount of buying or selling at reasonable price changes. Liquidity is one of the most important characteristics of a good market.

LISTED STOCK: The company which is traded on a securities exchange, and for which a listing application and a registration statement, giving detailed information about the company and its operations, have been filed with the Securities and Exchange Commission, unless otherwise exempted, and the exchange itself. The various stock exchanges have different standards for listing. Some of the guides used by the New York Stock Exchange for an original listing are national interest in the company, a minimum of one million shares outstanding with at least 700,000 shares publicly held among not less than 2,000 shareholders including at least 1,700 round-lot stockholders. The publicly held common shares should have a minimum aggregate market value of $12 million. Normally the company should have earning power of over $2 million annually before taxes and of over $1.2 million after all charges and taxes.

LOAD: The portion of the offering price of shares of open-end investment companies which covers sales commissions and all other costs of distribution. The load is incurred only on purchase, there being, in most cases, no charge when the shares are sold (redeemed).

LOCKED IN: An investor is said to be locked in when he has a profit on a security he owns but does not sell because his profit would immediately become subject to the capital gains tax. (See: *Capital Gain*)

LONG: Signifies ownership of securities. "I am long 100 U.S. Steel" means the speaker owns 100 shares. (See: *Short Position; Short Sale*)

MANAGEMENT: The Board of Directors, elected by the stockholders, and the officers of the corporation, appointed by the Board of Directors.

MANIPULATION: An illegal operation. Buying or selling a security for the purpose of creating false or misleading appearance of active trading or for the purpose of raising or depressing the price to induce purchase or sale by others.

MARGIN: The amount paid by the customer when he uses his broker's credit to buy a security. Under Federal Reserve regulations, the initial margin required in the past 20 years has ranged from 40% of the purchase price all the way to 100%. (See: *Broker's Loan; Equity; Margin Account; Margin Call*)

MARGIN ACCOUNT: An account which permits the customer to use a broker's credit, to the degree allowed by the prevailing margin requirements, to purchase securities. To open a margin account the customer must sign a margin agreement which authorizes his broker to lend to himself or to other brokers any securities carried in the account. (See: *Margin*)

MARGIN CALL: A demand upon a customer to put up money or securities with the broker. The call is made when a purchase is made; also if a customer's equity in a margin account declines below a minimum standard set by the Exchange or by the firm. (See *Margin*)

MARKET ORDER: An order to buy or sell a stated amount of a security at the most advantageous price obtainable after the order is represented in the Trading Crowd. (See: *Good Till Canceled Order; Limited Order; Stop Order*)

MARKET PRICE: In the case of a security, market price is usually considered the last reported price at which the stock or bond sold.

MATCHED AND LOST: When two bids to buy the same stock are made on the trading floor simultaneously, and each bid is equal to or larger than the amount of stock offered, both bids are considered to be on an equal basis. So the two bidders flip a coin to decide who buys the stock. Also applies to offers to sell.

MATURITY: The date on which a loan or a bond or debenture comes due and is to be paid off.

MEMBER CORPORATION: A securities brokerage firm, organized as a corporation, with at least one member of the New York Stock Exchange who is a director and a holder of voting stock in the corporation. (See: *Member Firm*)

MEMBER FIRM: A securities brokerage firm organized as a partnership and having at least one general partner who is a member of the New York Stock Exchange. (See: *Member Corporation*)

MEMBER ORGANIZATION: This term includes New York Stock Exchange member firm *and* member corporation. The term "participant" when used with reference to a member organization includes general and limited partners of a member firm and holders of voting and nonvoting stock in a member corporation. (See: *Member Corporation; Member Firm*)

MIP: Monthly Investment Plan. A pay-as-you-go method of buying New York Stock Exchange listed shares on a regular payment plan for as little as $40 a month, or $40 every three months. Under MIP the investor buys stock by the dollars' worth—if the price advances, he gets fewer shares and if it declines, he gets more shares. He may discontinue purchases at any time without penalty. The commission ranges from 6% on small transactions to slightly below 1½% on larger transactions. (See: *Dollar Cost Averaging; Odd-Lot Dealer*)

MORTGAGE BOND: A bond secured by a mortgage on a property. The value of the property may or may not equal the value of the so-called mortgage bonds issued against it. (See: *Bond; Debenture*)

MUNICIPAL BOND: A bond issued by a state or a political subdivision, such as county, city, town or village. The term also designates bonds issued by state agencies and authorities. In general, interest paid on municipal bonds is exempt from federal income taxes.

MUTUAL FUND: (See *Investment Trust*)

NASD: The National Association of Securities Dealers, Inc. An association of brokers and dealers in the over-the-counter securities business. The Association has the power to expel members who have been determined guilty of unethical practices. NASD is dedicated to—among other objectives—"adopt, administer and enforce rules of fair practice and rules to prevent fraudulent and manipulative acts and practices, and in general to promote just and equitable principles of trade for the protection of investors."

NEGOTIABLE: Refers to a security, title to which is transferable by delivery. (See: *Delivery; Good Delivery*)

NET ASSET VALUE: A term usually used in connection with investment trust, meaning net asset value per share. It is common practice for an investment trust to compute its assets daily, or even twice daily, by totaling the market value of all securities owned. All liabilities are deducted, and the balance divided by the number of shares outstanding. The resulting figure is the net asset value per share. (See: *Assets; Investment Trust*)

NET CHANGE: The change in the price of a security from the closing price on one day and the closing price on the following day on which the stock is traded. In the case of a stock which is entitled to a dividend one day, but is traded "ex-dividend" the next, the dividend is considered in computing the change. For example, if the closing market price of a stock on Monday— the last day it was entitled to receive a 50-cent dividend—was $45 a share, and $44.50 at the close of the next day, when it was "ex-dividend," the price would be considered unchanged. The same applies to a split-up of shares. A stock selling at $100 the day before a 2-for-1 split and trading the next day at $50 would be considered unchanged. If it sold at $51, it would be considered up $1. The net change is ordinarily the last figure in a stock price list. The mark $+1\frac{1}{8}$ means up $1.125 a share from the last sale on the previous day the stock traded. (See: *Ex-Dividend; Point; Split*)

NEW ISSUE: A stock or bond sold by a corporation for the first time. Proceeds may be issued to retire outstanding securities of the company, for new plant or equipment or for additional working capital.

NONCUMULATIVE: A preferred stock on which unpaid dividends do not accrue. Omitted dividends are, as a rule, gone forever. (See: *Cumulative Preferred*)

"NOT HELD" ORDER: A market or limited-price order marked "not held," "disregard tape," "take time," or which bears any such qualifying notation. An order marked "or better" is not a "not held" order.

NYSE COMMON STOCK INDEX: A composite index covering price movements of all common stocks listed on the "Big Board." It is based on the close of the market December 31, 1965, as 50.00 and is weighted according to the number of shares listed for each issue. The index is computed continuously by the Exchange's Market Data System and printed on the ticker tape each half hour. Point changes in the index are converted to dollars and cents so as to provide a meaningful measure of changes in the average price of listed stocks. The composite index is supplemented by separate indexes for four industry groups: industrials, transportation, utilities and finances. (See: *Averages*)

ODD LOT: An amount of stock less than the established 100-share unit or 10-share unit of trading: from 1 to 99 shares for the great majority of issues, 1 to 9 for so-called inactive stocks. (See: *Round Lot; Inactive Stock*)

ODD-LOT DEALER: A member firm of the Exchange which buys and sells odd lots of stock—1 to 9 shares in the case of stocks traded in 10-share units and 1 to 99 shares for 100-share units. The odd-lot dealer's customers are commission brokers acting on behalf of their customers. There are one or more odd-lot dealers ready to buy or sell, for their own accounts, odd lots in any stock at any time. There are at least four representatives of odd-lot dealers at each of the 18 active trading posts on the floor of the New York Stock Exchange. Odd-lot prices are geared to the auction market. On an odd-lot market order, the odd-lot dealer's price is based on the first round-lot transaction which occurs on the floor following receipt at the trading post of the odd-lot order. The usual differential between the odd-lot price and the "effective" round-lot price is 12½ cents a share for stock selling below $55, 25 cents a share for stock at $55 or more. For example: You decide to buy 20 shares of ABC common at the market. Your order is transmitted by your commission broker to the representative of an odd-lot dealer at the post where ABC is traded. A few minutes later there is a 100-share transaction in ABC at $10 a share. The odd-lot price at which your order is immediately filled by the odd-lot dealer is $10.125 a share. If you had sold 20 shares of ABC, you would have received $9.875 a share. (See: *Commission Broker; Dealer; Inactive Stock; Round Lot; Transfer Tax*)

OFF-BOARD: This term may refer to transactions over-the-counter in unlisted securities, or, in a special situation, to a transaction involving listed shares which was not executed on a national securities exchange. (See: *Over-the-Counter; Secondary Distribution*)

OFFER: The price at which a person is ready to sell. Opposed to bid, the price at which one is ready to buy. (See: *Bid and Asked*)

OPEN-END INVESTMENT TRUST: (See: *Investment Trust*)

OPEN ORDER: (See: *Good Till Canceled Order*)

OPTION: A right to buy or sell specific securities or properties at a specified price within a specified time. (See: *Puts and Calls*)

ORDERS GOOD UNTIL A SPECIFIED TIME: A market or limited-price order which is to be represented in the Trading Crowd until a specified time, after which such order or the portion thereof not executed is to be treated as canceled.

OVERBOUGHT: An opinion as to price levels. May refer to a security which has had a sharp rise or to the market as a whole after a period of vigorous buying which, it may be argued, has left prices "too high." (See: *Technical Position*)

OVERSOLD: An opinion—the reverse of overbought. A single security or a market which, it is believed, has declined to an unreasonable level. (See: *Technical Position*)

OVER-THE-COUNTER: A market for securities made up of securities dealers who may or may not be members of a securities exchange. Over-the-counter is mainly a market made over the telephone. Thousands of companies have insufficient shares outstanding, stockholders or earnings to warrant application for listing on a stock exchange. Securities of these companies are traded in the over-the-counter market between dealers who act either as principals or as brokers for customers. The over-the-counter market is the principal market for U.S. government bonds and municipals. (See: *NASD; Off-Board*)

PAPER PROFIT: An unrealized profit on a security still held. Paper profits become realized profits only when the security is sold.

PAR: In the case of a common share, par means a dollar amount assigned to the share by the company's charter. Par value may also be used to compute the dollar amount of the common shares on the balance sheet. Par value has little significance so far as market value of common stock is concerned. Many companies today issue no-par stock but give a stated per-share value on the balance sheet. Par at one time was supposed to represent the value of the original investment behind each share in cash, goods or services. In the case of preferred shares and bonds, however, par is important. It often signifies the dollar value upon which dividends on preferred stocks, and interest on bonds, are figured. The issuer of a 3% bond promises to pay that percentage of the bond's par value annually. (See: *Capitalization; Transfer Tax*)

PARTICIPATING PREFERRED: A preferred stock which is entitled to its stated dividend and, also, to additional dividends on a specified basis upon payment of dividends on the common stock.

PASSED DIVIDEND: Omission of a regular or scheduled dividend.

PENNY STOCKS: Low-priced issues often highly speculative, selling at less than $1 a share. Frequently used as a term of disparagement, although a few penny stocks have developed into investment-caliber issues.

PERCENTAGE ORDER: A market or limited-price order to buy (or sell) a stated amount of a specified stock after a fixed number of shares of such stock have traded.

POINT: In the case of shares of stock, a point means $1. If General Motors shares rise 3 points, each share has risen $3. In the case of bonds a point means $10, since a bond is quoted as a percentage of $1,000. A bond which rises 3 points gains 3% of $1,000, or $30 in value. An advance from 87 to 90 would mean an advance in dollar value from $870 to $900 for each $1,000 bond. In the case of market averages, the word point means merely that and no more. If, for example, the Dow-Jones Industrial Average rises from 470.25 to 471.25, it has risen a point. A point in the averages, however, is not equivalent to $1. (See: *Averages*)

PORTFOLIO: Holdings of securities by an individual or institution. A portfolio may contain bonds, preferred stocks and common stocks of various types of enterprises.

PREFERRED STOCK: A class of stock with a claim on the company's earnings before payment may be made on the common stock and usually entitled to priority over common stock if company liquidates. Usually entitled to dividends at a specified rate—when declared by the Board of Directors and before payment of a dividend on the common stock—depending upon the terms of the issue. (See: *Cumulative Preferred; Participating Preferred*)

PREMIUM: The amount by which a preferred stock or bond may sell above its par value. In the case of a new issue of bonds or stocks, premium is the amount the market price rises over the original selling price. Also refers to a charge sometimes made when a stock is borrowed to make delivery on a short sale. May refer, also, to redemption price of a bond or preferred stock if it is higher than face value. (See: *Corner; Short Sale*)

PRICE/EARNINGS RATIO: The current market price of a share of stock divided by earnings per share for a 12-month period. For example, a stock selling for $100 a share and earning $5 a share is said to be selling at a price/earnings ratio of 20 to 1.

PRIMARY DISTRIBUTION: Also called primary offering. The original sale of a company's securities. (See: *Investment Banker; Secondary Distribution*)

PRINCIPAL: The person for whom a broker executes an order, or a dealer buying or selling for his own account. The term "principal" may also refer to a person's capital or to the face amount of a bond.

PRIOR PREFERRED. A preferred stock which usually takes precedence over other preferreds issued by the same company.

PROFIT TAKING: Selling to take a profit, the process of converting paper profits into cash.

PROSPECTUS: A circular which describes securities being offered for sale to the public. Required by the Securities Act of 1933.

PROXY: Written authorization given by a shareholder to someone else to represent him and vote his shares at a shareholders' meeting.

PROXY STATEMENT: Information required by SEC to be given stockholders as a prerequisite to solicitation of proxies for a security. Subject to the requirements of the Securities Exchange Act.

PRUDENT-MAN RULE: An investment standard. In some states, the law requires that a fiduciary, such as a trustee, may invest the fund's money only in a list of securities designated by the state—the so-called legal list. In other states, the trustee may invest in a security if it is one which a prudent man of discretion and intelligence, who is seeking a reasonable income and preservation of capital, would buy.

PUTS AND CALLS: Options which give the right to buy or sell a fixed amount of a certain stock at a specified price within a specified time. A Put gives the holder the right to sell the stock; a Call the right to buy the stock. Puts are purchased by those who think a stock may go down. A Put obligates the seller of the contract to take delivery of the stock and pay the specified price to the owner of the option within the time limit of the contract. The price specified in a Put or Call is usually close to the market price of the stock at the time the contract is made. Calls are purchased by those who think a stock may rise. A Call gives the holder the right to buy the stock from the seller of the contract at the specified price within a fixed period of time. Put and Call contracts are written for 30, 60 or 90 days, or longer. If the purchaser of a Put or Call does not wish to exercise the option, the price he paid for the option becomes a loss.

QUOTATION: Often shortened to "quote." The highest bid to buy and the lowest offer to sell a security in a given market at a given time. If you ask your broker for a "quote" on a stock, he may come back with something like "45¼ to 45½." This means that $45.25 is the highest price any buyer wanted to pay at the time the quote was given on the floor of the Exchange and that $45.50 was the lowest price which any seller would take at the same time. (See: *Bid and Asked*)

RALLY: A brisk rise following a decline in the general price level of the market, or in an individual stock.

REALIZING: (See: *Profit Taking*)

RECORD DATE: The date on which you must be registered on the books of a company as a shareholder in order to receive a declared dividend or, among other things, to vote on company affairs. (See: *Delivery; Ex-Dividend; Transfer*)

REDEMPTION PRICE: The price at which a bond may be redeemed before maturity, at the option of the issuing company. Redemption value also applies to the price the company must pay to call in certain types of preferred stock. (See: *Callable*)

REFINANCING: Same as refunding. New securities are sold by a company and the money is used to retire existing securities. Object may be to save interest costs, extend the maturity of the loan, or both.

REGISTERED BOND: A bond which is registered on the books of the issuing company in the name of the owner. It can be transferred only when endorsed by the registered owner. (See: *Bearer Bond; Coupon Bond*)

REGISTERED REPRESENTATIVE: Present name for the older term "customers' man." In a New York Stock Exchange member firm, a Registered Representative is a full-time employee who has met the requirements of the Exchange as to background and knowledge of the securities business. Also known as an Account Executive or Customer's Broker.

REGISTERED TRADER: A member of the Exchange who trades in stocks on the Floor for an account in which he has an interest.

REGISTRAR: Usually a trust company or bank charged with the responsibility of preventing the issuance of more stock than authorized by a company. (See: *Transfer*)

REGISTRATION: Before a public offering may be made of new securities by a company, or of outstanding securities by controlling stockholders—through the mails or in interstate commerce—the securities must be registered under the Securities Act of 1933. Registration statement is filed with the SEC by the issuer. It must disclose pertinent information relating to the company's operations, securities, management and purpose of the public offering. Securities of railroads under jurisdiction of the Interstate Commerce Commission, and certain other types of securities, are exempted. On security offerings involving less than $300,000, less information is required.

Before a security may be admitted to dealings on a national securities exchange, it must be registered under the Securities Exchange Act of 1934. The application for registration must be filed with the exchange and the SEC by the company issuing the securities. The application must disclose pertinent information relating to the company's operations, securities and management. Registration may become effective 30 days after receipt by the SEC of the certification by the exchange of approval of listing and registration, or sooner by special order of the Commission.

REGULAR WAY DELIVERY: Unless otherwise specified, securities (other than governments) sold on the New York Stock Exchange are to be delivered to the buying broker by the selling broker and payment made to the selling broker by the buying broker on the fourth business day after the transaction. Regular way delivery for government bonds is the following business day. (See: *Delivery; Transfer*)

REGULATION T: The federal regulation governing the amount of credit which may be advanced by brokers and dealers to customers for the purchase of securities. (See: *Margin*)

REGULATION U: The federal regulation governing the amount of credit which may be advanced by a bank to its customers for the purchase of listed stocks. (See: *Margin*)

RETURN: (See: *Yield*)

RIGHTS: When a company wants to raise more funds by issuing additional securities, it may give its stockholders the opportunity, ahead of others, to buy the new securities in proportion to the number of shares each owns. The piece of paper evidencing this privilege is called a right. Because the additional stock is usually offered to stockholders below the current market price, rights ordinarily have a market value of their own and are actively traded. In most cases they must be exercised within a relatively short period. Failure to exercise or sell rights may result in actual loss to the holder. (See: *Warrant*)

ROUND LOT: A unit of trading or a multiple thereof. On the New York Stock Exchange the unit of trading is generally 100 shares in stocks and $1,000 par value in the case of bonds. In some inactive stocks, the unit of trading is 10 shares.

SCALE ORDER: An order to buy (or sell) a security which specifies the total amount to be bought (or sold) and the amount to be bought (or sold) at specified price variations.

SCRIP: A certificate exchangeable for stock or cash before a specified date, after which it may have no value. Usually issued for fractions of shares in connection with a stock dividend or split or in reorganization of a company. For example, a stock dividend might amount to only ⅓ share so scrip is issued instead of a stock certificate for ⅓ share. Not traded on New York Stock Exchange. (See: *Stock Dividend*)

SEAT: A traditional figure of speech for a membership on a securities or commodity exchange. Price and admission requirements vary.

SEC: The Securities and Exchange Commission, established by Congress to help protect investors. The SEC administers the Securities Act of 1933, the Securities Exchange Act of 1934, the Trust Indenture Act, the Investment Company Act, the Investment Advisers Act, and the Public Utility Holding Company Act.

SECONDARY DISTRIBUTION: Also known as a secondary offering. The redistribution of a block of stock some time after it has been sold by the issuing company. The sale is handled off the New York Stock Exchange by a securities firm or group of firms and the shares are usually offered at a fixed price which is related to the current market price of the stock. Usually the block is a large one, such as might be involved in the settlement of an estate. The security may be listed or unlisted. (See: *Exchange Distribution; Investment Banker; Primary Distribution; Special Offering; Syndicate*)

SELLER'S OPTION: A special transaction on the Stock Exchange which gives the seller the right to deliver the stock or bond at any time within a specified period, ranging from not less than five business days to not more than 60 days. (See: *Delivery*)

SELLING AGAINST THE BOX: A method of protecting a paper profit. Let's say you own 100 shares of XYZ which has advanced in price, and you think the price may decline. So you sell 100 shares short, borrowing 100 shares to make delivery. You retain in your security box the 100 shares which you own. If XYZ declines, the profit on your short sale is exactly offset by the loss in the market value of the stock you own. If XYZ advances, the loss on your short sale is exactly offset by the profit in the market value of the stock you have retained. You can close out your short sale by buying 100 shares to return to the person from whom you borrowed, or you can send them the 100 shares which you own. (See: *Hedge; Short Sale*)

SERIAL BOND: An issue which matures in relatively small amounts at periodic stated intervals.

SHORT COVERING: Buying stock to return stock previously borrowed to make delivery on a short sale.

SHORT POSITION: Stocks sold short and not covered as of a particular date. On the New York Stock Exchange, a tabulation is issued a few days after the middle of the month listing all issues on the Exchange in which there was a short position of 5,000 or more shares, and issues in which the short position had changed by 2,000 or more shares in the preceding month. This tabulation is based on reports of positions on member firms' books. Short position also means the total amount of stock an individual has sold short and has not covered, as of a particular date. Initial margin requirements for a short position are the same as for a long position. (See: *Margin; Up Tick; Short Sale*)

SHORT SALE: A person who believes a stock will decline and sells it though he does not own any has made a short sale. For instance: You instruct your broker to sell short 100 shares of ABC. Your broker borrows the stock so he can deliver the 100 shares to the buyer. The money value of the shares borrowed is deposited by your broker with the lender. Sooner or later you must cover your short sale by buying the same amount of stock your borrowed for return to the lender. If you are able to buy ABC at a lower price than you sold it for, your profit is the difference between the two prices—not counting commissions and taxes. But if you have to pay more for the stock than the price you received, that is the amount of your loss. Stock exchange and federal regulations govern and limit the conditions under which a short sale may be made on a national securities exchange. (See: *Margin; Premium; Up Tick*)

SINKING FUND: Money regularly set aside by a company to redeem its bonds, debentures or preferred stock from time to time as specified in the indenture or charter.

SPECIAL BID: A method of filling an order to buy a large block of stock on the floor of the New York Stock Exchange. In a special bid, the bidder for the block of stock—a pension fund, for instance—will pay a special commission to the broker who represents him in making the purchase. The seller does not pay a commission. The special bid is made on the floor of the Exchange at a fixed price which may not be below the last sale of the security or the current bid in the regular market, whichever is higher. Member firms may sell this stock for customers directly to the buyer's broker during trading hours.

SPECIAL OFFERING: Occasionally a large block of stock becomes available for sale which, due to its size and the market in that particular issue, calls for special handling. A notice is printed on the ticker tape announcing that the stock will be offered for sale on the floor of the Exchange at a fixed price. Member firms may buy this stock for customers directly from the seller's broker during trading hours. The price is usually based on the last transaction in the regular auction market. If there are more buyers than stock, allotments are made. Only the seller pays a commission on a special offering. (See: *Secondary Distribution*)

SPECIALIST: A member of the New York Stock Exchange who has two functions: First, to maintain an orderly market, insofar as reasonably practicable, in the stocks in which he is registered as a specialist. In order to maintain an orderly market, the Exchange expects the specialist to buy or sell for his own account, to a reasonable degree, when there is a temporary disparity between supply and demand. Second, the specialist acts as a broker's broker. When a commission broker on the Exchange floor receives a limit order, say, to buy at $50 a stock then selling at $60, he cannot wait at the particular post where the stock is traded until the price reaches the specified level. So he leaves the order with the specialist, who will try to execute it in the market if and when the stock declines to the specified price. At all times the specialist must put his customers' interests above his own. There are about 350 specialists on the New York Stock Exchange. (See: *Book; Limited Order*)

SPECIALIST BLOCK PURCHASE: Purchase by the specialist for his own account of a large block of stock outside the regular market on the Exchange. Such purchases may be made only when the sale of the block could not be made in the regular market within a reasonable time and at reasonable prices, and when the purchase by the specialist would aid him in maintaining a fair and orderly market. The specialist need not fill the orders on his book down to the purchase price.

SPECIALIST BLOCK SALE: Opposite of the specialist block purchase. Under exceptional circumstances, the specialist may sell a block of stock outside the regular market on the Exchange for his own account at a price above the prevailing market. The price is negotiated between the specialist and the broker for the buyer. The specialist need not fill the orders on his book down to the purchase price.

SPECULATION: The employment of funds by a speculator. Safety of principal is a secondary factor. (See: *Investment*)

SPECULATOR: One who is willing to assume a relatively large risk in the hope of gain. His principal concern is to increase his capital rather than his dividend income. The speculator may buy and sell the same day or speculate in an enterprise which he does not expect to be profitable for years. (See: *Investor*)

SPLIT: The division of the outstanding shares of a corporation into a larger number of shares. A 3-for-1 split by a company with one million shares outstanding would result in three million shares outstanding. Each holder of 100 shares before the 3-for-1 split would have 300 shares, although his proportionate equity in the company would remain the same, since 100 parts of one million are the equivalent of 300 parts of three million. Ordinarily splits must be voted by directors and approved by shareholders. (See: *Stock Dividend*)

STOCK AHEAD: Sometimes an investor who has entered an order to buy or sell a stock at a certain price will see transactions at that price reported on the ticker tape while his own order has not been executed. The reason is that other buy and sell orders at the same price came in to the specialist ahead of his and had priority. (See: *Book; Specialist*)

STOCK CLEARING CORPORATION: A subsidiary of the New York Stock Exchange which acts as a central agency for security deliveries and money payments between member firms of the Exchange.

STOCK DIVIDEND: A dividend paid in securities rather than cash. The dividend may be additional shares of the issuing company, or in shares of another company (usually a subsidiary) held by the company. (See: *Ex-Dividend; Split*)

STOCKHOLDER OF RECORD: A stockholder whose name is registered on the books of the issuing corporation. (See: *Record Date; Ex-Dividend; Ex-Rights*)

STOP LIMIT ORDER: A stop limit order to buy becomes a limit order executable at the limit price, or at a better price, if obtainable, when a transaction in the security occurs at or above the stop price after the order is represented in the Trading Crowd. A stop limit order to sell becomes a limit order executable at the limit price or at a better price, if obtainable, when a transaction in the security occurs at or below the stop price after the order is represented in the Trading Crowd.

STOP ORDER: A stop order to buy becomes a market order when a transaction in the security occurs at or above the stop price after the order is represented in the Trading Crowd. A stop order to sell becomes a market order when a transaction in the security occurs at or below the stop price after the order is represented in the Trading Crowd. A stop order may be used in an effort to protect a paper profit, or to try to limit a possible loss to a certain amount. Since it becomes a market order when the stop price is reached, there is no certainty that it will be executed at that price. (See: *Limited Order; Market Order*)

STOPPED STOCK: A service performed—in most cases by the specialist—for an order given him by a commission broker. Let's say XYZ just sold at $50 a share. Broker A comes along with an order to buy 100 shares at the market. The lowest offer is $50.50. Broker A believes he can do better for his client than $50.50, perhaps might get the stock at $50.25. But he doesn't want to take a chance that he'll miss the market—that is, the next sale might be $50.50 and the following one even higher. So he asks the specialist if he will stop 100 at ½ ($50.50). The specialist agrees. The specialist guarantees Broker A he will get 100 shares at 50½ if the stock sells at that price. In the meantime, if the specialist or Broker A succeeds in executing the order at $50.25, the stop is called off. (See: *Specialist*)

STREET: The New York financial community concentrated in the Wall Street area.

STREET NAME: Securities held in the name of a broker instead of his customer's name are said to be carried in a "street name." This occurs when the securities have been bought on margin or when the customer wishes the security to be held by the broker.

SWITCH ORDER—CONTINGENT ORDER: An order for the purchase (sale) of one stock and the sale (purchase) of another stock at a stipulated price difference.

SWITCHING: Selling one security and buying another.

SYNDICATE: A group of investment bankers who together underwrite and distribute a new issue of securities or a large block of an outstanding issue. (See: *Investment Banker*)

TAX-EXEMPT BONDS: The securities of states, cities and other public authorities specified under federal law, the interest on which is either wholly or partly exempt from federal income taxes.

TECHNICAL POSITION: A term applied to the various internal factors affecting the market; opposed to external forces such as earnings, dividends, political considerations and general economic conditions. Some internal factors considered in appraising the market's technical position include the size of the short interest, whether the market has had a sustained advance or decline without interruption, a sharp advance or decline on small volume and the amount of credit in use in the market. (See: *Overbought; Oversold*)

THIN MARKET: A market in which there are comparatively few bids to buy or offers to sell or both. The phrase may apply to a single security or to the entire stock market. In a thin market, price fluctuations between transactions are usually larger than when the market is liquid. A thin market in a particular stock may reflect lack of interest in that issue or a limited supply of or demand for stock in the market. (See: *Bid and Asked; Liquidity; Offer*)

TICKER: The instrument which prints prices and volume of security transactions in cities and towns throughout the United States within minutes after each trade on the floor.

TIME ORDER: An order which becomes a market or limited-price order at a specified time.

TIPS: Supposedly "inside" information on corporation affairs.

TOPPING OUT: This term can be applied to the general market, to a group of stocks or to an individual issue, and it signifies that an uptrend is, or appears to be, coming to an end.

TRADER: One who buys and sells for his own account for short-term profit. (See: *Investor; Speculator*)

TRADING CROWD: Members of a stock exchange assembled at a trading post to effect buy and sell orders. (See: *Trading Post*)

TRADING FLOOR: (See: *Floor*)

TRADING POST: One of 18 horseshoe-shaped trading locations on the floor of the New York Stock Exchange at which stocks assigned to that location are bought and sold. About 75 stocks are traded at each post. (See: *Inactive Post*)

TRANSFER: This term may refer to two different operations. For one, the delivery of a stock certificate from the seller's broker to the buyer's broker and legal change of ownership, normally accomplished within a few days. For another, to record the change of ownership on the books of the corporation by the transfer agent. When the purchaser's name is recorded on the books of the company, dividends, notices of meetings, proxies, financial reports and all pertinent literature sent by the issuer to its securities holders are mailed direct to the new owner. (See: *Delivery; Registrar; Street Name*)

TRANSFER AGENT: A transfer agent keeps a record of the name of each registered shareowner, his or her address, the number of shares owned, and sees that certificates presented to his office for transfer are properly canceled and new certificates issued in the name of the transferee. (See: *Delivery; Registrar; Transfer*)

TRANSFER TAX: A tax imposed by New York State when a security is sold or transferred from one person to another. The tax is paid by the seller. The current New York State tax is imposed at rates of from 1¼ to 5 cents a share based on the selling price of the stock. The tax is 1¼ cents on shares selling for less than $5; 2½ cents on shares selling for $5—9.99; 3¾ cents on shares selling for $10—19.99 and 5 cents for shares selling at $20 or more. There is no tax on transfers of bonds.

TREASURY STOCK: Stock issued by a company but later re-acquired. It may be held in the company's treasury indefinitely, reissued to the public, or retired. Treasury stock receives no dividends and has no vote while held by the company.

TURNOVER: The volume of business in a security or the entire market. If turnover on the New York Stock Exchange is reported at five million shares on a particular day, five million shares changed hands. Odd-lot turnover is tabulated separately and ordinarily is not included in reported volume.

TWO-DOLLAR BROKER: Member on the floor of the New York Stock Exchange who executes orders for other brokers having more business at that time than they can handle themselves, or for firms who do not have their Exchange member-partner on the floor. The term derives from the time when these independent brokers received $2 per hundred shares for executing such orders. The fee is paid by the broker and today it varies with the price of the stock. (See: *Commission Broker*)

UNDERWRITER: (See: *Investment Banker*)

UNLISTED: A security not listed on a stock exchange. (See: *Over-the-Counter*)

UNLISTED TRADING PRIVILEGES: On some exchanges a stock may be traded at the request of a member without any prior application by the company itself. The company has no agreement to conform with standards of the exchange. Companies admitted to unlisted trading privileges prior to enactment of the Securities Exchange Act of 1934 are not subject to the rules and regulations under that Act. Today admission of a stock to unlisted trading privileges requires SEC approval of an application filed by the exchange. The information in the application must be made available by the exchange to the public. No unlisted stocks are traded on the New York Stock Exchange. (See: *Listed Stock*)

UP TICK: A term used to designate a transaction made at a price higher than the preceding transaction. Also called a "plus tick." A stock may be sold short only on an up tick, or on a "zero plus" tick. A "zero plus" tick is a term used for a transaction at the same price as the preceding trade but higher than the preceding different price.

Conversely, a down tick, or "minus" tick, is a term used to designate a transaction made at a price lower than the preceding trade. A "zero minus" tick is a transaction made at the same price as the preceding sale but lower than the preceding different price.

A plus sign, or a minus sign, is displayed throughout the day next to the last price of each company's stock traded at each trading post on the floor of the New York Stock Exchange (See: *Short Sale*)

VOTING RIGHT: The stockholder's right to vote his stock in the affairs of his company. Most common shares have one vote each. Preferred stock usually has the right to vote when preferred dividends are in default for a specified period. The right to vote may be delegated by the stockholder to another person. (See: *Cumulative Voting; Proxy*)

WARRANT: A certificate giving the holder the right to purchase securities at a stipulated price within a specified time limit or perpetually. Sometimes a warrant is offered with securities as an inducement to buy. (See: *Rights*)

WHEN ISSUED: A short form of "when, as and if issued." The term indicates a conditional transaction in a security authorized for issuance but not as yet actually issued. All "when issued" transactions are on an "if" basis, to be settled if and when the actual security is issued and the Exchange or National Association of Securities Dealers rules the transactions are to be settled.

WIRE HOUSE: A member firm of a stock exchange maintaining a communications network linking either its own branch offices, offices of correspondent firms or a combination of such offices.

WORKING CONTROL: Theoretically ownership of 51% of a company's voting stock is necessary to exercise control. In practice—and this is particularly true in the case of a large corporation—effective control sometimes can be exerted through ownership, individually or by a group acting in concert, of less than 50%.

YIELD: Also known as return. The dividends or interest paid by a company expressed as a percentage of the current price—or, if you own the security, of the price you originally paid. The return on a stock is figured by dividing the total of dividends in the preceding 12 months by the current market price—or, if you are the owner, the price you originally paid. A stock with a current market value of $40 a share which has paid $2 in dividends in the preceding 12 months is said to return 5% ($2.00 ÷ $40.00). If you paid $20 for the stock five years earlier, the stock would be returning you 10% on your original investment. The current return on a bond is figured the same way. A 3% $1,000 bond selling at $600 offers a return of 5% ($30 ÷ $600). Figuring the yield of a bond to a maturity calls for a bond yield table. (See: *Dividend; Interest*)

Selected Readings: A Bibliography

By Sylvia Mechanic

THE STOCK MARKET AND HOW IT WORKS

Cooke, Gilbert
  The Stock Markets. 1964 Schenkman Publishing Co., Mass.
  $11.25
  Designed primarily to meet the needs of the undergraduate student taking a course in the stock market, this readable text should prove of value to all who are interested in the basic workings of the stock exchanges in America.

Leffler, George Leland
  The Stock Market, 3rd ed. 1963 Ronald Press, N.Y. $8.50
  Introduces new chapters on investment banking, foreign stock markets and local exchanges.

Shultz, Birl E.
  The Securities Market, and How It Works. Rev. ed. 1963 Harper & Row, N.Y. $8.00
  A complete updating and revision of one of the standard

This is a suggested list of readings prepared for use in conjunction with the course on "Securities and Investing" offered by the Investors' Information Program of the New York Stock Exchange. It is not intended to be a complete listing. The items included are generally available in leading Business Libraries. Out-of-print books have been omitted. The prices given are as of 1967 and of course are subject to change. Miss Mechanic is Business Librarian of the Brooklyn Public Library.

books on the workings of the New York Stock Exchange. Starts with a history of the Exchange and concludes with a chapter on customer protection.

Sobel, Robert
The Big Board: A History of the New York Stock Market. 1965 Free Press, N.Y. $7.95
This is perhaps the first "full-scale history of this great financial complex." An excellent bibliography and analytic index make this a book for further use.

LEARNING TO INVEST

Barnes, Leo
Your Investments. 1967 Prentice-Hall, N.J. $4.95
How to select a stock, mutual fund or closed-end investment company and how to choose the right time to buy and sell securities are only a few of the subjects covered in this popular guide. Revised annually.

Crane, Burton
The Sophisticated Investor. Rev. ed. 1964 Simon and Schuster, N.Y. $4.95
The former stock market columnist for *The New York Times* explains timing, chart reading and growth stocks. Includes a glossary of terms clearly defined.

Finley, Harold M.
Everybody's Guide to the Stock Market. Rev. ed. 1965 Regnery Co., Ill. $4.95
Defines words and terms used in the financial world, explains the Dow theory and discusses "blue chips" and "growth stocks." Illustrated by hypothetical cases, charts and graphs.

Fisher, Philip A.
Common Stocks and Uncommon Profits. Rev. ed. 1960 Harper & Row, N.Y. $4.50
For the larger investor who has the time and money to wait for accruement from long-term growth stocks. Author bases his opinion on more than 20 years of successful investment experience.

Fortune editors
Fortune's Guide to Personal Investing. 1963 McGraw-Hill

Book Co., N.Y. $4.50
The editors present in book form their series of articles on
investing which originally appeared in *Fortune* starting September, 1961. T. A. Wise contributes many of the highly
readable and informative chapters.

Graham, Benjamin
The Intelligent Investor. Rev. ed. 1965 Harper & Row, N.Y.
$5.95
Intended mainly for working analysts and advanced students.
Points out recent economic changes which affect the values
of various types of securities. Considers the needs of "de-
fensive" as well as "enterprising" investors.

Kahn, Lotte
Women and Wall Street. 1963 Macfadden-Bartell, N.Y.
$.60
An executive for one of the member firms of the New York
Stock Exchange, Mrs. Kahn addresses her advice to the
women.

Kamm, Jacob O.
Making Profits in the Stock Market. Rev. ed. 1966 World
Publishing Co., Ohio $4.95
A simply presented handbook covering the basic principles
of investing.

Loeb, Gerald M.
The Battle for Investment Survival. Rev. ed. 1965 Simon
and Schuster, N.Y. $5.95
Hardboiled, realistic advice on the difficulties of succeeding
in Wall Street. It promises no short cuts to wealth but,
rather, is a straightforward interpretation of investment
techniques.

McLane, Helen J.
The Investment Club Way to Stock Market Success. 1963
Doubleday & Co., N.Y. $.95
A step-by-step explanation of the fundamentals of investing
in stocks through club participation. Included is a listing of
the state laws affecting investment clubs.

Stabler, C. Norman
How to Read the Financial News. 10th rev. ed. Harper &
Row, N.Y. $4.95
A good starting point for the inexperienced investor. In-

cludes chapters on the securities and commodity markets, puts and calls, mutual funds and the workings of the various regulatory agencies. A basic book in the field.

Yarmon, Morton
  Invest Smartly. 1961 Charles Scribner's Sons, N.Y. $3.50
  For the beginner. Gives terminology, varieties of investments available and suggests the best investments for individual needs.

TEXTBOOKS ON INVESTMENT THEORY AND PRACTICE

Badger, Ralph E.
  Investment Principles and Practices. 5th. ed. 1961 Prentice-Hall, N.J. $12.65
  Revision of a basic book which first appeared in 1928. Special attention is given banks and insurance companies as fields of investment. There is also a comprehensive treatment of the principles and factors underlying the investment policies of individuals, financial institutions and trust funds.

Clendenin, John C.
  Introduction to Investments. 4th ed. 1965 McGraw-Hill Book Co., N.Y. $8.50
  Covers a wide variety of topics including life insurance, real estate, trusts, tax planning and savings institutions. Questions and problems, and suggested further readings enhance the value of this book as an introduction to the whole area of securities and investments.

Graham, Benjamin
  Security Analysis: Principles & Techniques. 4th ed. 1962 McGraw-Hill Book Co., N.Y. $14.50
  Comprehensive text covering the general field and broad problems of investment policy, techniques of appraisal and standards of measurement for investment securities.

FOR THE MORE EXPERIENCED INVESTOR

Edwards, Robert D. and Magee, J.
  Technical Analysis of Stock Trends. 1958 John Magee, Inc., Springfield, Mass. $13.00
  Emphasis on charts, Dow Theory, sensitivity indexes for the investor with a basic knowledge of common terms and procedures.

Granville, Joseph
Granville's New Key to Stock Market Profits. 1963 Prentice-Hall, N.J. $12.50
The author of the more basic *A Strategy of Daily Market Timing for Maximum Profit* discusses a new technical tool he has developed for gauging the pulse of the trading cycle. His "On Balance Volume Theory" offers the stock trader a new way to improved performance and profits.

Jiler, William J.
How Charts Can Help You in the Stock Market. 1962 Trendline, Inc., N.Y. $10.00
One of the few complete texts devoted to the role of charts and their analysis. Author also discusses such market indicators as the Odd-Lot Index, Short-Interest Ratio, Barron's Confidence Index and others.

Lerner, Eugene (ed.)
Readings in Financial Analysis and Investment Management. 1963 Richard D. Irwin, Inc., Ill. $8.75
A distinguished and far-reaching collection of articles from the *Financial Analysts Journal.* The contributors are leading security analysts and portfolio managers. This is a valuable handbook for professionals.

Schultz, Harry D.
Bear Markets: How to Survive and Make Money in Them. 1964 Prentice-Hall, N.J. $12.50
Author describes many of the techniques which he feels will assist the investor during a "bear" or falling market.

Weaver, Mark
The Technique of Short Selling. 1963 Investors' Library, N.J. $4.50

SELECTED REFERENCE BOOKS

Investors interested in reading more about specialized services and techniques of investing will do well to consult the reference sections of their libraries. Suggested are:

Encyclopedia of Stock Market Techniques. 2nd ed. rev. 1965 Investors Intelligence, N.J. $24.95
Forty-two chapters, each written by a specialist in the field, cover such areas as: I. Technical patterns and indicators, II.

Buying on the fundamentals, III. Specialized investing techniques.

Low, Janet
The Investor's Dictionary. 1964 Simon and Schuster $4.95
A most useful volume encompassing the many specialized terms used in the investing field. Definitions average about 100 words, but longer ones are included to explain more involved concepts. Author at times injects a humorous touch.

McNierney, Mary A. (ed.)
Directory of Business and Financial Services. 6th ed. 1963 Special Libraries Association, N.Y. $6.50
Included in this basic index are some 1,560 individual listings with brief description, publisher, price and frequency for each. An invaluable tool.

Walter, H. C.
Investment Information and Advice: A Handbook and Directory. 2nd ed. 1964 Fir Publishing Co., N.Y. $6.95
Another basic index in the field, this book has a listing of investment advisers who are registered with the SEC as well as an enumeration of the published sources of advisory and factual information. Other features make this a prime source book in the field and one which all serious investors should be familiar with.

Index